Jose Maria Sison

Imperialism in Various Global Regions

Sison Reader Series
Book 19

Julieta de Lima
Editor

Copyright © 2023
by International Network for Philippine Studies (INPS)

Published by
International Network for Philippine Studies (INPS)

Cover and Book Design by Ricardo Lozano

Table of Contents

Foreword	1
Third World Countries Oppose US Monopoly of IMF-WB Affairs	3
ASEAN — Still Another Military Alliance	9
Can ASEAN Be an Instrument for Economic Independence and Development?	11
The United States and the Third World	15
Message to the International Congress against the World Economic Summit	27
Message of Solidarity to the People's Conference against Imperialist "Globalization"	35
Accelerated Destruction of Productive Forces	41
Fight Imperialist Globalization and Wars	47
On US Intervention in the Philippines and Korea	51
On Revolutionary Struggles in Imperialist and Oppressed Countries	55
War, Imperialism and Resistance from Below	59
Condemn Imperialism and the G8 Big Swindle, Demand Cancellation of All Neocolonial Debts	65
ILPS Condemns the Terrorism and Barbarism of Al Qaeda and the Imperialists	71
ILPS Denounces UN Millennium Development Goals as Scheme to Aggravate Imperialist Plunder and Poverty	73
UN Security Council and Peacebuilding Commission Are Instruments of Imperialist Aggression and Plunder	77
Reform of UN Security Council Seeks to Reinforce Imperialist System of Aggression and Plunder	79
Statement against US Monopoly Control of Information and Communications	83
Junk the WTO! Resist Imperialist Plunder and War!	87
International Conference Towards a Just and Lasting Peace against Imperialist War and Plunder	95

Global Trends, Challenges and Opportunities after 9/11	101
ILPS Decries US Hypocrisy on the Russian-Georgian Conflict, Demands US Imperialism and NATO to Get Out of Caucasus	111
ILPS Statement on the Closing of the US Base in Kyrgyzstan	115
Keynote Address to the International Conference on Education, Imperialism and Resistance	117
Capitalist Crisis Makes Socialism Necessary	123
Intensify the Struggles of the Proletariat and Peoples against Imperialism and Reaction	129
Intensify the Struggle against Imperialist Exploitation and Plunder to Attain Development and End Poverty	135
Notes on the International Situation	139
We Unite to Fight Imperialism	143
A Review of Ray O. Light's Book: "US Democracy": the US Empire's Indispensable Myth	149
Note on the Occupy Movement	155
On the Growing Violent Conflict in Egypt	157
No to US Bases, Intervention and Plunder! Fight the US Imperialist Agenda in Asia-Pacific Region	161
ILPS Condemns US for Instigating Coup Scheme, Demands Respect for the Sovereignty of Venezuela	165
On Obama's Visit to East Asia	167
Foundations and Motivations of Imperialist Aggression and Most Important Tasks of the People in the Struggle	175
Strengthen the Unity of the Peoples of Asia and Africa against US-Led Neocolonialism: Fight for National Sovereignty	185
On China's Expansion and the US Pivot to East Asia	189
US Uses Japan to Strengthen its Hegemony in Asia	191
On the International Situation	195
ILPS Statement on US Imperialism's Drive to Annihilate the DPRK	201

We Salute and Support the DPRK and the Korean People
Stand against US Nuclear Threats, Sanctions and Provocations 203

Study Marx to Resist Imperialism 207

Author's Preface to Strengthen the People's Struggle
against Imperialism and Reaction 211

Latin America and the Anti-imperialist Movement 215

Message to Comrade Gabi Fechtner and the Youth in
Mass Education on Imperialism during Whitsun 219

World Situation: An Outline 223

The World Capitalist System Is Bankrupt and Breaking Down,
Causing the Resurgence of the World Proletarian Revolution 229

Terrorist Crimes of Trump and US imperialism Turn
the Peoples of the Middle East against Them 233

An Update on the International Situation 235

On the International Situation, Covid-19 Pandemic
and the People's Response 245

On the Relations of the Philippines
with US and Chinese Imperialism 253

US-led Wars and Types of Weapons in the Era of Modern Imperialism 263

On the World Situation 319

Foreword

Sison Reader Series book 19, Imperialism in Various Global Regions consists of Jose Maria Sison's writings (articles, speeches, statements, interviews and messages) from 1976 to 2022 on the workings of imperialism led by the United States worldwide as well as on the resistance of peoples, nations and countries against various kinds of impositions by the imperialists.

It details how the imperialist impositions are carried out through the instrumentality of the International Monetary Fund (IMF) World Bank (WB) or the International Bank for Reconstruction and Development (IBRD), the World Trade Organization (WTO) and such other multilateral and bilateral agreements and arrangements and how these impositions reduce underdeveloped countries to be basically producers and exporters of raw materials and importers of finished products from the capitalist countries.

It also reveals how the US dictate the policies governing the world capitalist system through the Group of 8, OECD, the IMF, World Bank, WTO, NATO, the UN Security Council, and numerous bilateral and regional treaties and agreements with other countries as well as how individually and collectively, directly and through multilateral agencies like the IMF and World Bank, they have imposed on other countries economic and political policies which impoverish and humiliate the people.

However, the imperialist impositions have incited the resistance and anti-imperialist struggles that include the the building of revolutionary parties of the proletariat to lead the anti-imperialist and democratic struggles in the imperialist and in the dominated countries, and promoting and strengthening proletarian internationalism and international anti-imperialist solidarity of peoples. Read as a whole the book points the way for defeating imperialism and its anti-people impositions.

Julieta de Lima
Utrecht, The Netherlands
August 30, 2023

Imperialism in Various Global Regions

Third World Countries Oppose
US Monopoly of IMF-WB Affairs
Ang Bayan, Special Issue, October 20, 1976

The International Monetary Fund (IMF) and the International Bank for Reconstruction and Development (World Bank) held their 31stjoint annual meeting in Manila last October 4 to 9. Attending the meeting were 1,288 delegates including the boards of directors of the two banks, the finance ministers and central bank governors of 128 member countries and representatives of several international organizations and observer countries.

Since their establishment under the auspices of the United Nations soon after World War II, the IMF and the World Bank have been under the firm control of US imperialism which holds the controlling shares. Both banks have always been used to promote the political and economic hegemony of the United States not only over other capitalist countries but mainly over the developing countries now collectively called the third world.

Under the pressure of the third world people and countries, this year's meeting focused on the problem of poverty which has worsened as a result of the protracted and deep going crisis of the world capitalist system. Except for a handful of development countries, the members of the two banks are developing countries to which the developed countries shift their crisis.

To shift the crisis, characterized by inflation and recession, the United States and other developed countries have deliberately caused currency devaluations in developing countries, reduced imports and set up tariff barriers, hiked prices of manufactured goods, pressed down prices of raw materials and used "aid" to promote foreign investments, unequal trade and debt slavery.

As a result, the economies of third world countries tied to the world capitalist system are in chaos. Their total outstanding debt from the imperialist banks has reached the astronomical sum of US$230 billion. The total balance of payments deficits of non-oil producing developing countries came to US$34 billion in 1975. These are expected to increase further this year.

The intensification of imperialist plunder and exploitation has prodded the third world countries to united in defense of their state sovereignty and economic rights against US imperialism and the other superpower, Soviet social-imperialism. Since 1974, when they adopted at the sixth special session of the United Nations General Assembly the Declaration and Program of Action on the Establishment of a New International Economic Order and at another meeting the Charter of Economic Rights and Duties of States, the developing countries have rapidly strengthened their unity and determination to fight for their legitimate interests.

The just-concluded conference inevitably became an occasion for the confrontation between the representatives of US imperialism and those of developing countries.

Imperialist threats

Delivering the IMF annual address, Johannes Witteveen as IMF managing director did not even pay lip service to the plight of the developing countries. He tried to place in a good light the monetary and financial policies and techniques by which the developed countries have not been able to solve their own economic crisis but which they have used to exploit the developing countries further. Worst of all, he threatened the developing countries with stiffer terms of borrowing and urged them to concentrate on raw-material production for the developed countries.

The IMF takes the guise of looking after the monetary and financial stability of its member countries and providing immediate and temporary relief from balance of payments deficits in order to keep foreign trade going. The facilities available for the purpose are the gold tranche, the four ordinary credit tranches, the facility for compensatory financing, the buffer stock financing facility and the oil facility.

In extending "aid" to developing countries, the IMF imposes such requirements as a "favorable climate" for foreign investments, removal of restrictions on profit remittances by foreign investors, liberalization of imports from the United States and other developed countries, acceptance of onerous foreign loans not only from the IMF but also from the World Bank and the private imperialist banks and adoption of a policy of raising the local tax burden.

IMF resources are most used and manipulated by US imperialism to maintain its economic and financial supremacy. Capitalist countries, like Italy and Great Britain, have also made large drawings to meet their balance of payments problems. The developing countries come last in the extension of IMF resources and get loans at the most onerous terms.

Burdened by accelerated profit remittances, increasingly lopsided trade of raw-material exports and manufacture imports and increasingly heavy debt servicing, the developing countries continuously suffer from balance of payments deficits that put them into deeper indebtedness and heavier impositions of the IMF.

Delivering the World Bank annual address, Robert S. McNamara as World Bank president spewed a lot of rhetoric and data about the poverty of developing countries but went no further than asking the developed countries for more "development assistance" for the developing countries. Of course, he

Third World Countries Oppose US Monopoly of IMF-WB Affairs

did not touch on the fact that foreign loans from the imperialists are precisely the cause of underdevelopment. Speaking on the scarcity of funds in his bank, he merely wanted to justify its increasingly onerous terms for loans.

The World Bank and its affiliate the International Development Association (IDA) are supposed to extend "soft loans" (long-term at low interest rates) to the developing countries upon recommendation of the IMF. But in fact these loans are onerous because of the excessive payments required for administration costs, feasibility studies, foreign experts, technical services, personnel training abroad and commodities that have to be purchased from the United States and other developed countries belonging to the Organization of Economic Cooperation and Development (OECD).

The basic scheme of the IDA is to orient the developing countries towards US investments and trade policies, limit the governments of these countries to infrastructure and other nonindustrial projects (including an expensive birth-control campaign), stimulate a climate for US and other foreign investments and demand counterpart funds, which together with foreign loans, divert local resources from genuine development of a self-reliant national economy.

The International Finance Corporation (IFC) is the affiliate of the World Bank which specializes in barefaced financing for US-owned and US-approved business projects. It extends loans at commercial rates. A comparison of the lending capital of IFC with that of IDA will show that the interest of US imperialism lies not in the genuine development of the developing countries but in their exploitation and plunder.

Aside from making possible loans from the IDA and IFC, the World Bank arranges for larger and more burdensome loans for its developing client-states from commercial banks, mainly US. To cover up the chief role of US commercial banks, the World Bank mixes them up in ostensibly multilateral groups of banks called "aid consortia." For instance, there is the "aid consortium" for the Philippines, supposedly Paris-based but composed mainly of US and Japanese banks, with the former as the largest creditor.

US finance secretary William E. Simon, who headed the US delegation, echoed the speech of Witteveen and threatened a tighter credit situation for the third world countries. Engaging in a sham debate with McNamara, he rebuffed the idea that the lending capital of the World Bank be increased and in that regard the developed countries increase their contributions to the bank. Instead, he demanded that the bank should operate and make profits on its present capital base and raise its interest rates.

Simon made a political diatribe against the Organization of Petroleum Exporting Countries (OPEC) in a futile attempt to drive a wedge between it and the other third world countries. He tried to blame the oil producing countries of the third world for the world inflation and demanded that they give more assistance to the oil-importing developing countries.

5

The third world stand

Mohammed Yeganeh, Iranian state minister and chairman of the OPEC governing committee, took up the cudgels for the oil-producing countries. He pointed out that Simon exaggerated the income of the oil-producing countries and that many of these countries are suffering balance of payments problems. He pointed to the OPEC special fund of US$800 million to assist oil-importing countries of the third world.

The oil prices increases since the oil embargo that followed the October war in 1973 have been necessitated in the first place by the spiraling prices of manufactures and food imported by the oil-producing countries of the third world. Until now, oil prices like those of other raw materials from the developing countries keep on falling behind the prices of imports from the developed countries. Thus, the oil-producing countries together with other third world countries have called for a system of price indexation.

The oil-producing countries are righteously asserting their sovereign rights over their natural resources. An increasing number of them are trying to wrest back ownership of their oil resources and control production so as to conserve these against wastage and profit-making by the giant US cartels. To promote their independence, they are trying to build national industries, develop agriculture and strengthen their national defense.

The anti-imperialist stand of the OPEC gave impetus in 1974 to the 6thspecial session of the UN General Assembly that put out the declaration and program of action on the establishment of a new international economic order. Instead of being taken in by the continuous anti-OPEC propaganda of US imperialism, many developing countries have organized raw-material producers' organizations patterned after the OPEC in an effort to protect themselves from the world capitalist crisis and from impositions of the imperialists.

Marie-Christiane Gbokou, finance minister of the Central African Republic, spoke for the African delegations. She charged that the debilitating effects of inflation and recession in recent years have caused a progressive deterioration in the terms of trade of the poorest among the poor countries. She also charged that the United Nations, the IMF and World Bank are veritably exclusive clubs of the rich countries because the poor countries are excluded from decision-making.

It is the long-standing demand of the third world countries that reform in the international financial and monetary system be tackled on an equal footing among all countries and that monopoly of decision-making in restricted boards must come to an end.

A.H. Jamal, Tanzanian finance and planning minister, derided the second amendments to the articles of agreement of the IMF as a tragedy. He said that there was no guarantee of protection for developing countries from the floating rate policy of the IMF and that the second amendments grant the prerogative to developed countries to make further amendments.

The second amendments deal with exchange arrangements, reduction in the role of gold, changes in the characteristics and expansion of the special drawing right, expansion of the IMF financial operations and transactions, the possible establishment of a council of governors, and minor changes in a number of organizational aspects. Not a single one of these is of any benefit to the developing countries.

It was the fascist dictator Marcos who was most enthusiastic about these as he in his keynote address uncritically announced his full approval and even urged other countries to also approve them. Cesar Virata, Philippine finance secretary, also abused the role of the Philippines as host to the IMF-World Bank meeting as he maneuvered the "Group of 24," a section of the third world, to issue a communiqué that went no further than echo McNamara's line. The main demand of the communiqué was one for the replenishment of World Bank funds by the developed countries, aside from merely expressing disappointment over the fact that balance of payments deficits of non-oil producing countries of the third world are rising fast, that lending rates are becoming tougher and that access of the raw material exports to the developed countries is more difficult than ever.

The Philippine fascist authorities have consistently played the role of US imperialist agents and of trying to dilute the demands of the third world at every turn. At the third ministerial meeting of the Group of 77, now composed of 110 member countries, in Manila last January, they maneuvered to push aside such demands of the third world as nationalization of foreign assets, control of US multinational corporations, cancellation of debts, price indexation and the like.

At any rate, US imperialism has become so bankrupt that it vigorously opposed the demands in the Manila Declaration and Program of Action at the fourth session of the United Nations Conference on Trade and Development (UNCTAD) in Nairobi, Kenya. The demands included: (1) adoption of an integrated program for commodities; (2) debt relief through rescheduling of payments; (3) preferential treatment for semimanufactures and manufactures; and (4) a revised patent system and a code of conduct in technology to ensure efficient transfer.

On the main question of integrated program of commodities, the United States counter proposed a system of individual commodity agreements and an international resources bank. By these, the developing countries can still be played off against each other but all of them would be tied to a bank similar to the IMF and World Bank.

While pretending to support the integrated program for commodities, the other superpower counter proposed a system of medium and long-term commodity agreements by which it could first bait in the developing countries and then subsequently make obnoxious impositions. Its relations with India and Egypt are instructive. The IMF-World Bank meeting ended, with the third world countries unsatisfied and determined to make ever stronger demands in forthcoming forums. US imperialism found itself more isolated than even before within the two financial institutions which had long been its bulwark.

So exasperated was Rama Mohammed Hanif Khan, finance minister of Pakistan, that at one point in the meeting he presented a resolution calling for a conference of all the third world countries at the highest level to take stock of the situation with the view of devising an appropriate strategy for looking after their own interests in the struggle between the poor and rich countries.

The Pakistani representatives, together with a big number of representatives from other third world countries, called for the ouster of those agents of the Chiang clique impersonating China in the IMF. The representatives of the Socialist Republic of Vietnam also took the occasion to denounce the United States for reneging on its pledge to help in the healing of the wounds of war in Vietnam and demanded the release of frozen Vietnamese accounts and assets in US banks.

While the third world people and countries are determined to oppose US imperialism, they are wary of the other superpower and are ever determined to promote their own national independence and self-reliant efforts rather than become subservient to either of the two superpowers. The third world is developing rapidly as the main force against imperialism, colonialism and hegemonism.

ASEAN — Still Another Military Alliance
Ang Bayan, Vol. IX, No. 9, July 15, 1977

The long-rotten corpse of the Southeast Asia Treaty Organization (SEATO) was finally buried last June 30. But the Association of Southeast Asian Nations (ASEAN) has emerged as its more clever replacement.

ASEAN leaders always make it a point to insist that the regional association of the Philippines, Indonesia, Thailand, Malaysia and Singapore is not a military alliance and is not an instrument of US imperialism. But in the same breath, they express as their main concern the suppression of the people's revolutionary movement in their respective countries. When they talk of military "self-reliance," they mean dependence on US military supplies and the continued presence of US military bases in the region, especially in the Philippines.

The Declaration of ASEAN Concord, put out at the Bali conference in February 1976, explicitly gave first place to the call for security, stability and counterinsurgency over the question of regional economic cooperation and the catchphrase of "peace and neutrality."

Within the framework of the ASEAN, there is open common agreement for the member-governments to exchange military expertise and intelligence and to carry out joint military undertakings on the basis of bilateral agreements.

The Philippine government has sought to isolate and crush the Moro people's struggle for national self-determination through bilateral agreements with Malaysia and also with Indonesia. The Marcos fascist regime is eager to succeed in this regard so that it can use more manpower and supplies against the entire Filipino people and the New People's Army led by the Communist Party of the Philippines.

Malaysia has actually helped the Philippine government in reducing if not cutting off supplies from abroad for the Bangsa Moro Army headed by the Moro National Liberation Front. Moreover, both Malaysia and Indonesia have helped the Philippine government in anti-MNLF diplomatic maneuvers among member-governments of the Islamic Conference.

The Philippine and Indonesian reactionary navies coordinate their patrols in the border waters of the Philippines and Indonesia, with the express intention of guarding against the revolutionaries.

Currently, the Philippine and Indonesian reactionary armed forces are conducting joint military exercises which involve amphibious landings, land maneuvers and reconnaissance under the cover of "civic action." The site for the current joint exercises is Unidos, Aklan and that for the next will be Surabaya, Java. These sites are already quite far from the Philippine-Indonesian borders.

Very much in the news for quite some time are the repeated joint military campaigns of the Malaysian and Thai reactionary armed forces against the revolutionary forces in the border provinces of Malaysia and Thailand. Malaysia and Singapore have also continuously cooperated to suppress the Malayan revolutionaries of various nationalities.

In every ASEAN member-state, there is an intensification of anti-communist and antipeople campaigns of suppression. There is the obvious agreement within the ASEAN that these are a concomitant of diplomatic and trade relations, including relations with China and the Indochinese countries.

ASEAN has definitely taken the place of SEATO. The former may even prove to be more effective as a military instrument of US imperialism than the latter if the revolutionary forces do not join up to at least expose and condemn its character as a counterrevolutionary instrument.

Unlike ASEAN, SEATO failed to make use of bilateral military agreements among Southeast Asian countries. It was hamstrung by conflicts between the United States and other member states. US imperialism had to undertake aggressive military actions solely or mainly on its own.

As developing countries still bound to US imperialism, the ASEAN states cannot truly be self-reliant militarily. Their rapidly increasing expenditures for military personnel, material and operations are bound to undermine their respective governments.

US imperialism may consider itself smart for being able to pass on to ASEAN states the burden of facing up to the people's revolutionary armed struggles. But only for the time being. Eventually, the people's war will win in the unliberated parts of Southeast Asia.

ASEAN has been in a frenzy of activities as a result of the decline of US imperialism in Southeast Asia, particularly its defeat in Indochina; the worsening crisis of the world capitalist system; the intensifying contention between US imperialism and Soviet social-imperialism; and the rise of the third world countries and peoples as the main force against the superpowers.

ASEAN is a holding-out instrument for US imperialism in Southeast Asia as the struggle of the two superpowers intensifies and both are drawn to a head-on collision in Europe and its periphery.

At the same time, the revolutionary people of Southeast Asia are taking the initiative under conditions that are increasingly° favorable to them. From the Philippine revolutionary standpoint, the anticommunist and antipeople military aspect of ASEAN must be opposed.

However, one foreseeable cause for an adjustment of policy in this regard would be the actual or impending outbreak of a world war between the two superpowers. Should Soviet social-imperialism provoke or initiate the war, there would be a clear need to further broaden the united front against it.

Can ASEAN Be an Instrument for Economic Independence and Development?
Ang Bayan, Vol. IX, No.9, July 15, 1977

The member-states of ASEAN are economic appendages of the world capitalist system. It will take a revolution to emancipate and properly develop the economy of any of the ASEAN states.

The Philippines, Indonesia, Thailand, Singapore and Malaysia are basically producers and exporters of raw materials and importers of finished products from the capitalist countries. Singapore is practically only a trading post.

All the member-states of ASEAN are controlled by the foreign monopoly capitalists through direct investments and loans. US imperialism lords over all of them.

There are a few important agricultural and mineral raw materials which are exported by one or more of the ASEAN states and imported by the other ASEAN states from elsewhere. These are petroleum, rice, corn, sugar, tin and copper.

But the exchange of these products among the ASEAN members cannot be made to their common advantage because these are controlled by foreign investors and traders who profit more by keeping the pattern of exchanging them with finished products from the capitalist countries.

There are a number of manufactured products exportable from one or more of the ASEAN states and imported by the other ASEAN states from elsewhere. These are cement, specific pharmaceuticals, metal fabrications, agricultural equipment and tools, processed food, paper, rubber products, chemical products, ceramic and glass wares and even reassembled cars.

It is in this kind of trading that the foreign investors and traders are interested so long as it does not tend to remove the pattern of raw-material exports to and finished-product imports from the capitalist countries. As a matter of fact, it is one of the motives of US imperialism in having ASEAN organized in 1967 to promote regional "free trade" and "complementation."

It can be added that US imperialism is also interested in exchanging some goods manufactured in one ASEAN state for raw materials from another. The point is for US imperialism to derive superprofits from the cheap raw materials and cheap labor power available in ASEAN states,

In line with the call for ASEAN industrial projects in the 1976 Declaration of ASEAN Concord, the economic ministers of ASEAN have agreed to establish five regional industrial projects, one in each member-state. Each project would fulfil not only the national requirements of the host country but also a portion of the requirements of the other member-states.

The five ASEAN industrial projects are: urea for Indonesia, another urea for Malaysia, soda ash for Thailand, diesel engines for Singapore, and phosphate fertilizer for the Philippines. These are assigned according to the availability of raw materials in each country,

The capital cost of each project is estimated at over US$800 million. The host country is responsible for 60 percent and the other countries, 10 percent each.

Each country is obliged to own 30 percent of the equity assigned to it but is also allowed to sell 70 percent to the private sector. In this manner, the foreign investors, especially US and Japanese, can control the ASEAN industrial projects. The board of directors of each project would be composed of the representatives of the owners of shares of stocks.

The foreign monopoly capitalist, especially US and Japanese, are also expected to provide loan capital for the equipment and services that have to be obtained from outside the region. This is one more way for the foreign monopolies to tighten their control over the projects.

Of course, in the first place, the raw materials that are the base for the various projects are already under the control of foreign capital. These are natural gas for urea; rock salt for soda ash; and sulfuric acid (as a byproduct of copper smelting) for phosphate fertilizer. Singapore for its part will merely assemble the knocked-down parts of diesel engines from outside the region.

Despite the advantages made available to the foreign monopoly capitalists, the proposed ASEAN industrial projects have run into a snag and have not gone beyond the stage of "prefeasibility" studies.

Although they have another list of industrial projects to recommend for establishment, the ASEAN foreign ministers are preoccupied mainly in their Singapore meeting this month with the difficulties of the traditional exports from ASEAN states as a result of trade restrictions by their capitalist trading partners.

ASEAN states are troubled by increasing trade deficits and balance of payments problems. Thus, the frantically push for talks with Japan, Australia and New Zealand next month and then with the United States in September.

Their previous talks on trade with the European Economic Community in Brussels last April has not at all diminished ASEAN trade worries.

The crisis of the world capitalist system has compelled the ASEAN states to broaden their diplomatic and trade relations in order to dispose of their raw material exports.

For several years already, the prices of these exports have been pressed down too hard in their traditional markets. And worse, the traditional trading partners have cut down on their purchases from ASEAN states, except in the case of oil from Indonesia and Malaysia.

In trying to widen the market for their exports, the ASEAN states have gone so far as to develop relations with countries that they would otherwise avoid, such as socialist China and the social-imperialist Soviet Union.

While their grave situation drives them to have relations with Soviet social-imperialism, the ASEAN states find common cause with the rest of the third world countries. The third world demands a new international economic order and looks for a way out from the dilemma of putting off the US pan only to fall into the Soviet social-imperialists fire.

Imperialism in Various Global Regions

The United States and the Third World
Conference on US Imperialism in the 1990s
Sheffield University
April 22, 1988

It is an honor and privilege to be among the main speakers and participants in this conference of distinguished intellectuals and activists who are decided on studying and discussing the nature, policies, actions and tendencies of US imperialism as well as the necessary self-strengthening and responses of all those anti-imperialist forces interested in national liberation, democracy, socialism and world peace.

There are problems for a speaker in discussing so large a subject as US imperialism and the third world in only thirty minutes. But such problems are not really confounding if we agree at the outset that my task is to present the essentials of the subject and provide some light to further discussion among the conference participants.

I propose to trace first the peak and decline of the United States as an imperialist power; and the rise of the national liberation movements and states in the third world. Then,I shall deal with the problems and prospects of the third world.

I. Peak and decline of US power

In the course and aftermath of World War II, the world capitalist system was severely weakened. The violent crisis of the system provided the conditions for the emergence of several socialist countries and the unprecedented upsurge of national liberation movements in the colonies and semicolonies.

But the United States stood out as the supreme capitalist power. Its productive capacity had been greatly expanded due to the war. It presided over new financial arrangements at Bretton Woods. It undertook to spearhead the reconstruction of the devastated economies of Western Europe and Japan.

It had a monopoly of the atomic bomb. It had an excessive supply of conventional weapons as well as an overcapacity for producing these. It was easy for the United States to pose as the No. 1 defender of the world capitalist system and No. 1 policeman of the world.

It was the undisputed economic and military leader of the Western alliance. It built subsidiary military alliances and military bases all over the world with the declared objective of first rolling back and then containing "communism"--the shorthand for the socialist countries and the national liberation movements.

The United States was a major initiator of the United Nations and was able to take for itself built-in privileges to enhance its scheme of Pax Americana. It mouthed peace but whipped up the cold war. It mouthed freedom but sought to subvert the socialist countries, crush the newly established people's democracies and the national liberation movements and take the place of the old colonial powers.

The proclivity of the United States for unnecessary and excessive violence was demonstrated in the atomic bombing of Hiroshima and Nagasaki. US strategists continue to celebrate this wanton massacre of civilians as an exemplary action to deter Soviet expansionism, so-called. The next major show of US military strength was the US war of aggression in Korea. But at this early instance, the United States was forced to a stalemate by the forces it sought to defeat and humiliate.

Up to a point in the 1960s, the United States was able to keep itself at the peak of its power and override its own internal crisis as well as the crisis of the world capitalist system. The American big bourgeoisie had seemingly inexhaustible outlets for its surplus capital in military production and overseas military bases, in the reconstruction of Western Europe and Japan, in the takeover and exploitation of colonies and semicolonies, in the production of consumer goods based on old and new technologies, in further urbanization, in space technology, and some amount of social alleviation.

But from the late 1960s onwards, a convergence of forces started to dramatically work against the United States. The economy was being overheated by military production which did not result in ultimate gains for the country. Relative to other sectors of the economy, the military-industrial complex was making profits. But the US economy as a whole could make no ultimate gains from the resources it was pouring into and wasting in the US war of aggression in Vietnam.

The phenomenon of stagflation emerged, driven by cost-push rather than demand-pull factors. The world became tighter for the United States because other capitalist countries it had helped to reconstruct under the Marshall Plan had recovered their productive capacity and had become competitors. The overstretched military bases and personnel all over the world was in fact a big drain on resources and a provocation to the peoples of the world.

The wanton circulation of overvalued US dollars was resented in Western Europe and confidence in it was shaken. The United States did not have enough gold at its fixed official price to back up US dollars in circulation. At the onset of the 1970s the United States unpegged the price of gold , detached the dollar from its gold backing and proclaimed that US industrial products backed the US dollar.

Nixon had to announce his doctrine of Victimizing the Vietnam war as the Vietnamese and other Indochinese people relentlessly waged resistance and advanced against every escalation of the US war of aggression. American public opposition to high US casualty and wastage of resources in the war persuaded Washington to accept defeat and withdraw in 1973.

The thrust of US policy for most of the 1970s pushed through the IMF and the World Bank the so-called second development decade involving the extension of large amounts of foreign loans to the third world countries in order not only to cover their growing trade deficits but more importantly to artificially create the demand for the industrial products of the capitalist countries and revive the stagnating world capitalist system.

Available for lending was the glut of Eurodollars and subsequently the petrodollars. The 1973 oil crisis was a shock to the United States and the capitalist countries because the producers of one strategic raw material asserted themselves and went against US dictates. But the petrodollars were deposited mainly in the banks of capitalist countries and fitted into the scheme of pump priming the world capitalist system with foreign loans to third world countries.

The United States decelerated in the 1970s its high-tech military spending relative to the Soviet Union thus allowing the latter to catch up with it and achieve overall military parity. The United States even hoped to reap larger profits by selling weapons rather than by using them in outright wars of aggression.

Much earlier in the fifties, the Soviet Union had broken US nuclear monopoly and taken the lead in space technology. The nuclear stalemate would be underscored after the Soviet Union achieved second-strike capability and the nuclear race became one of multiplying the capacity for annihilating the human race several times over.

Some US publicists complained of the so-called isolationist policy of the United States under the Carter administration and clamored for more military spending and aggressiveness. In fact, the ideology of national security continued to ride high on the doctrine of indirect military assistance through so-called economic assistance to repressive regimes in the third world.

The United States continued to suffer a big drain on its resources by making large military deliveries to both Israel and Egypt, both of which did not have the means to pay. And it would lose a big customer like Iran whose autocratic regime fell because of several factors including high-speed military purchases.

Eventually at the close of the 1970s, neo-Keynesianism had to be dropped in favor of monetarism on a global scale. The third world debtor countries were clearly unable to pay back the loans that they had been getting. To extend to them ever larger amounts of new loans without end would be to give away goods and services for free. International credit tightened in accordance with the capitalist rules of the game.

Riding to power by harping on the line of restrengthening the United States and getting ahead in the arms race, Reagan went on a trillion-dollar spending spree for high-tech military weapons. Because he cut back taxes to please big business, the way left for him to raise resources was to attract foreign funds by raising interest rates and go into outright foreign borrowing by issuing more overvalued dollars.

The illusion of renewed prosperity from the 1979-82 recession was created as the United States went into high-tech military production and financed imports from West Germany, Japan and the handful of "newly industrializing countries". In only a few years' time, the United States turned from being the biggest creditor to being the biggest debtor of the world by incurring huge budgetary and trade deficits.

For a short time, the United States looked smart in countering the deflationary trend from 1979 to 1982 with high spending. But in the case of the third world countries, their accumulated foreign debt was driven up by the high interest rates set by the United States. By taking cheap the manufactured goods of Western Europe and Japan, the United States undermined its own capacity to produce tradeable goods.

US budgetary and trade deficits have already resulted in serious consequences, like the first dollar plunge in 1985 and the unprecedented Black Monday stock market crash which wiped out US$3.2 trillion. These are harbingers of worse events for the US and the world capitalist system.

The United States can improve its productive capacity in tradeable goods and go on a trade offensive only at the expense of its capitalist allies and the few newly industrializing countries. As the eminent Paul Sweezy has pointed out, the trade surpluses of Japan and West Germany are the other side of US trade deficits.

Since there are limits to expanding their own capitalist economies without new foreign markets, Western Europe and Japan tend to become independent of the United States and seek to run ahead of it in developing economic relations with the socialist countries. Japan tends to be more obedient to the United States because of its dependence on the US market. But the United States itself is already strained by the special trade accommodations to Japan and the newly industrializing countries and by the burden of worldwide military spending from which it seeks relief by pushing the sharing of costs with Japan and Western Europe.

The United States is caught in the absurd position of being obsessed with the arms race and wasting its resources on the old anticommunist crusade but providing "security" to the initiatives of its capitalist allies in developing economic relations with the socialist countries and outselling the United States itself.

Even as it is more a symbolic than substantial step towards nuclear disarmament, the treaty between the United States and the Soviet Union on medium and shorter-range missiles induces the countries of Western Europe to consider their own economic and security interests independently of the United States.

The United States and the Third World Conference on US Imperialism

By pursuing the policy of peaceful co-existence of states irrespective of ideology and social system as well as the objective of economic development with the help of technology transfer from the crisis-ridden capitalist countries, the Soviet Union, China and other socialist countries are seeking to develop diplomatic, economic and cultural relations; restrain the aggressive impulses of US imperialism, stop the arms race, and ease tensions among states.

With its military capacity to overkill humanity and launch aggression, US imperialism is still a dangerous beast. But it must also be recognized that it has been politically incapable of launching any large-scale war of aggression since its defeat in the Vietnam war.

The Vietnam syndrome is still at work within the United States. Capitalist allies of the United States are no longer obedient to its dictates as in previous decades although they remain committed to the fundamental principles of capitalism, which unite them but which also put them in competition.

Whatever are the developments in the strategic relations of the United States with other capitalist countries and with the socialist countries, the general run of third world countries are suffering from and struggling against various degrees of oppression and exploitation by the United States and other capitalist countries.

II. The rise of the third world

The continents of Asia, Africa and Latin America have been both the boon and bane to the United States. They are a boon insofar as the United States can still exploit a number of countries as sources of raw materials, fields of investment, market for manufactures and as debtors up to a certain point. They are a bane insofar as the United States can no longer exploit at will an increasing number of countries assertive of their political and economic independence.

The third world (as the shorthand for the underdeveloped, less developed or developing countries of Asia, Africa and Latin America) is simultaneously a source of superprofits for the United States and a well-spring of resistance to US imperialism by independent states and national liberation movements.

Since the end of World War II, there have been two major phases in the rise of the third world states with varying degrees of independence from the United States and other capitalist powers. The first phase involved those countries in which national liberation movements had been able to take advantage of World War II in strengthening themselves and which either realized their independence through armed struggle or received formally the grant of independence from a colonial power through a compromise.

The new states included the people's democracies of China and the parts of Vietnam and Korea which basically completed the national democratic revolution and proceeded to socialist revolution; the states like India, Pakistan, Indonesia, Burma, Sri Lanka, Ghana and Guinea, which strove to enhance

19

their independence by being assertively nonaligned; and the more blatant semicolonies like the Philippines, South Korea and South Vietnam.

The second phase involves those countries in which the national liberation movements are removed from the conditions of a world war but have been favored by the ceaseless crisis of capitalism, by the existence of previously successful national liberation movements and by the growth of socialist countries. Either real independence has been achieved through armed struggle in varying degrees and forms or formal independence has been conceded by the colonial power in the face of national liberation movements.

There have been at least a dozen third world countries in which the national liberation movements have been able to achieve their objectives through armed struggle. And there have been more countries to which formal independence has been conceded and which are still in the process of achieving real and complete independence.

Cuba was the first country to assert its independence from US imperialism and take the road of socialist revolution not only in Latin America but also in the entire second major phase of the rise of independent third world states since the end of World War II.

In the same phase, Algeria, the Congo and Kenya were among the first to obtain independence by force of arms and negotiations with the colonial powers in Africa. In the 1960s and 1970s, the colonial system in Africa went into a process of collapse under the direct and indirect pressure of armed struggle in several countries.

In completing their struggles for national liberation, the Vietnamese, Laotian and Cambodian peoples waged the revolutionary armed struggle that directly defeated, debilitated and caused US imperialism to decline on a world scale. They have given the United States the most telling lesson on the futility of aggression.

At the core of the struggle for national liberation in the third world has been the peoples' determination to wage revolutionary armed struggle against the worst oppression and exploitation by a foreign power and the local reactionaries. But the armed revolutionary movement--though the most effective--is not the sole form of action for enhancing independence. The third world states already enjoying varying degrees of independence have used coordinated political, economic and other actions to promote independence and the success of national liberation movements.

The Bandung Conference of 29 Afro-Asian states in April 1955 was the very first attempt of third world states to concentrate their collective will for the all-round independence of each country and a common stand against foreign domination. The five principles of peaceful coexistence were laid down in this conference.

Up to the early sixties, the Bandung Conference inspired not only the trend of independence among Afro-Asian states but also the peoples' solidarity movements in Asia, Africa and Latin America. In 1961, independent third world states found a venue for further consensus and collective action in the Non-aligned Movement (NAM) which was launched in Belgrade. Most of the 25 states attending the summit conference came from the third world, including one from Latin America--Cuba.

Third world unity was dramatically demonstrated in the United Nations in 1972 when countries of Asia, Africa and Latin America gave the overwhelming vote for the restoration of the legitimate rights of China; and isolated the United States in that most respectable organization of states.

Algeria assumed the chairmanship of the NAM in 1973 and presided over the delegations of 75 countries, sixty of which were headed by chiefs of state. The Algiers summit led to the summoning of the Sixth Special Session of the UN General Assembly in 1974. This session passed the Declaration of the Establishment of a New International Economic Order and the Program of Action on the Establishment of a New International Economic Order.

The Declaration upheld sovereignty as a right of states and supported the right of countries to adopt the economic and social system they find most appropriate, these rights extending to the use of the natural resources, freedom from foreign domination and equality in trade based on fair prices for all commodities.

The Program of Action identified the issues to act on such as those involving commodity trade, food, transportation, insurance, monetary reform, industrialization, transfer of technology, regulation of multinational corporations, strengthening of the UN system and the Charter of Economic Rights and Duties of States adopted by the UN General Assembly.

Under the chairmanship of Algeria, the Nonaligned Movement was also made more effective by the formation of the 74-member Coordinating Bureau consisting of the representatives of 36 African, 23 Asian, 12 Latin American and three European countries.

By March 1983, at the New Delhi conference, the NAM attained a membership of 101 countries. This is the well-known automatic majority which has caused the United States a lot of worries both within and outside the United Nations.

Distinct from NAM, which has been concerned with third world affairs more in a political and all-round way, there is the Group of 77 which focuses on the economic sphere. The embryonic group emerged in 1963 and was behind the convening of the United Nations Conference on Trade and Development (UNCTAD I) in Geneva in 1964. The Group of 77 took full shape in Algiers in October 1967 when it convened to codify a common third world position in international economic negotiations, particularly those to take place in UNCTAD II in New Delhi in 1968.

Until now, the charter issued by the Group of 77 at the Algiers conference provide the basic guidelines for the third world position in North-South negotiations. In 1984, the Group of 77 grew to a membership of 126 countries.

Imperialism in Various Global Regions

To cite a recent document, the Final Act of UNCTAD VII in 1987 assesses the critical world economic situation and formulates broad policies and measures on the issues of resources for development, commodities, international trade and the problems of the least developed countries; but fails to provide specific policies and measures to satisfy the demands of the third world countries, specially in the areas of debt and international trade.

III. Problems and Prospects of the Third World

Definitely, the third world countries are not lacking in a recognition of their common interests, problems and aspirations and in global and regional forums to express them and agree on some level of coordinated actions regarding North-South and South-South relations. But the old world dominated by US imperialism and its capitalist allies persists Third World states may have the trappings of political independence. But they are still in need of economic independence.

Third world countries are generally backward, agrarian, preindustrial and dependent on raw-material production for export. Most of them depend on the world capitalist market and are susceptible to its vagaries. They are victims of finance capital at its worst.

The pseudodevelopment scheme intended to pump prime the world capitalist system in the 1970s has overloaded the third world countries with debts which have only served to deepen and aggravate economic backwardness of most and the lopsided growth of even the few so-called newly industrializing countries. The loans for the third world were used in the main for facilitating the sale of structural steel and construction equipment for building infrastructures, agricultural and milling facilities; cars, computers and home appliances for the well-to-do; and the like.

The multinational firms got the superprofits on overpriced supplies; the bureaucrats, their part of the loot; and the military, bigger budgetary allocations and share of private business.

The current accumulated foreign debt of the third world countries is more than US$1.0 trillion and is half of their combined gross national product. In the worst cases of indebtedness, debt servicing eats up sixty to 90 percent of export income. The annual net capital outflow from the third world to the capitalist countries keeps on growing mainly through debt service.

The third world countries have no way of paying their foreign debt because of their retrogressive economic base and because the terms of trade for their raw-material exports have continuously deteriorated. Commodity prices are now depressed to their lowest level in fifty years. These countries have to keep on begging for rescheduling of debts and have to suffer more onerous credit terms. The indebtedness is growing larger even as new loans have dwindled.

22

The United States and the Third World Conference on US Imperialism

As earlier pointed out, the US policy of deficits and high interest rates has accelerated the enlargement of the third world debt. Also, the US policy of imposing free flow of foreign exchange, unrestricted profit remittances, currency devaluations, import liberalization, wage cuts, privatization, conversion of foreign loans to equity and all sorts of foreign investment incentives have wrought havoc on third world economies.

The extreme economic exploitation that the third world countries is undergoing has recoiled upon the United States and other capitalist countries. Because most third world countries are being sucked dry of their blood, their capacity to buy goods and services from the capitalist countries is decreasing. The third world debt problem is drastically constricting the world capitalist market even as the particular winners in the capitalist game are raking in profits and interests as never before.

To make matters worse, the United States itself has imposed itself on the world capitalist system as the biggest single debtor through wanton military spending and luxury consumption. Attempts of the United States to revive its productive capacity in tradeable goods, outsell its capitalist allies and cut down its trade deficits will further constrict the world capitalist system.

In this regard, the handful of so-called newly industrializing countries (South Korea, Mexico, Brazil and the like), which enjoy special trade accommodations in the US market, have begun to encounter economic difficulties and are facing the prospect of the United States cutting down its imports because of its serious trade deficits, growing foreign debt and its desire to revive its own productive capacity and promote its own exports.

Economic difficulties have resulted in widespread social unrest in most third world countries. These provide favorable conditions for the rise of revolutionary movements, especially in third world countries dominated by the United States through colonial, neocolonial, fascist and racist regimes and such reactionary classes as the comprador big bourgeoisie and the landlord class. The toiling masses of workers and peasants as well as the middle social strata in the third world have no choice but to fight for their liberation.

The revolutionary movements in the third world play an even more important role in changing the balance of strength between the forces of anti-imperialism and imperialism in the entire world. They can overthrow pro-imperialist reactionary states and build new states that are completely independent; or push the existing states to become more politically independent of US imperialism and press for a new international economic order.

The scheme of the United States to impose its will on third world countries through neocolonial economic manipulation and use the low intensity conflict to put down popular resistance or subvert independent states can only serve to expand and intensify the anti-imperialist movement.

The low-intensity conflict ploy of the United States is as condemnable as it is callous and vicious. But it is actually a manifestation of the continuing political

23

inability of the United States to launch any war of aggression on the scale of the Vietnam war. The revolutionary forces of Central America, especially Nicaragua and El Salvador, are currently exposing the limits of US capabilities for the peoples of the entire world to see.

As current trends indicate, US power will be caught in the third world in the 1990s by a pincer of revolutionary movements and states increasingly taking a militantly independent stand.

Progressive forces of the third world will be able to avail themselves of the increasingly divergent and contradictory interests and positions of the capitalist countries. The workers' revolutionary movement and the peace movement in the capitalist countries will be able to resurge at some point in the worsening of the economic and political crisis.

The socialist countries shall have become stronger economically. They shall be in a position to be of greater help to the third world, unless the spirit of proletarian internationalism is lost in the course of accelerating economic construction and achieving national and personal affluence.

There is no irreconcilable contradiction between the revolutionary movements and the progressive states adhering to the policy of peaceful coexistence. The revolutionary movements in the third world have a just cause in fighting for national liberation, democracy and socialism; and can achieve victory on a self-reliant basis. Upholding peaceful coexistence among states means preventing foreign domination, interference, intervention and aggression; and averting war among states and the nuclear annihilation of mankind.

The demand for the peaceful relations of the United States and the Soviet Union, nuclear disarmament and termination of the arms race, the easing of tensions among all states in conflict and the development of diplomatic, economic and cultural relations among states does not mean the surrender and squelching of the people's revolutionary struggle for national liberation and democracy in third world countries.

Under conditions of peaceful coexistence among states, the forces of national and social revolution and the entire people in every third world country can easier win one victory after another. It is perfectly the sovereign right of the people in any country to change their social conditions without foreign interference.

To cite a few ongoing armed revolutionary struggles, those of the people of Palestine, South Africa, Namibia, El Salvador, Chile, Guatemala and the Philippines must proceed. All the oppressed nations and peoples of the world must rise against oppression and exploitation, expand and intensify their revolutionary struggles and advance to win total victory.

There is the reality of US imperialism dominating third world countries and interfering in their internal affairs. It is the obligation of the third world countries and peoples themselves to frustrate and terminate US domination and

The United States and the Third World Conference on US Imperialism

interference. It is as well the duty of all truly independent states and peoples to condemn US imperialism and extend moral and material assistance to those who are victimized by this scourge of mankind and are struggling against it.

Imperialism in Various Global Regions

Message to the International Congress against the World Economic Summit

Message to the International Congress against the World Economic Summit
July 8, 1992

I am deeply pleased to be invited to the International Congress Against the World Economic Summit. And I wish to thank the organizers of the congress.

It is regrettable that I cannot come because the Dutch authorities refuse to give me a laissez passer. As an asylum-seeker in the Netherlands, I have experienced what kind of democracy the class rule of the big bourgeoisie allows.

In the bourgeois world, there is so much media hype against the ways of the Stasi. But in fact, my application for political asylum has been denied twice on the basis of intelligence reports that my lawyer and I cannot look at. The third and final denial in the Netherlands will prompt a further appeal to the European court.

The Manila authorities subjected me to torture, solitary confinement, prolonged illegal detention and other acts of persecution. And they have canceled my passport without due process since 1988 and have offered the prize money of one million pesos for my head, dead or alive, since 1989. And yet the Dutch authorities claim that I cannot be granted asylum because the Manila authorities want me for prosecution and not for persecution. This is what I call word play against the reality of persecution.

Now, I cannot come to Munich even after applying for a laissez passer long before this congress. There is a wall of official silence against my application for this permit to travel. I am told only informally that the right to travel, free speech and other liberties can be negated to prevent me from attending a congress that opposes a sacred thing like the G-7 Summit.

So much for explaining my inability to come to the congress against my will. However, no one can stop me from sending you this message and from requesting a compatriot to participate in your discussions.

The International Congress

Obviously, the challenge that you are making to the G-7 Summit is seriously being taken in view of the fact that bourgeois governments have been obstructing your work and the participation of people from various countries.

At any rate, you have succeeded in convening the congress. I congratulate you wholeheartedly and wish you further success. I hereby convey my warmest regards to all participants.

The congress is highly significant. The people of the world look up to it as an effort to make a critical comprehension and analysis of and militant opposition to several major events unleashed in this year by the world's chief exploiters and oppressors for the purpose of making propaganda and further rationalizing the exploitation and oppression of the people of the world.

I refer to the bourgeois celebration of the quintennial anniversary of the Columbus expedition, the attempt of the worst plunderers of the world's human and natural resources, the main polluters of the world, to misrepresent themselves as the champions of ecology and development and of course the latest G-7 Summit, which is a grand cabal to exact more profits from the blood and sweat of the people.

The congress is made more significant by your determination to promote and help bring about lines of communication and a common understanding among the peoples of the world in the developed countries and in the client-states or neocolonies, against imperialism and neocolonialism and their reactionary agents.

The Filipino people and all progressive forces in the Philippines are in solidarity with you. They share with you the common understanding of the capitalist process of oppression and exploitation; and the common resolve to struggle against these.

They regard the Columbus expedition as the start of the process of bloody conquest and colonization, augmenting the primitive accumulation of capital in Europe and laying the foundation for modern imperialism and neocolonialism. The Filipino people have been subjected to this process and cry out for liberation from the colonial legacy and all the rigors of neocolonial subjugation.

They reject the misrepresentation of the last 500 years as a period of the West civilizing and developing the world. They condemn colonialism, slavery, feudalism, racism, the degradation of entire peoples and the women, clericalism and the destruction of entire cultures and all the current evils of monopoly capitalism and neocolonialism. They celebrate the unceasing resistance of the people of the Americas and farther afield, with whom they have the common experience of suffering and struggle for justice and freedom.

The Filipino people are united with all the peoples in the world in taking a common stand against the capitalist despoliation of the human and natural resources. Inherent to their anti-imperialist stand is the protection and the wise and healthy utilization of the environment. Like all victims of imperialist plunder, the Filipino people have contempt for the crocodile tears of the big bourgeoisie at the Earth Summit.

They are vigilant and opposed to the notion that the issue of ecology is decided by the worst plunderers and destroyers of the environment, that economic development is all decided by these hypocrites and deceivers and that environmental protection is a matter of the poor and underdeveloped countries begging for funds from the unconscionable extractors of superprofits.

The G-7 Summit aims to override the growing contradictions among its members by agreements to widen and intensify the exploitation and

Message to the International Congress against the World Economic Summit

oppression of the people of the world. It is therefore appropriate to denounce it where it is held, both through the indoor discussions of the Congress and through a militant mass action.

The Group of Seven

The Group of Seven is the most despicable combination of countries that has plotted and acted against the people in the entire history of mankind. In the last two decades, they have aggravated underdevelopment and poverty in the third world countries as well as directly and indirectly in the bureaucrat capitalist-ruled countries, which labeled themselves as socialist.

Individually and collectively, directly and through multilateral agencies like the IMF and World Bank, they have imposed on other countries economic and political policies which impoverish and humiliate the people. They have propelled the ever deteriorating terms of trade against the producers of raw materials and slightly-processed goods. They have plunged all these into indebtedness and they are now earning more from debt service than from dividends on productive investment.

And now that they are confronted with the problem of a prolonged world recession and are afflicted with internal contradictions and contradictions among themselves, they seek to devise more cruel and more deceptive ways of exploiting the peoples of the world, including those in capitalist countries.

The internationalization of capital has limits after all. These have been obvious since more than a decade ago when there was a shift from neo-Keynesianism to monetarist policy. The large shift of policy and all the economic restructuring done have only deepened the capitalist crisis of overproduction. The more the Group of Seven strains to solve the fundamental problems of capitalism at the greater expense of the people, the greater is the resistance that can arise.

There has been no end to the fact that all the client-states of the Group of Seven have been overburdened by foreign debt, the most conspicuous manifestation of their economic travail. Coming on top of the utter bankruptcy of most third world and East European countries at the end of the seventies has been the continued abuse of the international credit system by no less than the United States and by further lending to such new loan-clients as China, India and the Soviet Union in that chronological order in the eighties.

But from 1989 to 1991, the Group of Seven and the entire world capitalist system appeared to be triumphant over so-called socialism. So long as bureaucrat capitalism is misconstrued as socialism, capitalism can make the empty boast that it has prevailed over socialism and seems to make a big gain through an ideological offensive against revolutionary forces.

But in fact, the restoration of capitalism had gone on since the 1950s in the former Soviet Union and Eastern Europe. Now that the socialist mask is off the face of bureaucrat capitalism, the Group of Seven is expected to assume full responsibility for all the economic mess in the aforementioned countries and to ante up the loans with no certainty of payback. But driven by its obsessive greed, the Group of Seven prefers to dump finished goods on the client-states and de-industrialize them.

Also in the 1989-91 period, specifically in the year of 1991, the US-led global capitalist alliance was able to demonstrate its high-tech military power, murder 300,000 Iraqi people and devastate Iraq. Since then, there has been much gloating over the supposedly unchallenged hegemony of the US and over the supposed overcoming of the Vietnam syndrome.

But in fact, the Gulf war has exposed the limits of the neocolonialist techniques of economic and financial manipulation and political dictation as well as the persistence of the violent and aggressive nature of imperialism which comes to the fore whenever necessary. A client-state like Iraq became unwieldy in the hands of the US because of the high costs of the Iran-Iraq war and Iraq's own assertion of national interest against the imperialist oil interests. Consequently, the US and other capitalist powers shifted from the superficial civility of neocolonialism to the violence of imperialism.

Major contradictions in the world

In this year, we are in full view of several major contradictions in the world which are becoming more and more conspicuous.

First, all major capitalist powers like the US, Germany and Japan are individually in serious economic trouble.

The US continues to be overburdened by its huge budgetary and trade deficits due to military overspending and by overconsumption. Germany has a serious case of indigestion; the costs for absorbing East Germany are exceedingly heavy. The recent bursting of the financial bubble in the Tokyo stock market shows how Japan is so vulnerable to shifts in US economic policy.

In each capitalist country, the tax burden is increasing, the wage level is always being pressed down and social benefits are being cut back. The big bourgeoisie is already springing out racism and neo-fascism in order to augment the traditional bourgeois parties in the attempt to confuse the people.

Second, the contradictions within the Group of Seven and among all the capitalist countries are intensifying. The controversial issues are in all fields: industrial policy, finance, trade, spheres of influence and security matters. The continuing strategic decline of the US is being taken advantage of by its capitalist competitors.

The US wants to reduce the costs of its war machinery and revive its industrial competitiveness. Thus, both Germany and Japan are being pushed to build up their war machineries and aggressive capability and to engage in overseas military involvement under the banners of the UN and the old as well as new regional and bilateral alliances.

Message to the International Congress against the World Economic Summit

The emergence of new armed conflicts, the continuance of old ones and, of course, the inevitable rise of the people's armed resistance to imperialism and client-states on a widescale are now the main concern of the strategic planning by the capitalist powers which are cooking up various forms of military combinations in the wake of the disintegration of the Soviet Union.

Third, the contradictions between the capitalist powers and the client-states exist even as for the time being it looks like the hegemony of the US as well as that of the US-led alliance is difficult or impossible for any country to challenge.

As the crisis of the world capitalist system worsens and social unrest and resistance of the people are engendered, every reactionary ruling clique in the client-states is unstable and is vulnerable to an armed opposition even within the ruling system.

In fact, we see the ever increasing use of violence in the change of regimes in Asia, Africa, and Latin America. And we will see more and more of this in Eastern Europe and in the former Soviet Union. The illusion of democratization and peace under the aegis of imperialism and with the drumbeating by the pro-imperialist petty bourgeoisie is already giving way to more repressive regimes and further on to popular resistance.

Fourth, the contradictions between the people of all the client states and the capitalist powers are bound to intensify because the basic social problems are being aggravated and the domestic ruling classes are increasingly afflicted by the violent competition for power on the basis of a dwindling sociology-economic base for mutual accommodation.

The increasing possibility of successful armed revolutions led by the working class party arises from the widespread social unrest and turmoil that continue to occur in several countries and continents at the same time.

There are still proletarian revolutionary parties like the Communist Party of the Philippines, which are determined to win an armed revolution and carry out socialist revolution as the consequences of a new democratic revolution. The former Soviet Union and Eastern Europe are not getting as much manna as previously expected from the gods of capitalism and are in fact being de-industrialized. They are in social turmoil and have become hotbeds of ethnic conflicts, coups d'etat and civil wars. The political and economic chaos can ultimately lead to the reemergence of armed revolution.

Fifth, the contradiction between the big bourgeoisie on the one hand and the proletariat and people on the other is bound to intensify as the competition among the capitalist powers intensify upon a dwindling world capitalist market.

The capitalist crisis of overproduction is actually being accelerated by high technology and by the shrinkage of the world market due to the penury and indebtedness of the client states. In the rush to become more efficient and more profitable, the monopoly capitalist firms are now disemploying both blue collars and white collar, with the latter becoming more and more vulnerable to replacement by computers, and are forcing smaller firms into mergers and bankruptcies.

At the moment, the crisis within the advanced capitalist countries is not yet acute enough to cause any uprising. That is because the monopoly bourgeoisie can still exploit the client states. Widespread discontent can arise if the recession becomes a depression and the depression that has long been with most client-states generates armed resistance and social upheavals.

The Philippine revolutionary struggle

There can be no debate whatsoever that the chronic domestic crisis of the semicolonial and semifeudal society in the Philippines is ever worsening and providing the fertile ground for the protracted people's war during the last twenty three years.

This domestic crisis arises from the exploitative nature of the economy and the joint class dictatorship of the comprador big bourgeoisie and the landlord class and is of course generated by the world crisis of capitalism.

The extraction of superprofits from the Philippines by the US, Japanese, German and other multinational firms, the huge budgetary and trade deficits and the crushing foreign and domestic public debt are ceaseless in impoverishing the people and making their lives miserable. These incite the people to join the armed revolution.

In their ideological offensive, the imperialists have been trying to demoralize the people and the revolutionary forces in the Philippines by insisting that the movement for national liberation and democracy is hopeless because the world capitalist system is now without any strong socialist challenge and that the collapse of so-called socialism in Eastern Europe and the Soviet Union have made anti-imperialist and socialist movements helpless and pointless.

The response of the Filipino people and the revolutionary forces is as follows:

1. Like the rest of the people of the third world, the Filipino people have always been under capitalist domination since a long time ago. They have no choice but to fight imperialism and all reaction if they are to hope for any better life.

2. It has been demonstrated in history that genuine revolutionary parties of the proletariat have successfully carried out new democratic revolutions and undertaken a socialist revolutions. The great theoretical challenge for proletarian revolutionaries is how to prevent the undermining and betrayal of socialism and continue the socialist revolution after some decades.

3. The ruling parties and regimes that disintegrated in the Soviet Union and Eastern Europe have been anti-socialist for several decades even as they masqueraded as communist and socialist. In fact, the nomenclatura and apparatchiks continue to prey on the people as barefaced bourgeois, using bureaucratic privileges and doing more private business than ever.

Message to the International Congress against the World Economic Summit

4. In those countries, where bureaucrat capitalism has sought to further strengthen private capitalism by privatizing public assets, the economy and social life in all other respects have further deteriorated. The current conditions of these unabashed client-states of the Group of Seven are a further indictment of capitalism.

5. The ever worsening crisis of the world capitalist system is now clearly pointing to the rise of revolutionary resistance on an unprecedentedly wide scale sooner than later.

The domestic crisis in the Philippines is not all there is to favor the armed revolution. The crisis of the world capitalist system continues to worsen and favor the armed revolution in the Philippines.

A new element in the crisis in the Philippines is the current ascendance of a military figure (General Ramos) to the presidency of the Manila government on the basis of a fraudulent claim on less than a quarter of the electoral vote. He is a notorious puppet of the US and butcher of the Filipino people.

Under the Marcos regime he was the chief planner and implementor of repression. And under the Aquino regime he pushed the US-instigated total war policy. He has represented the continuity of the the fascist military organization and he now represents the militarization of the ruling political system, from top to bottom. This is a manifestation of the deterioration and desperation of the ruling system.

As Filipino revolutionaries say, "This fascist brute has a long record of trying and failing to suppress the revolutionary movement. It is easier to fight and beat such an enemy with his fangs immediately showing than one with lipstick." The new regime is expected to escalate armed counterrevolution and human rights violations but it shall have a lesser capability to deceive the people than Mrs. Aquino even as he is also known as a psywar expert.

The perseverance of the revolutionary forces in armed struggle guarantees the continuance of the general tendency of the ruling system to disintegrate. Economic and political resources of the reactionaries from within and from outside the Philippines for maintaining bureaucratic operations and suppressing the armed revolution are dwindling. The very obstinacy of every ruling clique in carrying out armed counterrevolution has become self-defeating.

The factionalization of the ruling classes and the reactionary armed forces is continuing. The resources for accommodation among political and military factions of the ruling system are more than ever limited. In fact, the entire ruling system has no way to solve its all-round bankruptcy.

The Filipino people are more than ever determined to strengthen their revolutionary forces. They are building their leading proletarian party, their people's army, their mass organizations, their united front and their organs of political power. These forces are growing in strength and advancing through the rhythm of expansion and consolidation; and are in the process of steadily supplanting the power of the imperialists and reactionaries in more and more areas in the Philippines.

At present, the armed revolution that is now going on in the Philippines is in the forefront of the revolutionary movement of the peoples of the world. The Communist Party of the Philippines, the New People's Army and the National Democratic Front are holding high the torch of armed revolution as social turmoil is now spreading in the world and the people are urged by the ever deteriorating conditions to take the road of revolutionary resistance.

I hope that the Filipino compatriot who will participate in the discussions in the forum will be able to shed more light on the content of this message and learn from the exchange of information and views with the other participants in the congress. Thank you.

Message of Solidarity to the People's Conference against Imperialist "Globalization"
November 19, 1996

Warmest greetings of solidarity to all the organizers and participants of the People's Conference Against Imperialist Globalization!

I wish to express my admiration to you for holding this conference and for standing up against the Asia-Pacific Economic Cooperation (APEC) leaders' summit, headed by the United States and Japan. By standing up for the rights and interests of the proletariat and peoples of the world, your conference is diametrically opposite to the APEC, the imperialist states and neocolonial client-states and the multinational firms and banks that use them.

Your conference is also radically different from the so-called parallel NGO conferences that are in fact under the shade of the APEC and whose main role is to deck themselves out as the alternative to the revolutionary movement for national liberation and democracy against imperialism and the local reactionaries.

I am confident that you will succeed in analyzing and criticizing the exploitative, destructive and deceptive character of imperialist "globalization" and inform the broad masses of the people so that they shall be further aroused, organized and mobilized to uphold and defend their rights and interests against imperialism and all reaction.

It is of crucial importance to stress the need for the revolutionary struggle of the people in the face of the destructive character of the imperialist states and their supermonopolies as they use high technology and the most rapacious forms of finance capital in order to extract superprofits and accumulate capital and in the process further exploit and oppress the proletariat and peoples of the world.

After the Keynesian decades of "development" which promoted infrastructure-building and the overproduction of raw materials in underdeveloped countries and also after the collapse of revisionist regimes based on state monopoly capitalism, the US and other centers of monopoly capitalism appear to face no formidable resistance to their intensification of monopoly capitalist exploitation under the signboard of neoliberalism. Your conference can be significant as an encouragement to revolutionary resistance.

We are still in the era of imperialism and proletarian revolution. The uneven development of the world capitalist system has become more gross than ever before. Look at how monopoly capitalism is ravaging the third world and the former Soviet bloc countries. Look at the worsening social conditions in the industrial capitalist countries and the intensifying cutthroat competition among the monopoly capitalists and capitalist powers.

It is utterly deceptive of the imperialist states and their neocolonial client-states in the APEC to tout "free market economies", "free competition" and "free trade" in order to camouflage the reality and workings of monopoly capitalism and to impose on the oppressed peoples and nations worse conditions of neocolonial dependence and subservience to monopoly capitalism.

US monopoly capitalism has always used the liberal slogan of "free market place of goods and ideas" to confuse people. But in recycling this slogan today, it is bringing down drastically the level of economic development in more than 90 percent of the countries of the world. It is trying to break down all barriers to its export of surplus goods and surplus capital and gives no leeway to its neocolonial client-states to make any pretense at economic sovereignty.

Principles of economic and political development drawn from history are obfuscated by assertions that transnational corporations (TNCs) have rendered useless and helpless the states in general and the role of the state in the economy, even as the monopoly bourgeoisie continues to use the imperialist states as well as neocolonial client-states to aggrandize itself and to further exploit and oppress the people.

A semicolonial and semifeudal country like the Philippines cannot attain the status of a newly-industrialized country (NIC) under a regime that shuns national industrialization, that liberalizes the importation of surplus manufactured and agricultural goods from the imperialist countries, that seeks to attract foreign investments for export-oriented manufacturing and that squanders domestic resources and foreign funds on upper-class consumption.

As well articulated in the Anti-Imperialist World Peasant Summit, the Philippines will not only remain agrarian but will sink to a lower level -that of a disjointed agrarian country, lacking in food self-reliance -while there is no land reform, the agricultural surpluses of the imperialist countries flood in, the agrichemicals, seeds and equipment are controlled by the MNCs and the land is further concentrated in the hands of the landlords and the corporations of all sorts.

The crisis of overproduction in the world capitalist system is driving the supermonopolies to accumulate constant capital and reduce variable capital to beat their competitors and raise their profits in their homegrounds. Thus, they cut down their domestic market through massive unemployment and cutbacks on social spending and unwittingly lower the national rates of productivity and profitability. Consequently, they seek to maximize their profits by exporting their surplus goods and surplus capital.

Capitalist competition within capitalist countries leads to larger monopolies and more intense competition among the capitalist countries. It is untrue as some theorists of imperialists globalization that monopolies have lost their national basing. There are indeed international combinations of monopoly firms and alliances of capitalist countries. But there is also the sharpening competition to redivide the world as the general crisis of capitalism worsens.

Message of Solidarity to the People's Conference

The United States is upsetting the balance of its relations with other imperialist countries by trying to take back previous accommodations granted to its favored allies during the Cold War. It wishes to solve its colossal debt and deficit problems by using its technological lead, reviving its manufacturing capacity and intensifying its export drive. It has been consolidating its national market and its regional market (like NAFTA) as well as penetrating the markets of its capitalist rivals. It is taking the initiative in APEC in order to keep Japan in tow, prevent it from taking its own initiative in the AFTA and EAEC and harmonize US-Japan partnership at the expense of other countries.

The Ramos regime can never attain the status of a NIC by imitating the earlier examples of the so-called four tigers of East Asia, especially two of them, Taiwan and South Korea, which have developed relatively more comprehensive economies. The regime conveniently forgets that these carried out land reform, accumulated capital from export-oriented manufacturing to build some basic industries and, most important of all, enjoyed special accommodation in the US market and were allowed to protect state and domestic investors for the overriding purpose of front-lining in the the anticommunist crusade.

It must be pointed out that today these "tigers" and their imitators are now altogether suffering from a crisis of overproduction in their type of products and are now facing declining rates of productivity and profitability. Moreover, they are all under pressure to open their domestic markets to the unrestricted inflow of consumer products and speculative capital from the imperialist countries.

In fact, all the countries hooked to export-oriented manufacturing in Southeast Asia, South Asia, Latin America and Central Europe are now confronted with increasing trade deficits and foreign debt. In the case of China, the misallocation of resources towards export-oriented manufacturing and import-dependent consumption of the new bourgeoisie has undermined the national industrial foundation previously established under socialism. Consequently, the US is requiring China to further liberalize its investment and trade policies in return for admission to the WTO.

The portfolio funds for the so-called emergent markets are meant more to finance budgetary and trade deficits, sustain luxury consumption among no more than the top ten percent of the population and enable the MNCs to finance their sale of consumption goods and the operation of labor-intensive sweatshop enterprises. These so-called emergent markets are no more than ten countries at every given time and are mostly within the ambit of APEC.

The imperialists and their neocolonial puppets are utterly reprehensible for propagating and enforcing the dogma that development is possible in underdeveloped or less developed countries only if they opt for "competitive" exports by keeping labor cheap and attracting foreign investments. The wage and living conditions of the workers are pressed down and a huge reserve army of labor is maintained. And yet 75 percent of the global flow of foreign direct investments is concentrated in the United States, Japan and the European Union and only 25 percent is in countries where superprofits can be drawn due to cheap labor and lower levels of economic development.

The APEC is one more device for imposing imperialist policies on the Philippines and the other neocolonial states. It tries to promote and accelerate trade and investment liberalization already gained bilaterally and through the multilateral agencies like the IMF, World Bank and WTO. The most interesting events in the APEC leaders' summit are not the individual action plans of the neocolonial puppets, which are obsequious to both the US and Japan, but the expressions of these two countries about their competition and anti-people collusion and the US message to China on US preconditions to her entry into the WTO.

Under imperialist domination, the Philippines has no other way to go but deeper into semicolonial and semifeudal status, weighed down by foreign and local debt, foreign trade deficits, budgetary waste of the proceeds of privatization, and heavier taxation on the people to countervail the reduction and elimination of tariff barriers.

No matter how high or low are the GDP growth rate and gross international reserves, it is far more important to consider the nature of the economy, the exploitation done by the foreign monopolies and the local reactionaries, the rising foreign trade deficit and real budgetary deficit (minus the window-dressing), the growing foreign and local public debt and the mounting flow of resources to the coercive apparatuses of the state and to bureaucratic corruption.

The raw-material exports of the Philippines have long been pressed down in the world market since the '70s and the low value-added products of export-oriented manufacturing are already in jeopardy in the global crisis of overproduction. The export of live human beings, which is actually the biggest earner of foreign exchange, is also tending to fall because of the global recessive trend and the growing restrictions imposed by foreign governments against migrant labor.

The objective conditions for the new-democratic revolution through protracted people's war are increasingly favorable in the Philippines. By intensifying the exploitation and oppression of the people of the Philippines and throughout the world, the US and other imperialists are generating the conditions for revolutionary resistance on an unprecedented global scale.

In analyzing, criticizing and condemning imperialist "globalization", your conference has the objective of helping to arouse, organize and mobilize the broad masses of the people. It is not to offer recommendations to the states in APEC as to how they can improve the methods of imperialist exploitation and avert revolutionary resistance.

The main targets of your conference are the imperialist states and the neocolonial puppet states, which altogether serve monopoly capitalism. I

Message of Solidarity to the People's Conference

presume that you condemn not only the anti-worker and anti-people agenda in the APEC leaders' summit but also the human rights violations and extraordinary costs inflicted on the Filipino people in order to prepare and stage this summit.

But you can also take a look at and condemn the special agents of monopoly capitalism who organize so-called alternative conferences which are dependent on funding from imperialist agencies and which pretend to criticize APEC within the limits of reformism but whose main objective is to seize the initiative from the national democratic movement.

The US-instigated low intensity conflict in the Philippines involves not only the most conspicuous forms of brutal actions but also psychological warfare. This involves the use not only of military and police thugs in mufti, special operations teams of the reactionary armed forces and religious fanatical cults but also certain foreign-funded "NGOs" operated by covert agents of US and Philippines intelligence agencies, together with Trotskyites, racketeers, revisionists, pseudo-socialists, bourgeois populists, pro-imperialist liberals and the jesuitical religio-sectarians.

I hope that your conference can draw up clearly the firm line of resistance against imperialist "globalization" and work out further cooperation through an international network of anti-imperialist forces. Of course, I also hope that the people's caravan from Manila to Subic and the nationwide protest actions of the people will be successful.

I wish you all the success in struggle now and in the future. Thank you.

Imperialism in Various Global Regions

Accelerated Destruction of Productive Forces
Message of Solidarity to the People's Conference against Imperialist Globalization
Vancouver, British Colombia, Canada
November 21, 1997

I wish to express my solidarity with all the participants in the People's Conference Against Imperialist Globalization: Continuing the Resistance, from November 21 to 25, as well as with those in the NO to APEC International Youth and Student Caucus on November 27.

I congratulate the NO! to APEC Coalition for its successful preparatory work and I wish the aforesaid conference and caucus the utmost success in continuing the resistance to APEC and the monstrosity that is imperialist globalization.

You hit the nail on the head when you speak of imperialist globalization. The monopoly capitalists, their political stooges in states and their reformist "civil society" apologists try to bamboozle people with the term "globalization" as if it were a brand-new fact of life that one cannot do anything about, except to adjust to it or at best plead to the monopoly capitalists and their states to reform and improve themselves.

Retrogressive meaning of "globalization"

"Globalization" is a term to which the imperialists and their camp followers attach a retrogressive meaning, denoting the hoary dogma of "free trade" and the entire antipeople train of liberalization, deregulation and privatization. The neoclassical and neoliberal terminology of free competition capitalism simply does not apply to the reality of monopoly capitalism and neocolonialism.

We are still very much in the era of imperialism and proletarian revolution, especially because of the betrayal of socialism in the Soviet Union since 1956 and in China since 1976 and the persistent predominance of monopoly capitalism. The higher technology that is now available and that further compresses the globe has a higher social character than the earlier electro-mechanical technology and is far more suitable to socialism than before. But unfortunately, the capitalist social relations and the private methods of appropriating the product of labor have become even more avaricious and antisocial.

As the imperialists use the term, globalization means a policy shift from Keynesian or social-democratic methods to neoliberal methods, or rather to the use of neoliberal jargon to rationalize the unmitigated greed of the monopoly capitalists. It is meant to disparage the idea and experience of state intervention for social welfare, economic development and coping with the crisis even within the world capitalist system and, most of all, to counter the cause of socialism.

The neoliberal bias disdains fiscal measures and favors the use of monetary measures in running the economy and letting the monopoly capitalists have the utmost free play in the market. At any rate, the monopoly capitalists still use both fiscal and monetary measures to aggrandize the monopoly capitalists.

It is untrue that there is a growing separation between the multinational corporations and banks on the one hand and the states on the other hand. States have always been the instrument of the ruling class, now the monopoly bourgeoisie. It is also untrue that multinational firms and banks have no national basing. National stockholders own and control each of them, even as their predatory operations are borderless.

The 18 chiefs of state in the APEC Summit are subdivisible into the representatives of a few imperialist states and the more numerous client-states. They are all servants of monopoly capitalism. Under the neoliberal policy shift, pushed vigorously by Reaganism and Thatcherism since the 1980's, these states shamelessly abandon social pretenses, accelerate the delivery of public resources to the monopoly capitalists and push corporate welfare at the expense of social welfare in the very centers of global capitalism and prevent economic development in the neocolonial hinterlands.

For a long time, until the 1970s, the traditional imperialists had to adopt the fiscal measures of state intervention in order to cope with the crisis of overproduction during the Great Depression, to run war economies in the course of World War II, to combat socialism and national liberation movements in the aftermath of World War II and subjugate Soviet monopoly bureaucrat capitalism in the Cold War.

Destructive character of "globalization"

In comparison, the neoliberal policy-shift is proving to be far more destructive to the forces of production and far more shortlived. In the last ten years, from 1987 to 1997, we have witnessed a series of worsening crises, the stock market crash of 1987, the debt crisis and hyperinflation in Latin America in the late 1980s, the Mexican peso collapse and the current economic and financial turmoil. Also within the last decade, the growth rate of all the OECD countries have fluctuated between 1 and 3 percent, despite the extremely speculative overvaluation of assets and the more than 30 times overvaluation of the real value of world output.

The national profit rates in the three global centers of capitalism, the United States, Japan and the European Union have drastically fallen. Winning monopoly firms maximize profits by putting in more capital into new technology

Accelerated Destruction of Productive Forces

and by downsizing their labor force, generating mass unemployment and increasingly utilizing untenured and part-time labor under the so-called flexible labor policy in both imperialist and client states.

The United States has relatively the strongest economy among the imperialist powers because it uses its technology lead and its politico-military strength and attracts funds into its stock and bond markets from the weaker and more stagnant imperialist economies. It benefits most from the investment and trade liberalization that it is pushing most vigorously under the WTO and through trade blocs like APEC and NAFTA.

However, the accumulated costs of the Cold War and imperialist preeminence as well as the decline of its client economies reduce and adversely affect the growth of the US economy. The United States is still suffering from a huge debt burden and trade deficits, even as its export drive has undercut Japan and the European Union and such old tigers as South Korea and Taiwan.

Since its economic bubble burst in 1990, Japan has continued to languish in economic decline, despite its exceptionally heavy deficit-spending on public works, shifting plants abroad, export of supplies for export-oriented manufacturing in East Asia, investments in US bonds and financing real estate speculation mainly through Honking banks. The European Union suffers from an official rate of unemployment at 12 percent and has adopted austerity measures.

Seventy to 75 percent value-added by multinational corporations is still being produced in the imperialist countries. The process of concentration through mergers and acquisitions, assisted by bankruptcies, continues unabated. Only 100 MNC's or 0.3 percent of the total number own one-third (US$1.8 trillion) of the total of foreign direct investments.

Seventy percent of the total global flow of direct investment is concentrated in the three global centers of capitalism and some neighboring countries. In turn, 30 percent is concentrated in only some ten so-called emergent markets, with East Asia taking the lion's share. Up to the eve of the current economic and financial turmoil which conspicuously started in Southeast Asia last July, the imperialist finance companies and multinational firms put their funds into the so-called emergent markets in Southeast and Northeast Asia because they could get here the highest rates of profit in the world.

Surplus capital from the global centers of capitalism went into financing in the client states of East Asia budgetary and trade deficits, privatization of state assets, importation of luxury goods, supply of components for low value-added export-oriented manufacturing, sale of telecommunication equipment, real estate development and other speculative activities. If the most conspicuous construction under Keynesian economics was that of public roads and bridge, that under neoliberal economics has been that of office and residential towers and golf courses.

43

Of course, the overborrowing and overspending by the "emergent markets" must come to a dismal end. Now, there is gross overproduction in low value-added, labor-intensive export-oriented manufacturing. The oversupply of garments surfaced in 1994, followed by that of consumer electronics in 1996. The old tigers also find their higher value-added products squeezed by the US export drive and the continuing decline of the Japanese economy.

The debt problem of Southeast Asia has gone from bad to worse at an accelerated rate. The causes have also gone from bad to worse. Whereas up to the late '70s the debt problem involved heavy borrowing and spending for infrastructure and expansion of raw-material production, it has now involved frenzied use of private speculative capital from abroad to sustain upper class consumption, real estate speculation and other antipeople and antidevelopment activities.

Obscurantism in the APEC

The current economic and financial turmoil now shaking the entire world capitalist system is inevitably the focus of discussion in the APEC summit. The summiteers are bound to expose themselves as obscurantists when they gloss over the rotten fundamentals of the world capitalist system, especially because of the neoliberal policy-shift, push further for trade and investment liberalization under the WTO and promote the entire range of prescriptions in the Multilateral Agreement on Investments from the OECD.

There is massive capital flight from the "emergent markets" in East Asia. Austerity measures are certain to be applied on them. They are being required to accept new conditionalities from the IMF in exchange for bail-out funds, now running at more than US$80 billion for a number of East Asian countries. The deterioration of economic conditions in the client-states in the Asia-Pacific region means further shrinkage of the market and a dwindling source of superprofits for the United States, Japan and the European Union.

The crisis of the world capitalist system is certain to worsen, pushing the imperialist powers to redivide the world because of the shrinking market and reduction of superprofits. The client states are also driven to compete with each other in producing goods for export and in pushing down wage and living conditions and producing goods for export.

Volatility in the world capitalist system is induced by a large bloat of speculative capital, including the daily flows of more than US$1.2 trillion through foreign exchange markets and US$55 trillion traded in the derivatives market. In the stock markets, the multinational corporations buy back their own stocks or engage in cross sales of stocks with their sister companies to conjure the illusion of recovery. But in real terms, they are losing markets and profits and have to reduce production.

All the while, the overwhelming majority of third world countries, which have been brought down economically by the global overproduction of raw materials

Accelerated Destruction of Productive Forces

since the late '70s continue to sink in further underdevelopment, poverty and civil strife. Foreign exploitative capital have gone only in trickles into these countries, in contrast to the large amount poured into East Asia since the late 80's. At any rate, they continue to be crushed by the debt burden and ever deteriorating terms of trade for their raw-material exports.

The former Soviet bloc countries have been plunged into third world conditions. The most rapid destruction of productive forces is demonstrated by Russia, where production has gone down by more than 40 percent since 1991. Surplus goods from the West rather than productive capital have been dumped on Russia, which now is more than ever dependent on the export of oil and other raw materials. In the former Soviet satellite countries, production has gone down in the range of 16 to 30 percent.

Capitalist crisis and proletarian revolution

The imperialist countries are themselves reeling from the crisis of their system and the class struggle between the monopoly bourgeoisie and the proletariat is coming to the surface. The old tigers and all the later "emergent markets" are in serious economic trouble fraught with social and political unrest. In Southeast Asia, the Filipino people are demonstrating to neighboring peoples that protracted people's war is possible and necessary. China which has gotten the lion's share of speculative capital for "emergent markets" has compradorized and made its economy lopsided, is now in economic decline and is vulnerable to renewed social turbulence.

In general, the third world countries and former Soviet-bloc countries are sinking deeper into lower levels of poverty and misery and discontent. The people in these countries suffer stagnation and destruction of productive forces and the worst forms of oppression and exploitation. They are weighed down by the global unemployment of more than one billion people and a debt burden of more than US$2 trillion. They have no way out but to wage revolutionary struggle.

Conditions in the world capitalist system are now comparable to those during the Great Depression and even worse in several respects. The stage is set for far worse capitalist crisis and interimperialist war as well as for proletarian revolution and national liberation movements in the 21st century. I am confident that in the revolutionary struggles of the proletariat and the people in the forthcoming century, the cause of national liberation, democracy and socialism will win victories greater than those in the 20th century.

I express my admiration for the organizers and participants of the People's Conference Against Imperialist Globalization for carrying on the criticism and repudiation of monopoly capitalism, the imperialist and client states and the reformists who use the slogan of "civil society" to inveigh against revolutionary mass struggles and who wish to keep the people within the confines of the capitalist system and neocolonialism. You help to light the way towards a new and higher level of revolutionary anti-imperialist struggle for national liberation, democracy and socialism.

Once more, I congratulate you. I hope that your conference will inspire more people to continue the struggle against imperialism. Thank you.

Fight Imperialist Globalization and Wars
Auditorium P. E. Jansen, Universite Libre de Bruxelles
Brussels, Belgium
December 15, 2001

Fellow activists and friends, from the people's organizations in the Philippines and from the International League of Peoples' Struggle, I convey to all of you militant greetings of solidarity!

I am glad to be in Brussels to witness and to be among the workers, youth, women and other people engaged in mass actions from 13 December onward in order to uphold their democratic rights and demand a better world.

I am honored to speak at this international meeting of solidarity with the people who struggle for justice and peace, against imperialist globalization and imperialist wars of aggression.

In accordance with my assignment, let me focus on the suffering, struggles and aspirations of the people of the third world.

The people of the third world constitute the overwhelming majority of the people of the world. They suffer the most acute forms of oppression and exploitation inflicted by the imperialists and the local reactionaries. They provide the cheap labor and the cheap raw materials, they absorb the surplus goods and the surplus capital and thereby yield superprofits to the imperialists.

By using the catchphrase "free market" globalization, the imperialists have accelerated their profit-taking from the third world and have devastated their economies. The multinational firms have used liberalization, privatization and deregulation to plunder human and natural resources and have placed the people under the crushing weight of the current global recession.

The people suffer impoverishment, mass unemployment, falling incomes, rising prices of basic goods, lack of such basic social services as medical care, education and housing, the degradation of women and the destruction of the environment. They are made to shoulder the costs of the bankruptcies, the budgetary and trade deficits, the foreign debt and devaluation of the currency. The economic ills kill people in large numbers. This is the daily violence of exploitation.

The people resist the imperialists and local reactionaries at first spontaneously and then in a conscious and organized way. In reaction to the growing protests of the people, especially the workers and peasants, the puppet regimes are escalating repression and their imperialist masters, especially the US, are unleashing wars of aggression as in Iraq, the former Yugoslavia and Afghanistan.

Imperialism in Various Global Regions

The US, European and Japanese imperialists are grandscale terrorists. They have committed monstrous acts of terror in the course of their interimperialist global wars and wars of aggression. Yet they have the gall to call the people waging revolution, the nations fighting for liberation and the countries asserting national independence as terrorists. They have gone so far as to witchhunt and repress their own nationals and immigrants by arbitrarily calling them terrorists.

As one who comes form the Philippines and Asia, I am keenly aware of the fact that the biggest terrorist in the entire history of mankind is US imperialism. It has been responsible for massacring and causing the death of millions of people in a long series of aggressive wars and campaigns of open terror, especially in Asia.

The US conquest of the Philippines involved the genocidal killing of 700,000 or one-tenth of the Filipino people at the beginning of the 20th century. Then, there were the massacres of millions in the wars of aggression against the Korean and the Vietnamese peoples. Remember all these as you look at how the imperialists are now murdering the people in Palestine and Afghanistan.

The people of the third world are waging all forms of struggle against oppression and exploitation. They undertake protest mass actions and wage revolutionary armed struggles. In the country from where I come, the people wage both legal and armed forms of struggle.

Like other peoples of the third world, they aspire for national liberation, democracy, social justice, peace and all-round progress. These can be attained only by fighting and ending the domination of the imperialists and the local reactionaries.

The people of the third world and the people of industrial capitalist countries need to unite and fight against imperialism, their common enemy. The revolutionary strength of the people in one part of the world redounds to the benefit of those in other parts of the world. All the people of the world aspire and strive for a world that is free, progressive, just and peaceful.

We are confident that we shall have a better future because the people are rising up as the imperialists and their agents escalate oppression and exploitation. The reign of greed and terror is what precisely incites the people to defend themselves and fight for a better world.

The general direction is for the mass struggles within countries, global regions and the world as a whole to reach higher levels of consciousness, militancy and revolutionary achievement. To carry forward such general direction, the International League for Peoples' Struggle has been founded this year.

I take this opportunity to invite your mass organizations to join the International League for Peoples' Struggle (ILPS), which is a broad democratic alliance. At the minimum, the ILPS seeks to cooperate with your organizations in acting on all major concerns of the people of the world.

Fight Imperialist Globalization and Wars

Let us all march together for a just peace and a better world against imperialist globalization and wars.

No Euro for war!

Stop the war of the rich versus the poor!

US and Europe out of Afghanistan!

NATO No, Euro Army No!

Solidarity with the Palestinian people!

Imperialism in Various Global Regions

On US Intervention in the Philippines and Korea
Keynote Speech at the Forum on US Intervention in the Philippines and Korea, An Evening of Resistance Broadcast by WBAI/Pacifica, New York City, July 16, 2003

First of all, let me thank all the organizers for inviting me to keynote this forum on US intervention in the Philippines and Asia. I feel greatly honored and deeply pleased to be among speakers who are knowledgeable about the subject, to speak before anti-imperialist activists, and to reach a great number of people through the electronic multi-media and further political work.

I admire and salute all the Korean and Filipino organizations for working together to expose and oppose US intervention and related evil acts in their respective countries. I also appreciate the relations of solidarity and cooperation that these organizations have developed with organizations of the American people and other peoples in the course of common struggle against imperialist plunder and war.

In the face of the worsening crisis of the US and world capitalist system, we can expect that the No. 1 imperialist power, which is at the same time the No. 1 terrorist force, will escalate the exploitation and oppression of the people of the world, and will generate all such monstrosities as chauvinism, racism, the violation of women's rights, fascism and wars of aggression.

The US has used 9-11 as the pretext for internationalizing the fascist provisions of the Patriot Act, for unleashing wars of aggression, for using weapons of mass destruction against the civilian population and social infrastructure, and for misrepresenting and demonizing as "terrorist" national liberation movements, countries assertive of national independence and leaders who take an anti-imperialist stand.

The Bush ruling clique is hell-bent on delivering tax cuts, public funds, contracts and subsidies to the monopoly bourgeoisie. It is pushing low-employment war production as the supposed stimulus to the crisis-stricken American economy. It is whipping up war hysteria and actually carrying out wars of aggression. These wars are aimed at seizing the sources of cheap labor and natural resources (especially oil), markets and fields of investment.

The dream of the "neoconservatives" around Bush is to build further an incomparable empire, a Pax Americana of unprecedented scale, by maximizing the use of the sole superpower position of the US and, of course, its high-tech weapons of mass destruction and mass distraction. A number of states is lined up as targets for aggression, intervention, blockade and pressure, in order to make them yield to the global hegemony of the US.

The US has used its war of aggression against Afghanistan to entrench itself further in Central Asia and ensure that the sources of oil and oil supply routes are under its control. It has used its second war of aggression against Iraq to gain direct control over the second largest oil reserves in the world and in effect over the OPEC and over global oil production, and to further subordinate the whole of the Middle East to the US-Israeli combination.

All the time that it has been carrying out its wars of aggression against Afghanistan and then Iraq, the US has been deploying US combat troops in the Philippines under the pretext of antiterrorism, and hurling threats against the Democratic People's Republic of Korea under the pretext of pushing non-proliferation of nuclear weapons. The hostile acts of the US against the Filipino and Korean peoples are interrelated. They have something to do with pushing US hegemony over the whole of East Asia.

Let me focus first on the US military intervention in the Philippines. The US is using its so-called war on terrorism in order to bring in military advisors, trainors and combat troops in violation of the 1987 constitution of the Manila government; to develop interoperability with the Filipino mercenary puppet troops; to elaborate on US military access rights through a logistical support agreement; to expand the facilities for the US air and naval forces; and to prepare the ground for the return of US military basing rights.

US strategists see the Philippines as the center of an arc, with one wing consisting of more developed countries in Northeast Asia (Japan, South Korea, North Korea and China) and another wing consisting of the underdeveloped but natural resource-rich countries in Southeast Asia. The US gives high priority to preparations for establishing US air and naval bases in Central and Far South Mindanao, and thereby acquiring a control point over the oil-producing and predominantly Muslim countries of Southeast Asia.

The US considers the Philippines as its most reliable vantage point because this is the country in Asia that it dominates the most – economically, politically and culturally. It is also the best located vantage point for the whole of East Asia. US military bases can oversee from here the movement of more than half of the global trade through the South China Sea.

The new shift in US military strategic thinking affects the Philippines and the rest of East Asia. The US is eager to establish small US military bases and outposts wherever possible, under the concept of forward deployment, which veers away from the previous concept of rapid deployment. The advance deployment of US forces on the ground are seen as effective facilitation of any subsequent deployment of large US military forces from their secure US bases at any time.

US military access and basing rights in the Philippines are considered of crucial importance. Through these the US can pose a serious military threat to China and the DPRK. A US military position of strength in the Philippines gains even more importance as the US moves towards the relative reduction

On US Intervention in the Philippines and Korea

of US military forces in Japan due to the rising clamor of the Japanese people for the dismantling of US military bases, and as it is also trying to redress the vulnerability of US military bases around Seoul and near the 38th parallel in Korea.

In keeping with its doctrine of preemptive strike (based either on accurate or Bush-style falsified intelligence) and with its cowardly style of raining missiles and bombs upon people and buildings from a great distance, the US has already announced plans of reshaping its military force deployment in East Asia in such a manner as to make the Philippines the main frontline against China and the DPRK, and Australia the main rear for US military forces.

It must be observed that the US is trying to persuade the DPRK to come to terms with US policy by using diplomacy with the participation of China. It is highly probable that the US is now using the subtle language of diplomacy to boast of having tightened its control over oil and having the ability to block the oil supply to the DPRK and even China. The US is already heard loudly proclaiming that it can move back its troops from the range of any DPRK military action, and that it can attack the DPRK from a distance with cruise missiles with nuclear warheads.

In the imperialist mode of thinking, especially that of Bush and his retinue of neoconservatives, high-tech weaponry can ultimately solve any problem that economic, financial and diplomatic manipulation cannot. But has high-tech weaponry solved the problem for the US in Afghanistan and Iraq? It was effective only for destroying fixed structures and pushing aside the incumbent government. The Taliban and Al Qaida are back in control of more than 40 percent of Afghanistan by waging guerrilla warfare.

And in Iraq, the anti-imperialist forces are also waging guerrilla warfare and are inflicting more and more casualties on the US occupation forces. But Bush and other high US officials are violently against bringing the US troops home. They have made clear that they will keep US troops in Iraq for a long while. The name of their game is occupation.

They cannot leave behind the oil fields and oil reserves, all the business projects of the US monopoly firms and the military bases for controlling the entire Middle East. The greed and arrogance of the Bush regime and US monopoly firms are placing the US in a quagmire reminiscent of Vietnam.

Are there ways for the Korean and Filipino peoples to frustrate US military intervention and related evil actions? Yes, of course.

The entire Korean people of both north and south can unite against US imperialism, against US military bases and US nuclear weapons in the south, and against the economic embargo and military threats of the US against the DPRK. It is fine that the DPRK is standing up firmly for national independence, peaceful reunification and socialist aspirations, and is ready to fight courageously with the omnipotence of the people and with some powerful weapons. The US cannot successfully launch a blitzkrieg against the DPRK with impunity, without grave consequences to the US and its most rabid followers, and without offending the Chinese and other peoples of the world.

The Filipino people can unite and raise the level of their revolutionary consciousness and fighting capabilities. In the face of the US and the Manila puppet government, the people are fortunate to have the Communist Party of the Philippines, the New People's Army, the National Democratic Front of the Philippines, the organs of democratic power and the mass organizations as the solid forces in the struggle for national liberation and democracy. The current form of people's war in the Philippines is extensive and intensive guerrilla warfare on the basis of an ever widening and deepening mass base. The hightech weaponry of the US is impotent against such popular resistance.

The Korean and Filipino peoples enjoy abundant support from all anti-imperialist and democratic forces and people of the world. The broad anti-imperialist solidarity is developing vigorously on a global scale. It is inspiring the people of the world to intensify their resistance for national and social liberation against imperialism and all reaction. The world disorder of today is the prelude to a new wave of social revolutions.

Thank you.

On Revolutionary Struggles in Imperialist and Oppressed Countries
Interview by David Hungerford
Utrecht, The Netherlands, December 25, 2003

Question: When you work in imperialist countries in support of revolutionary movements in oppressed countries, what are the specifically communist tasks?

Jose Maria Sison (JMS): Persevere in carrying out the ideological, political and organizational tasks for developing the revolutionary movement in the imperialist countries and for supporting the revolutionary movements in oppressed countries. You must have a home base for supporting the struggles of the people abroad.

The ideological tasks involve the propagation and application of Marxism-Leninism. Thus, you develop the proletarian vanguard and hardcore of the revolutionary movement. The political tasks involve arousing, organizing and mobilizing the proletarian, the semi-proletarian and petty bourgeois masses. Thus, you have the strength of the masses to win the battle for democracy, overthrow the monopoly bourgeoisie and establish socialism. The organizational tasks involve upholding democratic centralism and expanding the ranks of communists by drawing the most advanced from the mass movement.

Question: Could you explain further the relationship of revolutionary struggles in both imperialist and oppressed countries?

JMS: The revolutionary struggles in imperialist countries and those in oppressed countries interact and support each other. They have a common enemy in imperialism and reaction. Revolutionary work must be done in both imperialist and oppressed countries. The working class exists in every country and should take the lead in the revolutionary movement for the best possible revolutionary outcome in the era of imperialism and proletarian revolution. There must be proletarian internationalism among communist and workers parties, and revolutionary solidarity among the peoples.

Question: What is the main contradiction in the world today?

JMS: It is valid to say that the struggle between the people of the world and imperialism is the main contradiction. But we can make a more penetrating distinction of contradictions in the world. There is the contradiction between the imperialist powers and the oppressed peoples and nations. There is the contradiction among the imperialists. And there is the contradiction between the monopoly bourgeoisie and the proletariat within imperialist countries.

The contradiction between the imperialist countries and the oppressed peoples and nations is the main contradiction today. It is the most intense in terms of oppression and exploitation, and in terms of counterrevolutionary violence being unleashed, either one-sidedly or opposed by revolutionary violence.

Question: Does the focus of armed revolution change in terms of location?

JMS: Yes. In the early years of the 20th century, Lenin observed that after the bourgeois democratic revolutions in Western Europe, armed revolutions had shifted from the West to the East. The focus can change from continent to continent and from country to country. Lenin pointed out that if the revolutionary movement in oppressed countries develops, it helps the struggle in the imperialist countries.

Revolutionary struggle in the oppressed countries can help bring about the best conditions for armed revolution in the West. However, inter-imperialist wars have also given the workers in the West the opportunity to rise up. Mao was very confident that revolutions in the East would develop and help revolutions in the West. But revisionism has sabotaged the world proletarian revolution and caused big setbacks.

Question: What is the revolutionary role of the peasantry in the East?

JMS: The peasantry is the most numerous class in the predominantly agrarian East. It is a class that cries out for the democratic revolution to solve the land problem. The proletariat and its revolutionary party can and must bring about the worker-peasant alliance in order to win the bourgeois-democratic and socialist stages of the revolution. Stalin spoke of the peasantry as the reserve of the proletariat. Mao went further. He spoke of the peasantry as the main force, actively following the working class as the leading force.

Question: You once said in a forum that the revisionists opposed Mao's line of people's war but Reagan would use a kind of "people's war in reverse?" What do you mean?

JMS: The Soviet and other revisionists worshiped the high-tech military power of the Soviet Union. But Reagan had a strategy of people's war in reverse: the use of mass-based reactionary forces against the targets of imperialism. In Afghanistan, the mujaheddins had a religious kind of mass base against the Soviet occupation. In Angola, the UNITA had a tribal kind of mass base against the Soviet-supported government. There were the Contras in Nicaragua, who used a kind of religious and anti-communist mass base against the Sandinistas.

In every revolutionary situation, the US tries to form some kind of a reactionary mass base against the revolutionary mass base. In the Philippines, the US and the local reactionaries periodically use the elections in trying to draw the masses away from revolution. In the countryside they also field psywar experts in order to form anti-communist communities based on tribalism and religious cultism. Ahead of Reagan, Kennedy had the idea to use counter-

On Revolutionary Struggles in Imperialist and Oppressed Countries

guerrilla tactics by mimicking the revolutionary guerrillas. He tried to use the tribes in the central highlands in Vietnam against the Communists. But the big US defeat came anyway. Thus, the role of Kennedy as a pioneer in counterguerrilla tactics has been obscured.

Question: What is the status of people's war in the East right now?

JMS: At the moment, there are not too many people's wars led by Marxism-Leninism-Maoism. These are in India, Nepal, Peru, Philippines and Turkey. But they are very weighty in relation to what communist and workers' parties are doing in the West. These people's wars are directly answering the central question of revolution by seizing political power wave upon wave in the rural areas. People's war can and must be the effective counter to the wars of aggression, high-tech weapons of mass destruction, and the possibility of nuclear war.

Question: What is the role of the people of imperialist countries in relation to wars and the possible use of nuclear weapons?

JMS: The people of the imperialist countries, led by the proletariat, have a special mission of preventing the imperialists from waging wars and using nuclear weapons. When the people have sufficient organized strength, they can surround, weaken, isolate, and remove from power those officials who wish to launch wars of aggression and use nuclear weapons. Stockpiles of nuclear weapons were useless when the revisionist regimes were disintegrating. At the moment, there are no big nuclear powers blatantly threatening each other. But the Bush regime is planning to miniaturize nuclear weapons to make them more useable.

Question: After 9/11 the US has benefited much from further penetrating Central Asia. Is there any counter from Russia and China?

JMS: Indeed, the US has benefited much from intrusions in Central Asia. It is trying to outflank both China and Russia. These seem to be allowing the US to do what it wants. But in fact they take steps to prevent one-sided penetration. The Shanghai Cooperative Organization was originally an agreement to stabilize the borders of five countries: Russia, China, Kyrgyzstan, Uzbekistan and Tajikistan. But they are now undertaking joint military exercises under the guise of "relief and rescue operations". Russia and China are also setting up some military outposts in their Central Asian neighbors in connection with said exercises.

Question: To return to the question, how may revolutionaries in imperialist countries develop in connection with revolutionary struggles in oppressed countries?

JMS: When the imperialists engage in wars of aggression in the East, the revolutionaries and people in the West can rise up against such wars. They can condemn these wars as detrimental to the people at home and abroad. The solidarity and support that they extend to the revolutions in the East are ultimately useful and beneficial to the entire people of the world. But the revolutionary party of the proletariat must grow from within the imperialist country. It must lead, build and correlate with the mass movement. A small party can actually lead the mass movement and grow in stages. Such a party grows faster as the crisis worsens and the mass movement expands.

Go into the trade unions and communities. Lead the struggles there and recruit members into the revolutionary party. You can start with a few, go through a slow process of developing Party cadres and members through study and mass work. In a big crisis you can attract many people to the mass movement. From this you can draw more Party members than when the mass movement was nonexistent.

The Philippine Communist Party started with a few members. To increase, we required each of five members in a Party group to recruit five candidate members. It was five times larger every six months. In a short period of time, we became scores. When it was time to break away from the old party, which had degenerated into a revisionist party, the proletarian revolutionaries outnumbered the revisionists. Clarity of line is the first thing, and work among the masses follows quickly.

War, Imperialism and Resistance from Below
April 24, 2004

Dear colleagues, good afternoon!

Let me thank the Global Studies Association for inviting me to speak on the occasion of its Third Annual Conference. It is an honor to speak before a distinguished assembly of scholars.

For someone like me who is banned from entering the US, it is gratifying to be able to speak on an occasion like this.

I. The phenomenon of war as concomitant of imperialism

Let me speak first on the relationship of modern imperialism and war.

Free competition capitalism reached the apex of its development in several industrial capitalist countries from 1860 to 1870. At the end of the 19th century, monopoly capitalism or modern imperialism became dominant in the leading industrial capitalist countries.

Industrial capital had merged with bank capital to form the finance oligarchy. The export of surplus capital began to gain importance over the export of surplus goods. The imperialist countries and their monopoly firms formed international combinations (such as cartels, syndicates, trusts and so on) against the people and against each other.

Beyond the imperialist and colonial countries, the economic hinterland of the world was divided into colonies, semicolonies and dependent countries. These were coveted by the imperialist powers as markets, sources of cheap raw materials, fields of investment and spheres of influence.

After the frenzied acquisition of colonies by the chief European states in the years 1884-1900, the division of the world among imperialist and colonial powers became complete. No country could be found outside the clutches of modern imperialism and old style colonialism.

The manufacturing surpluses and the ensuing crisis of overproduction in imperialist countries impelled them to compete bitterly with each other, expand economic territory, and come into violent collisions that culminated in wars. Chauvinist calls and war hysteria became convenient for drawing away the consciousness of the working class, particularly the unemployed, from class struggle against the monopoly bourgeoisie.

Imperialism as the highest stage of capitalism in America and Europe, and later in Asia, became conspicuous through wars and the economic crisis in the period 1898-1914. The Spanish-American War (1898), the Anglo-Boer War (1899-1902), the Russo-Japanese War (1904-05), and the economic crisis of 1900 in Europe were the signal events in the appearance of modern imperialism on the stage of world history.

The competing protectionist drives of the imperialist powers prevailed over the pretenses at free trade. The crisis of overproduction sharpened the political and economic conflicts within each imperialist state and among the imperialist powers, and led to the first global interimperialist war from 1914 to 1918. However, these also provided the conditions for the rise of the first socialist country and encouraged the anticolonial struggles of the people in many countries.

After an alternation of crisis and boom in the aftermath of World War I, the Great Depression came upon the world capitalist system after the Crash of 1929. It was a prolonged crisis of overproduction and financial collapse. It exacerbated the contradictions among the imperialist powers and caused the second interimperialist war to break out. World War II was even more destructive than World War I. But it also resulted in the rise of several more socialist countries and a great wave of national liberation movements.

In 1948, the US launched the Cold War in order to contain and combat the challenge of socialism and the national liberation movements, and to counter the tendency of the US economy to slide into a crisis of overproduction. The Cold War was actually a series of hot localized wars. These included the big US wars of aggression in Korea and Indochina, the US-supported Israeli wars on Palestine, and the anti-Soviet wars in Angola, Ethiopia, Nicaragua and Afghanistan.

During the Cold War, the US instigated the overthrow of independent governments and propped up repressive puppet regimes, which unceremoniously killed people in great numbers. The massacre of at least 1.5 million Indonesians was a major campaign of repression intended to secure US, British and Dutch oil interests, and countervail the losing position of the US in Indochina. The death toll as a consequence of the daily violence of exploitation and the intolerable burden of foreign debt should also be taken into account in a complete reckoning.

The US could not solve the problem of stagflation within the framework of Keynesianism for several reasons. It served the interests of the military-industrial complex and thus obscured the cost-push effect and limited job growth in high military spending, especially for high-tech weaponry and space research and development. It wanted to wreak vengeance on the working class and pointed to wage inflation and state social spending as the cause of stagflation. Thus, the neoliberals and monetarists of the Chicago School went to town to replace the Keynesians.

Running parallel to the economic decline of the US, the phenomenon of modern revisionism and monopoly bureaucrat capitalism was undermining and degrading the socialist-labeled countries and pushing them towards open and unabashed adoption of capitalism. Afflicted by its own stagnation, corruption and military overspending, the Soviet Union was outplayed by the US in the contest of neocolonialism for hegemony over the newly-independent countries.

II. Imperialism: neoliberalism and neoconservatism

In the period of 1989-91, all the revisionist-ruled and pseudosocialist countries were in turmoil. The big bourgeoisie proceeded to legalize all previous ill-gotten private assets, and accelerated the open privatization of the most important and largest public assets. The Soviet Union collapsed. The bipolar world of the Cold War ended. The US emerged as the sole superpower.

There was the widespread notion that the end of the Cold War would result in "peace dividends" for humanity, especially in terms of more funds for poverty alleviation and socioeconomic development. But subsequent developments showed that the US became more rapacious and aggressive. The consensus in Washington to this day is to let the phoney free market of monopoly capitalism solve the problems of the world, and to let high-tech weaponry take out any "rogue state" or unwieldy client regime.

The disintegration of the Warsaw Pact provided the opportunity for the US and NATO to expand to Eastern Europe and to some former Soviet republics. The US and NATO were able to wage wars on Iraq and the former Yugoslavia. The US strengthened its position in the Middle East and built positions of strength on the southern flanks of Russia. Further, the US gained foothold in the Caucasus, Caspian sea region and Central Asia, all regions related to the overweening desire of the US to control the sources and routes of energy supply.

After the collapse of the Soviet Union, it became fashionable for some bourgeois propagandists to proclaim the end of history with capitalism and liberal democracy. In fact, the crisis of the world capitalist system was conspicuously worsening in the 1989-1991 period, as manifested by the bursting of the Japanese bubble economy, the stagnation of the German economy, and of course by the devastation of the economies of the former Soviet bloc countries and the third world countries.

The crisis of overproduction and financial collapses persisted in the world capitalist system throughout the 1990s. The US economy could shine only at the expense of its imperialist allies and the newly-industrializing economies. It continued to attract heavy doses of funds from abroad, especially from Europe, Japan and the oil-producing countries, due to high US interest rates and favorable rates of return on capital. It took the lead in the commercialization of high technology. It kept the US consumer market as "the market of last resort" of the entire world.

The moment of truth came for the US and entire world capitalist system in 2000. The high-tech bubble burst due to the global crisis of overproduction in high-tech goods. US industrial production plummeted. The financial meltdowns spread to the stock market and to the banks in the US and throughout the world. Until now, both the US and global economy are in a protracted state of stagnation and decline. Bankruptcies, production cutbacks and high unemployment rates continue to constrict the global market.

Neoliberalism has proven to be a futile policy for fixing the problems of the world capitalist economy. It has accelerated the concentration and centralization of capital in the imperialist countries, chiefly the US. And it has whipped up financial speculation far beyond the real economy in the imperialist countries and in so-called emerging markets or transition economies. Financial collapses have been terribly devastating.

In connection with the invasion and occupation of Iraq and other aggressive actions elsewhere, neo-conservativism as a policy direction in Washington has gained global notoriety. It projects a new American century, in which the US as sole superpower develops full-spectrum power, uses this to impose a Pax Americana on the world and launches preemptive wars in order to take out recalcitrant regimes and prevent any power from being able to rival and challenge the US.

The 9/11 attacks have given the so-called neoconservatives the pretext for claiming to wage a permanent war on terrorism and for seeking to deprive opponents of the US weapons of mass destruction. Indeed, the US went to war against Iraq in violation of the UN charter and UN Security Council resolutions by dishing out lies that Iraq had conspiratorial links with Al Qaeda and had weapons of mass destruction.

The real motives of the Bush regime and the so-called neoconservatives are to take over the second largest oil resources of the world in Iraq, keep secure the US dollar as the currency of oil transactions, increase US control over Saudi Arabia and the Organization of Petroleum Exporting Countries (OPEC), use US military bases in centrally located Iraq to control the entire Middle East, and remove Iraq as a threat to the US-Israeli collaboration.

Neoconservativism is apparently the unabashedly violent complement of neoliberalism. It adds the force of war to the myth of "free market" under modern imperialism. Both neoliberalism and neoconservatism are intended to expand US economic territory and to make the pretense at building a market economy and democracy.

III. Resistance from below

Let me speak of the anti-imperialist resistance from below.

We may count as forces of resistance from below those non-imperialist states that stand up to defend their national independence against imperialism.

War, Imperialism and Resistance from Below

In fact, the US has launched the most violent wars of aggression against such states, which have included Iraq, former Yugoslavia and Afghanistan in recent times. It has also emboldened and supported the Israeli Zionists to occupy Palestine and suppress the Palestinian resistance. As a consequence, we see the steady growth of armed and other forms of resistance in countries directly or indirectly attacked by the US.

During the first quarter of 2003, we saw the rising of millions of people in hundreds of cities all over the world. The biggest was on 15 February, when 30 million people rose up. The protest marches and rallies were reminiscent of those held at the peak of the people's resistance to the Vietnam war in the late 1960s and early 1970s.

The resurgence of mass protest actions against war and against imperialism in the imperialist countries reflects not only a high sense of solidarity of the people in such countries for other peoples but also the growing discontent over the crisis of the world capitalist system. The people are restive over high rates of unemployment, the reduction of social benefits, the deterioration of social services, and the highest priority given to corporate benefits and to military spending.

The Iraqi people are now waging a broad-based armed resistance of nationalists, communists, religious believers and various ethnic communities against the US occupation and the puppets, and are laying the basis for bigger protest actions in the US and in the world.

The American and other peoples of the world are now demanding the withdrawal of US troops and bases from Iraq. It is difficult for peaceful mass actions to compel the US to withdraw from Iraq. But as in the US war of aggression in Vietnam, the increasing US body bags from the Iraqi battlefield and the gigantic mass actions of the American and other peoples of the world can persuade the US to withdraw from Iraq.

Throughout the world, the broad masses of the people have been roused by the exploitative character of "free market" globalization and by the oppressive character of "the new world order". They detest and resist the ugly character and consequences of neoliberalism and neoconservatism. They are carrying out various forms of resistance, which are spreading and intensifying.

The most effective and most promising kind of resistance are the revolutionary armed struggles being carried out in such countries as the Philippines, Turkey, Nepal, India, Colombia and Iraq. There are also reemerging revolutionary forces of the oppressed nations and people that see the imperial overstretch of the US and are determined to wage armed revolution.

It is self-defeating for the US to have used cruise missiles and other weapons of mass destruction to take out regimes that are opposed to it, and also for it to have provocatively shown off its military strength in so many countries. Now, it has become clear that the US has nearly exhausted its deployable military forces by being absorbed in only Iraq and Afghanistan. It has also become

63

clear that high-tech weapons are ineffective against people's revolutionary forces that wage an armed resistance of fluid movement and offer no fixed targets to their enemy.

The resistance from below from the toiling masses of workers and peasants is the strongest, most inexhaustible and most important kind of resistance. The toiling masses are ever willing and eager to resist the most intolerable forms of oppression and exploitation, now surfacing under the current crisis conditions. The people's resistance is sustained and well-directed where there is a truly revolutionary party of the proletariat. The working class is still the principal agent for revolutionary change in the epochal struggle against imperialism.

So long as imperialism persists in oppressing and exploiting the people, the people's struggle for national liberation, democracy and socialism will continue. US imperialism and the local exploiting classes themselves create the crisis conditions which generate the people's resistance and pave the way for the revolutionary forces to arise. There is no stopping the wheels of history from moving, despite any curve, bumps or zigzags along the way.

Thank you.

Condemn Imperialism and the G8 Big Swindle, Demand Cancellation of All Neocolonial Debts
July 5, 2005

The G8 summit scheduled for July 6-8, 2005 in Scotland is being promoted by the big corporate media of the imperialist countries with much fanfare. The G8 promise of canceling debts of some US$40 billion for 18 Most Indebted Poor Countries (MIPC), upon the fulfillment of certain conditionalities, is being hailed as a "historic" deal and a "victory for millions."

The amount of debt promised to be canceled is a tiny fraction of the US$2.4 trillion total debt (2003 computation) of the "southern countries" or "third world countries" of Asia, Africa and Latin America. By merely making a promise of token debt cancellation, the imperialist creditors try to conceal their criminal responsibility for overloading the dominated countries with onerous anti-development loans, misrepresent themselves as charitable to the poorest countries which they in fact continue to squeeze and make acceptable the neocolonial system of exploiting the overwhelming majority of countries through international usury and "free trade".

It is misleading and in fact willfully criminal for the imperialists themselves and their camp followers to praise the G8 summiteers as being engaged in "debt relief" and "poverty reduction", as "making poverty history" and as providing charity to the MIPC for education, health, anti-AIDS campaign, disaster relief and infrastructure. For praising and praying to the G8 and seeking to deceive the people, the social democrats, the bourgeois liberals, the Trotskyites and NGO racketeers expose themselves as hired hacks of their imperialist masters.

False promises of G8 countries

G8 countries have repeatedly made false promises. But they have always failed to deliver even the little that they promise. In March 1999, Canada's Prime Minister, Jean Chrétien, said that Canada would act alone on debt relief if other G7 countries failed to respond to the needs of the severely indebted countries. US President Bill Clinton in September 1999 said that the United States would try to forgive all the debt that poor countries owed the US. Britain announced a plan in December 1999, to cancel 100 percent of the debt owed by 26 poor countries. None of these promises have been kept.

The latest G8 proposal is a big swindle because it carries with it conditionalities that prevent full availment of the debt cancellation. The character and scope of such conditionalities have precisely caused underdevelopment, poverty and further indebtedness in the countries the G8 are supposedly desirous of rescuing from poverty. These conditionalities include so-called measures against corruption and reforms that are designed to impose and apply neoliberal prescriptions of further investment and trade liberalization, privatization and deregulation. The client economies are further opened to foreign monopoly capital, which precisely causes underdevelopment, poverty, deficits and ceaseless local and foreign borrowing by the client state.

The G8 promise of debt cancellation being hyped by the big corporate media is calculated to make the monopoly capitalist countries look good while they lay the blame for poverty and misery on the people of the underdeveloped countries themselves. The culprits blame the victims for the crimes committed against them.

Many of the G8 countries have been responsible for the colonial rape of the countries of Africa, Asia and Latin America. They plundered the human and natural resources of these countries in their primitive accumulation of capital. Since direct colonial rule became largely a thing of the past, the former colonial powers (which had since industrialized using the wealth from colonial plunder) have continued the exploitation of these countries through neocolonialism using such subservient local stooges as the big compradors, landlords and bureaucrat capitalists who are given part of the spoils to perpetuate their control and dominance.

The G8 countries have a big responsibility for corruption in their client states. Aside from their historical role in creating the corrupt local ruling classes, the multinational firms and banks have been the sponsors and supporters of such corrupt politicians as Marcos, Mobutu and the rest of them for the behest loans and supply contracts that have thrust these countries into the vicious debt cycle. A large part of the borrowed money always ends up in the bank accounts of the puppet rulers, be these openly dictatorial or seemingly democratic. These puppets can "pay back" by taxing their people dry and begging for more loans at more onerous terms imposed by the G8 countries, the IMF and World Bank.

Foreign monopoly firms are efficient at corrupting the politicians in client states in order to capture juicy public works contracts and arms deals. The British government is even known to reward these firms by giving them tax breaks on these "commissions" paid abroad which are considered deductible expense.

In 1970, roughly 60 countries classified as low-income by the World Bank, owed US$25 billion in debt. By 2002, this was US$523 billion. Over the three decades from 1970 to 2002, US$550 billion has been paid in both principal and interest on US$540 billion of loans, and yet US$523 billion dollar debt burden remain.

66

The crushing debt burden of Africa

The following is a quote from the President of Nigeria: "All that we had borrowed up to 1985 or 1986 was around US$5 billion and we have paid about US$16 billion yet we are still being told that we owe about US$28 billion. That US$28 billion came about because of the injustice in the foreign creditors' interest rates."

The effects of the debt trap on the people of the third world are staggering. According to UNICEF data as many as five million children and vulnerable adults may have lost their lives in sub-Saharan Africa as a result of the debt burden since the late 1980s. Some 11 million children below five years old die each year around the world, not just Africa, due to similar conditions of poverty and debt.

The IMF and World Bank require poor countries to pay around 20 to 25 percent of their export earnings for debt repayment. Yet, no European country including Britain, France and Italy is repaying its loans at levels higher than 4 percent because they consider it unsustainable and bad for their economy.

Many of the proposals on debt relief coming from the imperialist countries and their instruments such as the G8, WEF and IMF and World Bank are a sham. The real solution is repudiation and cancellation of all the outstanding debts owed by third world countries. The reason is simple: these debts have been repaid many times over.

The "carrot" of debt cancellation is being dangled as a bargaining chip to wring more concessions on trade and investments. Debtor countries are told that they can only avail of debt cancellation if they institute neoliberal reforms such as trade and investment liberalization. These "reforms" have already wreaked havoc on the economies of these debtor countries.

In Senegal, tomato production used to provide peasant families with some kind of livelihood. After liberalization, the price for tomatoes was halved and tomato production fell from 73,000 tons in 1990 to only 20,000 in 1997 leaving many peasants without a cash crop. In Kenya, cotton production fell from 70,000 bales a year in the mid-1980s to less than 20,000 bales in the mid-1990s. Employment in textile factories fell from 120,000 people to 85,000.

Manufacturing industries have also been hit hard by trade liberalization. In Zambia, employment in manufacturing fell by 40 percent in just five years of trade liberalization. In Ghana, employment in manufacturing fell from 78,700 in 1987 to 28,000 in 1993. In Malawi, textile production fell by more than half between 1990 and 1996. Many firms producing soap and cooking oils went bankrupt and the poultry industry collapsed in the face of cheap imports.

Trade liberalization in third world countries follows this pattern. When trade is liberalized, imports of consumer goods rise sharply. Local producers are priced out of their markets by cheaper imports. Exports also tend to grow but not as much. Besides, third world countries tend to export similar primary commodities that flood the world market and result in the ever worsening prices for their exports. Over-all production falls as both producers for the local market and for export cannot stand the cutthroat competition. Any short-term gains to consumers from cheap prices are wiped out in the long term as their incomes fall and unemployment rises.

According to one study, sub-Saharan Africa lost US$272 billion in twenty years of trade liberalization. This would have been enough to wipe out the debt of all the countries in sub-Saharan Africa estimated at US$204 billion with still enough money to have every child in the region vaccinated and sent to school.

The oppressed peoples of the third world cannot pin their hopes on so-called solutions being offered by their oppressors. These do not solve their problems but aggravate them.

Solutions to the debt problem

The only solution is for the oppressed peoples and nations and the underdeveloped countries to uphold and exercise political independence and economic sovereignty against the impositions of the imperialists and their local puppets. They must resist the dictates and bullying of the imperialist powers who wish to impose social and economic policies through such imperialist instruments as the IMF, World Bank and WTO. They must repudiate and cancel all the odious and onerous foreign debts.

They must conserve the natural resource and use them wisely for national development. They must carry out national industrialization and land reform. They must thereby develop the economy, generate employment and expand the domestic market. They must satisfy the basic needs of the people. They must break away from the unequal exchange of their raw materials with the manufactured goods of the imperialist countries. They must set themselves from the superprofit-taking and international usury of imperialism.

We must expose the sham solutions being hyped by the imperialist governments and the imperialist media. We must also struggle against the erroneous ideas being peddled by the social democrats, bourgeois liberals, Trotskyites and NGO racketeers and reformists that try to make imperialism appear benevolent, reformable and palatable.

The oppressed peoples and nations are being incited to rise up in armed revolution by the fact that imperialism has reduced them to a life of poverty and misery, due to superprofit-taking and international usury. Half of humankind or 3 billion people live on less than US$2 per day and 1.1 billion of them live on less than one dollar day. To keep the people of the world captive, the US is spending US$500 billion this year on its military forces, while US$15 billion is estimated to be enough to alleviate poverty in the worst-case countries. Under the worsening conditions of oppression and exploitation, the proletariat and

Condemn Imperialism and the G8 Big Swindle

people of the world are bound to rise up in order to overthrow the system of imperialism.

Imperialism in Various Global Regions

ILPS Condemns the Terrorism and Barbarism of Al Qaeda and the Imperialists
July 9, 2005

We, the International League of Peoples' Struggle, consistently stand in active solidarity with the Palestinian, Arab and other peoples of the Middle East in their revolutionary struggle for national liberation and democracy and we condemn the grand scale terrorism that imperialist powers headed by the US and Britain have historically and currently carried out through plunder and wars of aggression. But we do not condone the terrorism perpetrated by the Al Qaeda even if such is of far lower scale.

In fact, we vigorously condemn the bombing attacks on ordinary people on three trains and in one bus on Thursday, 7 July 2005 in London and express our sympathy and support for the victims and their families and our solidarity with the entire people of various nationalities in England. The so-called Secret Organization of Al Qaeda in Europe has claimed responsibility of the attacks, which have resulted in the death of scores and injury to hundreds of people.

We are firmly opposed to violent attacks mainly or solely directed against ordinary people, such as those of 11 September 2001 in New York, USA or 11 March 2004 in Madrid, Spain. These are prohibited by the principles, standards and norms of civilization, as enshrined in the international law on human rights and humanitarian conduct toward civilians and captured combatants even under conditions of war. The crime of mass murder is clear and definable without the imperialists and their rabid puppets having to use their specious anti-terrorism laws and decrees to intimidate the people.

There is no justification for the mass murder of innocent civilians even if the perpetrators were to claim that they seek to avenge the massacres and other injustices inflicted on the people who believe in Islam by the medieval crusaders, the colonialists and the imperialists together with the Zionists. But why direct the bombings against the ordinary people and not against the imperialists, the rabid puppets and their armed minions?

We consider as reprehensible acts of terrorism and barbarism the violent attacks on ordinary people by those that proclaim themselves as the Al Qaeda and wave the flag of Islamic fundamentalism. We respect Islam and its believers but we oppose the retrogressive notions of theocracy, bigotry and communal barbarism.

Those who unleash violent attacks on ordinary people in the name of Islamic fundamentalism play into the hands of the imperialists, who use such attacks to justify and undertake wars of aggression, obfuscate the reality of imperialist terrorism, repress the people in imperialist countries and on a global scale in the name of counterterrorism and obstruct the anti-imperialist solidarity of the peoples.

Historically, imperialism has created and used Islamic fundamentalism as its tool in the anti-communist crusade in order to oppose the modern secular ideas of national liberation, democracy and scientific socialism. But the Al Qaeda brand of Islamic fundamentalism has since the 1990s taken a position and undertaken actions against the US and its allies, for occupying holy land in Saudi Arabia, grabbing a big part of Saudi oil income through overpriced military sales and other impositions and for collaborating with the Zionists against the Palestinian and Arab people.

However, the legitimate grievances of the people of the Middle East against imperialism are no justification for terrorist acts against the people in the homegrounds of imperialism. The correct path is to promote the anti-imperialist solidarity and struggle of the people living outside and inside the imperialist countries. Therefore, we denounce the terrorism of the perpetrators of the attacks on ordinary people in London.

At the same time, we consider as the far bigger terrorism and barbarism the concatenation of colonialism, imperialism and neocolonialism that the Western powers have imposed on the people of the Middle East and the rest of the world. The monsters have wrought havoc and destruction on the lives of billions of people the world over through daily plunder and wars of aggression.

The barbaric crimes that imperialism has committed against the people who believe in Islam are far greater than those crimes purportedly committed by the Al Qaeda in New York, Madrid and London. Now, the imperialists are further using the latter crimes as the pretext for whipping up anti-terrorist hysteria, stepping up war production, and adopting so-called anti-terrorist laws and measures that lead to the escalation of oppression and exploitation of the people in the imperialist countries and abroad.

In a manner of speaking, the imperialist macro-terrorists and the Al Qaeda micro-terrorists help each other. By its terrorist acts, the Al Qaeda pushes the imperialist countries towards militarism, fascism and wars of aggression. By launching wars of aggression against Afghanistan and Iraq, the US and Britain have provided to Al Qaeda wide fields for recruiting and developing its forces. At the same time, Bush and Blair have played to the hilt the anti-terrorist pretext to undertake the biggest and worst kind of terrorism and to continue their grip on political power.

The people inside and outside of the imperialist hands must steadfastly fight for national and social liberation against imperialism and reaction. They must join hands in frustrating the interactive terrorism of the imperialists and the Islamic fundamentalists. Both of them are barbarically hostile to and destructive of the people. Higher levels of social development are possible for humankind through revolutionary struggles for national liberation, democracy and socialism against imperialism and reaction.

ILPS Denounces UN Millennium Development Goals as Scheme to Aggravate Imperialist Plunder and Poverty
September 12, 2005

The scheduled high-level review of the Millennium Development Goals (MDGs) by the United Nations (UN) on 14-16 September is merely another attempt to further legitimize the sham being peddled by the UN and the international financial institutions (IFIs) under the auspices of the most predatory imperialist powers.

Far from promoting global economic and social justice, the MDGs is a shrewd scheme of the imperialist powers to distract attention from structural issues that are the root cause of the chronic and worsening poverty which afflicts billions of people around the world today. Worse, the MDGs is being used to promote the same policy prescriptions of imperialist globalization that have hastened and aggravated the massive destruction of livelihood and economic opportunities in poor countries where more than 1 billion people are forced to survive on less than US$1 a day.

Originally conceived by the imperialist countries through the Development Assistance Committee (DAC) of the Organization for Economic Cooperation and Development (OECD) in 1996 and picked up by the UN in its 2000 Millennium Declaration, the MDGs conveniently distorted the issue of poverty, and ignored its causes and conditions. Thus, it did not only set token and selective targets to eradicate poverty but also twisted the very concept of poverty eradication to accommodate the corporate agenda of imperialist globalization while avoiding such crucial demands as unconditional cancellation of debt of all poor countries, the reversal of World Trade Organization (WTO)-type international trade regime, and the reversal of International Monetary Fund (IMF)-World Bank-imposed neoliberal economic reforms.

The scale of debt in the poorest countries has so crippled their economies that development has become impossible because much of the limited resources are being deflected to debt servicing. In 2002, the level of debt of the poorest countries was almost 21 times its size in 1970. The international usury perpetrated by the IFIs has siphoned off US$550 billion in interest and principal payments for US$540 billion of loans, yet the poorest countries still owe foreign creditors US$523 billion as of 2002. [1]

The declaration last June of the Group of Seven (G7), the principal cabal of imperialist powers, to cancel 100 percent of the US$40 billion owed by 18 heavily indebted poor countries (HIPC) is a vain attempt to fend off criticisms on the sincerity of their much-ballyhooed 'making poverty history' publicity stunt. By imposing the terms of the debt cancellation including disastrous neoliberal reforms, the G7 initiative merely legitimized the odious and illegitimate debt incurred by the puppet regimes of these poor countries and debt which facilitated their economic plunder by imperialist corporations and banks.

In fact, the MDGs systematically makes semicolonial and colonial countries even more beholden to their imperialist patrons rather than promoting self-reliance through genuine national industrialization. While the MDGs commit to achieve universal access to primary education and improve health services, it promotes the same post-Washington consensus (i.e. liberalization, deregulation, and privatization plus 'good governance') policies that have, in the first place, intensified the bankruptcy and indebtedness of national governments in the Third World, and obliterated their capacity to provide vital social services including health and education. To finance such services, the rich countries promised to provide more aid money such as the US$5-billion Millennium Challenge Account (MCA) of the US. But the problem with the MCA is not simply the doubtful commitment of the US to the MDGs with the Bush administration's recent statement that it only supports the Millennium Declaration but not the specific targets of the MDGs.

Worse, poor countries have to first implement US-imposed preconditions including economic liberalization to have access to the MCA.

The liberalization of trade and investment, the drastic reduction in government spending on vital social services, the privatization and deregulation of strategic economic activities all have pushed the workers, peasants, urban and rural poor, indigenous people, women, youth, and other marginalized sectors not only in poverty but also in unspeakable desolation while generating unimaginable wealth and power for the few. According to the UN's Human Development Report 2005, in 1990, the average American was 38 times richer than the average Tanzanian while today, the average American is now 61 times richer.

It is clear from the onset that poor countries should never hope that the MDGs will truly address the issue of poverty precisely because the MDGs was designed to deodorize the imperialist plunder that has impoverished and dehumanized the people of the poor world. The MDGs runs counter to the peoples' fight against poverty precisely because it does not attend to the structural issues of global poverty, namely the neocolonial relations between the rich and the poor in terms of development cooperation, trade, diplomacy, etc. that is at the core of the permanent crisis of backwardness and poverty in the semi-colonies and colonies, but even perpetrates the exploitative relations between the semicolonies and colonies and their imperialist masters.

The only way to fight poverty is the assertion of the poor people's inalienable human right not simply to live but to live decently and this entails the struggle to bring to an end all structures of exploitation and poverty. At the minimum, this means freeing all the poor countries from the debt bondage without conditions, reversing all WTO and IMF-World Bank neo-liberal policies, and creating a global environment which recognizes and respects the sovereign right of poor countries and their people to determine their own development agenda and needs. Any effort to combat poverty should not be without these minimum requisites.

But we should recognize that these reforms will not be given to the poor on a silver platter by imperialist institutions including and even the UN. Like all the hard-earned victories of the people in the past, it can only be borne out by the militant and uncompromising struggle for national liberation, social justice and peace of the anti-imperialist movement. This is what the International League of Peoples" Struggle is striving to advance.

Imperialism in Various Global Regions

UN Security Council and Peacebuilding Commission Are Instruments of Imperialist Aggression and Plunder
September 13, 2005

The UN World Summit on September 14 to 16 has a pretentious and deceptive agenda, from supposedly solving global poverty, debt and development to reforming the UN's two major organs – the Security Council (SC) and the Economic and Social Council (ECOSOC). However, the real objective of US imperialism and its allies is to give United Nations (UN) imprimatur to the US invasion and occupation of Iraq and Afghanistan through the creation of a Peacebuilding Commission. This is consistent with the role that the UN has played throughout much of its 60-year history: an instrument to window-dress the bullying by the "great powers," notably the United States, of small and weaker developing states.

The Peacebuilding Commission is purportedly a mechanism to bring together "all stakeholders in and outside" the UN to "marshal resources and advise... comprehensive strategies for peacebuilding and conflict recovery" concerning "countries emerging from conflicts." In fact, it seeks to provide the United States with a political and economic mechanism that allows it to appear as exiting from Iraq but at the same time to retain military bases for directing the puppet regime and controlling the oil resources and all major business enterprises and contracts.

The "coalition of the willing" cobbled by the US has practically disintegrated and the US now finds itself sinking in the quagmire in Iraq. It has already achieved its primary objective in invading Iraq, which is to weaken and subjugate it on a long term basis. Before 1991 Iraq used to be a relatively strong client-state economically and strategically but it repeatedly showed disobedience to US dictates. Now, Iraq is in danger of disintegration as a nation-state and fragmentation into three smaller and weaker entities organized along sectarian lines. The US finds it convenient to use the UN in a futile attempt to cover and share with other countries the rising political and material costs of occupation and to counter the increasingly effective, broad-based resistance of the Iraqi people against US imperialist domination.

The US has no intention of relinquishing its paramount role in determining the strategic direction of post-Saddam Iraq. Through a powerful Organizational Committee that includes all the permanent members of the Security Council, the US is assured of a leading role in the Commission. Moreover, since membership in the Organizational Committee is based solely on the amount of regular and special contributions to the UN, this Commission, despite its pretended holy intentions, merely augments and reinforces the Security Council as an instrument of aggression and plunder in the Middle East and farther afield. The Peacebuilding Commission is intended to further unify the imperialist countries against the people within the frame of the US-instigated schemes of neoliberal globalization and escalating repression and aggression under the pretext of "war on terror". The US wants to avert the recurrence of recriminations among the Permanent Members in the run up to the US-UK invasion of Iraq.

The US has so wantonly violated the norms and instruments of international law and the principles and charter of the United Nations. The invasion of Iraq is only one of a long list of cumulative examples of such outlawry. The standing of the United Nations is at its lowest point in its sixty-year history. The much-hyped UN World Summit is touted as part of the attempt to rehabilitate the UN. But the Peacebuilding Commission is precisely nothing but the discredited Security Council in a more malignant and obnoxious form. It is in fact the corporate board of a Holy Crusade by the imperialist countries headed by the US in the 21st century in order to further dominate the Middle East and the rest of the world under the shibboleths of neoliberalism and sham democracy.

Reform of UN Security Council Seeks to Reinforce Imperialist System of Aggression and Plunder
September 14, 2005

Among the issues to be taken up at the UN World Summit from September 14 to 16 in New York is reform of the UN Security Council. While talk of reforming the Security Council has been going on since a long time ago, it was only in 1992 that serious steps were taken with a resolution by the Non-Aligned Movement calling for reform of the Security Council, followed by a resolution of the General Assembly asking the Secretary General to ask member states for written comments on Council reform. But the US and the imperialist powers with veto power in the UN Security Council and with financial control over the UN will allow only that of kind of reform which reinforces and favors the interests of imperialism against the people of the world and the client states.

Talk of reforming the UN Security Council has become louder precisely because this has become more active since the 1990s with the end of the Cold War and the decline in the use by permanent members of their veto power. The Security Council has deployed more "peacekeeping operations" since 1990 than during its first forty-five years. It has imposed more economic sanctions. It has acted on a wide range of international security issues, requiring almost daily sessions.

It is notable that such hyperactivity and common interest of the permanent members have involved conflicts or crises internal to states such as civil wars, all sorts of humanitarian crises and breakdown of central governmental authority rather than disputes between states. The Security Council has more than ever become an imperialist instrument of some of the permanent members to further political and military intervention in the internal affairs of weaker and smaller states in violation of their sovereignty. Also notable is the recent practice of the Security Council to "subcontract" enforcement of its resolutions to military forces of permanent members with the token participation of member states.

Events that have renewed and amplified the calls for reform of the Security Council are the UN interventions in Iraq in 1990, specifically the setting up of the inhuman sanctions regime that lasted almost until the US invaded Iraq in 2003, the sanctions against Libya in the aftermath of the Lockerbie bombing and the UN mission to Somalia. Many UN member states have questioned all these as going against the norms of international law and the wishes of the majority of the UN member states. Moreover, the United Nations and the Security Council have failed or refused to deploy civilian personnel and resources on other more urgent or unambiguous humanitarian cases, obviously maintaining double standards, again to promote the geopolitical imperialist aims and interests mainly of the US and some other permanent members.

The practice of "subcontracting" has often meant that the veto-wielding Security Council members use Council resolutions merely to provide legal cover for their own military operations against smaller or weaker countries. Notable examples are the Gulf War, Somalia and Haiti in the case of the United States. France and Russia have also resorted to the same tactic against countries within their sphere of influence. Permanent members contribute the least manpower to peacekeeping operations (with the exception of France) and they do not want their armed forces to be under direct UN command, with the US explicit in not allowing its forces to be commanded except by a US national.

While it has intervened in numerous cases involving internal problems of member states, the Security Council and the United Nations have chosen to ignore the many outstanding inter-states disputes in practically all continents. Thus while a world war like WW 1 or 2 has not happened, contrary to what the founders of the UN feared, the world today is far from having achieved the international peace and security envisioned in the Charter of the United Nations. The issues or problems on which the Security Council has chosen to act creates the impression that the only problems of the world now are 'weak' states and civil wars and humanitarian problems and that inter-state disputes rarely or no longer occur.

The problem of being rendered inutile whenever a big power is an interested party in an international dispute, continues to plague the Security Council today. The Security Council failed to play any significant role in ending the apartheid regime in South Africa, the Suez crisis in the 1950s, the US aggression and genocide in Vietnam in the 60s and 70s and the US military interventions in Nicaragua and El Salvador and the Soviet invasion of Afghanistan in the 1980s. The intervention by NATO in Yugoslavia which resulted in its break up and the recent invasion by the US of Iraq and the overthrow of the government of Saddam Hussein on imaginary charges of possession of weapons of mass destruction are the two latest examples of this problem.

Two major problems concerning international peace and security now confront the world. One is the failure of the United Nations and the Security Council to implement their resolutions on Palestine even after sixty years. The silence of the UN World Summit on this major global and historical problem of international peace and security renders ludicrous all talk of reform of the United Nations and the Security Council. The other is nuclear proliferation or more accurately the desire of the United States to maintain nuclear monopoly to enable it to play the role of globocop. This superpower is using the issue of nuclear proliferation as pretext to blackmail and intervene in the internal affairs of Iran and North Korea for example while allowing other states and itself to maintain a nuclear stockpile.

Reform of UN Security Council Seeks to Reinforce Imperialist System

Thus the problem of United States "unilateralism" on a host of issues, from its invasion of Iraq to its refusal to sign the Rome Statutes of the International Criminal Court to intransigence on international measures to ease global pollution to its continuing insistence on the Monroe doctrine of treating Central and Latin America as its own backyard, including the continuing economic and military blockade of Cuba, is one that the United Nations and the Security Council have to face head on if they are to become democratic and effective instruments for international peace and security and for strengthening the rule of law in international affairs.

The Security Council and the United Nations have become the tools for the intervention of imperialist powers in the affairs of other countries under the pretext of undertaking humanitarian missions, protecting human rights and effecting democratic regime change. It is currently using the pretext of protecting children in armed conflict to justify economic sanctions, military intervention and threats thereof. In this regard, the proposed creation of a Human Rights Council to replace the Human Rights Commission is futile while the imperialist states are not subject to the same yardstick of human rights as the rest of the world. It should be denounced as one more instrument for legitimizing the violation of the national sovereignty of other countries by the imperialist powers.

Reform of the Security Council that aggravates the unjust global authoritarian order against the poor or underdeveloped countries while it continues to allow the rich and powerful developed countries to flex their economic, political and military muscles and do as they please, subject only to the countervailing selfish interests of other powerful countries, presided over by the United States as globocop, is clearly unacceptable and should and will be resisted. Substantial reform of the United Nations and the Security Council should make them truly democratic, guaranteeing the rights of weaker states, allowing these to exercise the same rights and privileges as the strong states and countering the power of the imperialist states with the majority vote of all states in the UN General Assembly.

Suggestions by Germany, Japan, India and Brazil or the so-called G-4 to increase the number of permanent members would not necessarily make the Security Council become less of a tool of US and other imperialist powers. Neither would other reforms being considered, such as the adoption of permanent standing rules to make the operations or proceedings of the Council more transparent and reduce the undue advantage of the permanent members. It is extremely anomalous that permanent members engage in closed door meetings which do not have minutes or formal reports. Resolutions proposed by any of the permanent members are not circulated ahead of time but are presented as fait accompli. The regular report to the General Assembly required of the Council is often skimpy and incomplete. The resolutions of the Security Council are not subject to review by the World Court and are beyond check and balance.

81

Even if some reform of the Security Council were possible, it would not reduce the power of the imperialist states. Neither would the United Nations become an instrument for democracy and justice. The reform would only be cosmetic. The political power of the imperialists in the UN Security Council is meant to facilitate hegemony, aggression and plunder. The International Monetary Fund, the World Bank and the World Trade Organization will continue to squeeze the countries dominated by imperialism. The havoc wrought on the people by these three institutions in supposedly creating a global "neo-liberal" economic order has been immeasurable. The call to strengthen the Economic and Social Council (ECOSOC) to eventually displace the overwhelming role of these three institutions will amount to nothing more than a new package for the same poisonous substance.

No reform can be expected to change the character of the United Nations and its Security Council as instruments of imperialist power. A new and better world is possible only through the relentless struggles of the people of the world for national liberation, democracy and socialism. Only thus will the oppressive and exploitative structures of the world be replaced by new ones in the interest of the people.

The broad masses of the people and their forces for national and social liberation must intensify their struggle against imperialism and achieve greater victories in order to counter the use of the United Nations and its Security Council and the IMF, World Bank and WTO as instruments of imperialism and to build new international institutions for the benefit of the people. As of now, the dominant institutions are being used by the imperialist powers for repression, war and plunder. We need new institutions for upholding, defending and promoting national sovereignty, democracy, development, social justice and world peace.

Statement against US Monopoly Control of Information and Communications
November 16, 2005

The arrogance and drive for profit of the United States and other monopolists of information and communications technology (ICT) are well exposed in the World Summit on Information Society (WSIS). The impositions of the World Trade Organization (WTO) and World Intellectual Property Organizations render inutile any high-sounding rhetoric about freedom and equity in the WSIS Declaration of Principles.

As the supposed response of the United Nations (UN) on the growing gap between rich capitalist countries and poor countries on Internet access and ICT development, the second phase of the WSIS in Tunis is touted as the occasion to finalize Internet governance policies and the plan for the mobilization of resources to bridge the worldwide "digital divide."

The extent of the digital divide can be visualized in the September 2005 report of www.worldInternetstats.com, which shows that only 28 countries worldwide have more than 50 percent of their population connected to the Internet, while Internet penetration for other countries is only about 8.1 percent. This demonstrates that all other countries, excluding the 28 countries, have very inadequate ICT infrastructures.

It is not enough, however, to merely interpret this unequal development in ICT infrastructures as a "digital divide". More importantly, this must be viewed as a clear manifestation of the unequal economic development between capitalist countries and poor countries. The Economist.com has correctly pointed out that the deeper reason of the "digital divide," is, "Fewer people in poor countries than in rich ones own computers and have access to the Internet simply because they are too poor, (and) have other more pressing concerns, such as food, health care and security."

The WSIS Tunis summit is more concerned about Internet Governance (IG) and about balancing the dominance of US state power and its private monopolies in the industry on the one hand and the demands of Europe and China. It does not focus on the need to find solutions for the above hindrances to instant communications access, so that achievements may be possible in WSIS' avowed goal to build an open and free information society.

WSIS' approach to Internet governance is to treat uneven ICT development as a purely technical and regulatory concern. And yet the reality is that developed countries are making available through technological innovations alternatives to address these technical concerns of Internet governance.

For instance, in the management of the domain name system, the control of Internet Corporation for Assigned Names and Numbers (ICANN) or any other entity should not hinder the creation of additional top-level domains (.com, .org, .net). The use and management of country code top-level domains (.ph, .fr, .uk, .us) would be more fair if these were handed over to corresponding countries to allow these to exercise their sovereignty. The domain name system is being managed as if there is a scarcity of domain names, but in reality this scarcity is conjured by the current managers of domain names as a means for gaining more profit.

In terms of the allocation of IP addresses, the transition to Internet Protocol version 6 (IPv6) will solve the concern of using up all of IP addresses in the current Internet Protocol version 4. The Regional Internet Registries that will manage the allocation of these addresses should, therefore, not be discriminatory in allocating addresses to member countries.

However, the use of such technical alternatives and other upcoming discoveries are at the mercy of a very few developed capitalist countries that have the monopoly on ICT-related products and infrastructure. The direction of ICT development is still dictated by the monopolist agenda of those who own, have control over, and access to resources to pursue ICT research and development.

As for intellectual property rights (IPR) protection laws, there is, indeed, a need to give due recognition to innovators, inventors, researchers and other intellectuals for their contributions to new ideas, procedures and the like. But this should not allow the multinational firms in actual control of these rights to use them to impede and prevent the open and free access of this new information that may be beneficial to the people. The Trade-Related Aspects of Intellectual Property Rights (TRIPS) restricts this free access and gives more undeserved profits to entities that have the resource monopoly to do groundbreaking information and communications technology research.

IPR protection is governed by the Agreement on Trade-Related Aspects of Intellectual Property Rights and the WSIS adheres to the WTO's regulatory framework. Furthermore, WSIS recommends the development of Internet connectivity through Official Development Assistance (ODA), foreign direct investments and public-private big business ventures. This does not augur well for the poor and developing countries, given the exploitative and oppressive terms that they have suffered with regards to the conditionalities of ODA and such other foreign debt protocols.

In short, the WSIS is being used to facilitate and reinforce the WTO's onerous agreements that allow the unhindered market expansion of advanced capitalist countries to the third world where ICT-related industry is almost non-existent. And given that the main source of ICT equipment, software and services are from the richest countries, the poor underdeveloped countries are made the dumping ground of the consumerist technology surplus that may

Statement against US Monopoly Control of Information and Communications

be inappropriate to the real time needs of the countries concerned. Instead of having the opportunity to use ICT to help poor countries develop, ICT has become another "chain" that binds them to the control of the imperialist countries.

Any attempt, therefore, to make ICT fully accessible and beneficial to the majority of peoples of the world, should first and foremost address the imperialist plunder, the widespread poverty and uneven economic development of the different countries. To do so, it must not turn a blind eye on the monopoly control of ICT of only a few corporations from the imperialist countries; on the fact that accessibility to ICT is very much related to the political and economic system of each particular country; on the unequal and exploitative and oppressive economic and political relations of the rich and poor countries; and on the reality that the WTO — with the US and other monopolists in full control — and its agreements are mere instruments of monopoly capitalists that further impoverish billions of people in the majority of countries in the world.

The WSIS Tunis summit is bound to be used by the monopolists to further perpetuate their control over ICT. It is very much within the framework of keeping the US hegemony over ICT and harmonizing the relations of the monopoly firms in various imperialist countries at the expense of the underdeveloped countries. The US and other imperialist powers are motivated by the drive for monopoly profits and the use of ICT to propagate pro-imperialist ideas and block progressive ideas in the name of national security and counter-terrorism.

The WSIS' "dream" of an Information Society "where everyone can create, access, utilize and share information and knowledge", and where ICT can enable "individuals, communities and peoples to achieve their full potential in promoting their sustainable development and improving their quality of life" will just remain as it is: a dream.

Imperialism in Various Global Regions

Junk the WTO!
Resist Imperialist Plunder and War!
December 14, 2005

I am deeply pleased and honored to be given the task of opening this forum on Trade and War. Let me congratulate the Hongkong People's Alliance for successfully organizing and holding this People's Action Week on the occasion of the World Trade Organization (WTO) 6th Ministerial Conference. I extend warmest greetings of solidarity to the alliance and to all participants in this forum and in the week of protest actions here in Hongkong.

The theme of this forum, "Junk the WTO! Resist Imperialist Plunder and War" most appropriately encapsulates the demand and tasks of progressive forces all over the world with respect to the WTO. The people of the world, especially the toiling masses, must unite to demand the dismantling of the WTO and to resist imperialist plunder and war.

Historical background

The very essence of capitalism is the exploitation of labor in the process of commodity production. The capital in the hands of the capitalist class is congealed labor, originally taken away and alienated from the working class to further exploit it. New material values can be produced only by new inputs of living labor and not by "dead labor" in the form of capital. The capitalist class is driven to extract profits by minimizing wage costs, maximizing the surplus value over the wage costs and accumulating capital. This leads to the crisis of overproduction relative to the shrinkage of the market, as a result of the loss of jobs and incomes.

In a growing industrial capitalist society, the social wealth created by the working class is appropriated by the capitalist class. But the capitalists themselves compete and try to gobble each other up. From this process within "free competition capitalism" emerged and grew the monopolies in the latter part of the 19th century. The winning enterprises in the competition countered the tendency of the rate of profit to fall by resorting to the export of surplus goods and capital and the acquisition of cheap sources of raw materials and labor. Thus, the era of monopoly capitalism or imperialism began at the onset of the 20th century.

It was in the nature of the industrializing countries to consolidate their national markets and compete for economic territory beyond these. Upon the advent of modern imperialism, the world beyond the national borders of the capitalist powers had been completely divided as colonies, semicolonies or dependent countries. Conflicts easily arise among the capitalist powers because they always seek to expand economic territory at the expense of others. War erupts when they can no longer settle their differences amicably. Any number of capitalist powers can start war when they use their political and military strength to forcibly seize territory and thus redivide the world according to changes in the balance of economic and politico-military strength.

The series of capitalist crises in the last quarter of the 19th century gave rise to industrial-financial monopolies that gained control over entire economies, shifted the balance of power among the highly industrialized countries, and led to a scramble for territories at the end of the 19th century that was ultimately decided by wars (e.g. Japanese-Russo War, Boer Wars, and the Spanish-American War), and ushered the era of imperialism. These were followed by the most destructive wars in the history of mankind, the two successive world wars within the first half of the 20th century.

As history has proven, it is in the nature of modern imperialism to plunder natural resources and the social wealth created by the working class and the entire people of the world, to engage in repression and fascism and to unleash war either to subjugate entire countries and peoples or settle the conflicts of the imperialist countries over sources of raw materials, markets, fields of investment, spheres of influence and strategic points of control. Direct wars and proxy wars have arisen among imperialist powers after some periods of arranging their respective shares of the world.

The US emerged practically unscathed from the second world war and with its industries intact and greatly expanded was in the position to profit the most from postwar reconstruction. It became the No. 1 imperialist power in terms of economic and military power. It assumed the role of perpetuating the world capitalist system, containing the socialist states and opposing or coopting the national liberation movements. However, contrary to the wishes of the monopoly capitalists, the global wars considerably contracted the capitalist market as it had given rise to the socialist USSR, the East European states, the People's Republic of China, and the Democratic People's Republic of Korea. By the mid-20th century, the socialist system had encompassed one-third of the world population.

During World War II and shortly thereafter, the US economy was boosted by a large amount of public spending on war production that further expanded and fattened the military industrial complex. To justify further war production, the US embarked on the Cold War. This consisted of at least two major wars (Korea and Vietnam), several more proxy wars (especially in the Middle East and Africa), hundreds of military interventions and pocket wars in the entire third world, global troop and bases deployment and an expensive arms and space race with the USSR (especially nuclear ICBM systems) to contain the socialist challenge, suppress national liberation struggles and prop up fascist dictatorships and other repressive regimes.

Junk the WTO! Resist Imperialist Plunder and War!

Economic relations after world war II

The economic relations among countries and nations take form through trade (the exchange of goods and services) and finance (investments, loans, "aid" and other financial transactions). The legal fiction is that these are carried out on terms that are mutually agreed upon by equal and sovereign nations, and therefore mutually beneficial. In fact, the terms of trade and finance are always dictated by the stronger country to its advantage and invariably to the detriment of the weaker country.

After World War II, the US was determined to direct and control the world capitalist system through the Bretton Woods Agreements. It wanted to build an alliance of all the capitalist countries against socialist countries and to coopt the newly-independent countries and national liberation movements. It used a comprehensive range of political, economic, trade, financial and security policies for the purpose. To stem the wave of nationalism in the colonies and divert the anticolonial struggles from the socialist path, the imperialist powers led by the US granted nominal independence to their colonies but secured their or neocolonial hold on them through various lopsided economic, security and other treaties and arrangements.

The US plan in 1948 to establish the International Trade Organization was frustrated when the European powers objected to provisions that patently favored the US. In the absence of a global trade organization, trade issues were discussed and settled multilaterally through successive rounds of the General Agreement on Tariffs and Trade. Under the pretext of social and economic development, underdeveloped countries were pushed to avail of massive lending under the auspices of the IMF and World Bank. But the loans carried conditionalities that effectively stunted the growth of local industries and consigned the economies to a chronic state of backwardness, all the better to serve as sources of raw materials and cheap labor and as dumping ground for surplus products and capital. Thus were third world countries mired in chronic depression and debt and the resulting devastation of domestic productive sectors further deepened their dependence on monopoly finance capital.

The need for the imperialist powers to set up the WTO arose from the intensifying and insoluble crisis of overproduction. Average world GDP growth declined from 5.1 percent in 1945-70 to 3.8 percent in the 1970s (and only 3.1 percent for the industrialized countries). Stagflation as a consequence of huge federal state spending for the military and import-based consumerism had become a chronic phenomenon in the US since the full reconstruction of Japan and Western Europe in the late 1960s and the US accommodation of so-called newly industrializing economies (Taiwan, Brazil, etc.) with some manufacturing and exports to the US market in the 1970s and 1980s. These would steer the US towards lessening its manufacture of tradeable goods, overborrowing from abroad and becoming the world's biggest debtor from the 1980s onward.

Keynesianism had been credited for helping monopoly capitalism to cope with the Great Depression in the US and the continuing crises in most capitalist countries after WWII, More than New Deal pump priming, it was at first production stimulated by exports of supplies to the hungry war building industries of Japan and Germany and then full-blast participation in the war effort of the Allied Powers against the Axis Powers that brought the US out of the depression. Even then the civil works of Keynesianism could not solve fully the basic problem arising from the monopoly capitalists' drive to increase profit by reinvesting heavily in new machinery to increase productivity while pushing down wages, consequently contracting the market and resulting in overproduction. But Reagan and Thatcher in the 1980s blamed the crisis instead on rising wages and government spending on social benefits and services, and led the capitalist economies away from Keynesianism to monetarism and "neoliberalism".

Neoliberalism is anachronistic and deceptive. Its claim of "free market" globalization misrepresents monopoly capitalism as "free competition" capitalism. After the collapse of the Eastern European regimes in 1989-91 and the disintegration of the USSR in 1991, the monopoly capitalists carried out an ideological, political and economic offensive, proclaiming the "end of history" with the triumph of capitalism over socialism, and heralding an era of world peace, progress and prosperity with the full integration of the world into a single capitalist system.

The WTO was conceived, formed and operated as a major instrument in the hands of the imperialist powers to dictate on and dominate the weaker states and allow the monopoly capitalists to extract more superprofits from the world's toiling peoples. The WTO, more than any other prior imperialist device short of military intervention and wars of aggression, blatantly compels the weaker countries to accede to the negation and violation of their political and economic sovereignty. Since its establishment in 1995, it has been the main instrument for propagating the myth of "free market" globalization and pushing unequal trade agreements chiefly at the expense of the underdeveloped countries.

The WTO, currently encompasses 98.8 percent of the world population, with 147 member countries plus the European Union and 33 observer countries, including Russia and Vietnam, that are due to accede within five years. It purports to be a democratic institution where member states discuss and decide trade issues by consensus on the basis of equality and mutual benefit, mutual respect of national sovereignty and independence. In reality, the few imperialist states, acting in behalf of their respective monopoly capitalists, compel the weaker states to further open up their economies to imperialist plunder and they subject them to arm-twisting, blackmail and bullying. They

Junk the WTO! Resist Imperialist Plunder and War!

use economic as well as political sanctions on states for non-compliance with unequal "agreements". In this way, the biggest monopolists aim to overcome the chronic crisis of overproduction by shifting the burden of the crisis to the people of the world.

The WTO serves as a mechanism for the dominant imperialist powers to compel the underdeveloped countries as well as the retrogressive countries (the erstwhile newly-industrializing and socialist countries) to desist from upholding their economic sovereignty and protecting their economies from the assaults of foreign monopoly capitalism. Since the 1990s, some 130 countries have amended their constitution and enacted laws to further accommodate imperialist demands affecting labor, trade and other economic aspects. On the other hand, the US, Europe and Japan continue to use protectionist measures (prohibitions, restrictions, high tariff walls and subsidies) to develop and overdevelop their economies but prohibit other countries from using these to develop their own economies.

The main thrust of so-called free market globalization is the denationalization of the underdeveloped economies. The "neoliberal" policies of liberalization, deregulation and privatization have destroyed national barriers to the flow of imperialist trade and investments. They have removed government subsidies, antitrust laws, and social regulations to protect labor, women, children, the aged and the environment. They have delivered public assets and other resources to the foreign monopolies and their big comprador accomplices for privatization, private profit making and capital accumulation.

Rapid advances in high technology since the 1960s and 1970s (due to massive investments in R&D and retooling with the use of state monopoly capital, e.g., war technology -laser, nuclear, electronic, fiber optics and information technology) and the private appropriation and utilization of such technology in an environment of WTO-facilitated neoliberal "globalization" have further aggravated the inherent contradiction between the increasingly social character of production and the extremely rapacious monopoly capitalist appropriation of profit.

This has accelerated the overconcentration and overcentralization of capital in the advanced imperialist centers, chiefly in the US. Only 300 multinationals and big banks account for 70 percent of all foreign direct investments. The 100 biggest companies now control 70 percent of world trade. The 50 largest banks and financial companies control 60 percent of all global capital. The total assets of the three wealthiest persons in the world are greater than the GDP of the 48 poorest countries with a total population of 600 million.

While the imperialist powers conspire and collude to dominate and exploit the weaker economies, they cannot avoid intensifying their own conflicts within and outside the WTO, despite its supposed function to promote harmony among nations with respect to trade, by averting trade and shooting wars through the "rule of law", negotiations, consensus, settlements, and whenever necessary through a system of hearing grievances and imposing sanctions. But there is no escaping the laws of motion inherent to the capitalist system. The rules of the WTO can only mitigate for a while but cannot override the objective workings of these laws.

The trend after the collapse of the US "new economy"

In most of the 1990s, especially in the latter half of the decade, the US appeared to have established a "new economy" that was supposedly propelled by high technology and characterized by inflation-free full employment. It seemed as if the US would be able to override any crisis by being at the commanding heights of global high-tech production and finance as well as by being the sole global superpower. But eventually in 2000, the crisis of overproduction hit high-tech production in the US. The stock market collapsed at the head of a financial meltdown.

Like the rest of the world capitalist system, the US is economically recessive and stagnant. All types of products (including raw materials, basic industrial products, machine tools and high-tech products) are in relative oversupply. The economic and financial crisis has devastated and depressed the global economy. The US is suffering from huge trade and budgetary deficits and debts. Just as it did in the past, during the Great Depression, the two world wars and the entire Cold War period, US imperialism is now stepping up war production under the notion of military Keynesianism, promoting state terrorism on a global scale and unleashing wars of aggression.

Using the September 11, 2001 attacks as pretext, the US imperialists launched their so-called "war on terror". They accelerated their blatant acts of aggression and military intervention on a global scale. The invasion and occupation of Afghanistan and Iraq, the restructuring, upgrading and redeployment of the US armed forces, skyrocketing defense spending and the revival of costly defense programs such as the Anti-Ballistic Missile Defense Program and the Space Program, are all part of the "Project for a New American Century", hatched by US neoconservatives to consolidate US global hegemony by seizing strategic resources and territory, deterring, preempting and eliminating opposition and long-term rivals. In the process the US flagrantly violates international law, tramples on the rights of sovereign nations and peoples, wreaks havoc and destruction on civilian population centers and on the environment.

After nearly 11 years, the World Trade Organization has achieved exactly the opposite of what its proponents, the imperialist powers led by the US-claimed it would. It has aggravated poverty and misery instead of bringing progress and prosperity to the world's peoples. It has deepened instead of lifted the poor countries from their state of underdevelopment and exploitation. It has forced weaker countries to open up their economies to plunder by the stronger countries, instead of promoting equality and mutual benefit among nations. It has exacerbated the rivalry and competition among the imperialist powers and abetted aggression and war, instead of ushering in an era of harmony and world peace.

People's resistance

History shows that the people resist imperialist oppression and exploitation. Since the beginning of the 20th century, the world's peoples have stood up and fought against imperialist plunder and war. The working class has built political parties and trade union movements to realize immediate and long-term aims. It has led the people in national democratic and socialist revolutions on a global scale. Peoples in Asia, Africa and Latin America have waged wars for national liberation, either resulting in revolutionary victories or compelling the colonial powers to shift to semicolonial or neocolonial rule. Today, there is a forward interaction between the popular struggles in the imperialist and dominated countries.

Patriotic movements have arisen to uphold national and economic sovereignty against foreign intervention. Various social movements advocating people's rights, including self-reliant economic development, environmental protection, gender equality, cultural diversity and so on, have proliferated and exerted significant pressure on governments while raising the awareness of the public on various issues. Propelled by revolutionary movements as well as by legal protest and advocacy movements, countries have stood up to assert national sovereignty and independence against flagrantly one-sided impositions and onerous conditions and all sorts of threats and intimidation by the US and other imperialist powers.

The people of the world have established historically a certain high level of resistance against imperialism and reaction. Consequent to the betrayal of socialism by the modern revisionists and the disintegration of revisionist-ruled states, it would seem as if the US and other imperialists had scored a permanent victory over the socialist cause and all movements of national and social liberation. But the intensification of oppression and exploitation under such policy stresses as "free market" globalization, repression and fascism and imperialist wars of aggression drive the people to recall their revolutionary legacy, muster their capabilities, act on their current needs and demands and rise up resolutely to fight for their rights and interests.

We should avail ourselves of all forms of struggle in exposing and opposing imperialist plunder and war. We should do all we can to frustrate, if not defeat the schemes of the imperialist powers to pursue the Doha Round negotiations for further reducing agricultural and nonagricultural tariffs and other nontariff protection in third world countries, expanding the coverage of GATS to the service sector and thus privatize such social services as education, health, communications and water, and pursuing the Singapore issues relating to investments, competition policy, government procurement and trade facilitation. We must demonstrate our resolute opposition to imperialist plunder through the WTO.

Whatever is our success in exposing and opposing the objectives of the 6th Ministerial Conference, we should build on our gains to pursue further the long-term struggle against the WTO and neoliberal "free market" globalization by raising the consciousness of the world's peoples against imperialism and by organizing and mobilizing them for various anti-imperialist struggles. The struggles against WTO, against "neoliberal" globalization and against imperialist wars enhance and compliment each other. They combine naturally and most effectively within the framework of anti-imperialism.

The imperialists can and will continue to maintain the WTO and implement the neoliberal policies and measures of liberalization, deregulation, privatization and denationalization for some time as the crisis of overproduction worsens. They anticipate and react to the resistance of the people. And they increasingly use coercive force as deception fails to stop the advance of the people in their struggle for national and social liberation.

The US imperialists, their allies and puppets are hell-bent on unleashing state terrorism and wars of aggression for the purpose of attacking anti-imperialist social movements, national liberation movements and countries that assert national independence. It is therefore important and necessary that we strive to build international solidarity against imperialism and reaction and the broadest possible people's anti-imperialist united front in every country and region.

The epochal struggle between imperialism and the people is once again intensifying. Imperialism is bound to weaken further as the people of one country after another break free from the chain of imperialist exploitation and oppression. We are confident that we shall win greater victories in the struggle and rise to a new and higher level of revolutionary struggle and social achievement against imperialism and reaction. Ultimately, total victory belongs to the people.

International Conference Towards a Just and Lasting Peace against Imperialist War and Plunder
June 16, 2006

Let me express first of all the deep gratitude of the International Coordinating Committee and entirety of the International League of Peoples' Struggle to the Canada-based ILPS participating organizations and their conference secretariat and organizing committees for organizing this international conference towards a just and lasting peace against imperialist war and plunder.

We appreciate that this conference is meant to build on the previous work and resolutions of the two study commissions on ILPS Concern No. 1 (the cause of national liberation, democracy and social liberation) and Concern No. 4 (the cause of a just peace against wars of counter-revolution and aggression) to deepen our understanding of these two concerns and to renew and strengthen our resolve to carry forward the peoples' struggle.

The two concerns are necessarily linked. A just and lasting peace can be realized only with the people achieving national liberation, democracy and social liberation and defeating the wars of counterrevolution and aggression. Imperialism and reaction are culpable for the oppression and exploitation of the people, for state terrorism and wars. The people can obtain a just and lasting peace only by overcoming imperialism and reaction.

Imperialist plunder, crisis, repression and war of aggression

The monopoly bourgeoisie maximizes its profits right at the workplace by reducing the wage fund for the workers while increasing capital for the plant, equipment and raw materials. It always seeks to raise the rate of exploitation in order to improve its competitive position vis a vis rivals within the same industry in the same country and on an international scale.

Because the monopoly capitalists in various industries constantly seek to press down the wage level in order to raise their profitability, they ultimately decrease the purchasing power of the workers and reduce the market for their products. The result is a crisis of overproduction relative to the constricted market. Production cutbacks, mass layoffs and bankruptcies of companies ensue. Upon the breakdown of the real economy, the financial crisis takes the form of stockmarket crashes, an epidemic of bad loans, currency devaluation, and so on.

In the era of imperialism, the monopoly bourgeoisie seeks to counter the falling rate of profit and the economic and financial crisis in the metropolis by exploiting the working people in the economic hinterlands of the world, consisting mainly of countries described politically as semi-colonies and dependent countries or economically as underdeveloped and less developed. These are the sources of cheap raw materials and labor, markets for surplus goods, fields of investment for surplus capital and spheres of influence.

But the expanded field of exploitation leads to bigger and more bitter economic competition and political contentions among the imperialist powers. Economic and financial crises become more devastating, more frequent and more prolonged, generating repression and fascism, wars of counterrevolution and aggression and global wars among the imperialist powers that try to redivide the world, as in World War I and II.

As a result of inter-imperialist wars, new nation-states and socialist states have arisen. But still the imperialist powers jointly and separately have been able to impose neocolonial forms of exploitation and domination on most nations of the world. At the same time, the phenomenon of modern revisionism has undermined and paved the way for the restoration of capitalism in socialist states.

Since the 1980s, the US unleashed the policy of neoliberalism or "free market" globalization, which is a misnomer for the narrow character and selfish interests of monopoly capitalism. The main tool of the policy consists of the manipulation of the interest rates and the supply and flow of money to consumption of durable and nondurable goods and to whichever are the favored sections of production, such as high-tech weapons under Reagan, high-tech consumer products under Clinton and once more high-tech weapons plus major wars of aggression under Bush.

The policy objective is economic growth in terms of the growth of monopoly capital but certainly not in terms of employment and higher income for the working people. The neoliberal policy is aimed at solving the problem of stagflation by reducing regular workers in favor of part-timers, pressing down the wages of workers, attacking workers' rights and cutting back on social but certainly not military spending by government.

The monopoly firms and banks are given all the leeway to build up their resources and capacities through tax exemptions, denationalization of the economies of the underdeveloped countries, liberalization of trade and investments, privatization of public assets and deregulation against the protection of the workers, women, children and the environment.

Under the US-instigated policy of neoliberalism, the world capitalist system has hurtled from one crisis to a deeper and graver one in more than 25 years. The policy has not prevented but has served to accelerate the economic and financial crisis of the following in chronological order: the general run of raw-material exporting countries of the third world, the monopoly bureaucrat capitalism of the Soviet bloc and industrial overproducers like Japan, Germany and such so-called economic tigers as South Korea and Taiwan, the so-called emerging markets in the ex-Soviet bloc countries and ultimately the US.

In the latter half of the 1990s, the US appeared to have a "new economy" of overvalued assets, high speculation, high-tech production and constant growth without inflation until the high tech bubble burst in the year 2000. All along the US was attracting foreign funds to finance its frenzied overconsumption and huge trade deficits. It was the principal beneficiary of the accelerated concentration and centralization of monopoly finance capital under neoliberalism but finally became afflicted with economic and financial crisis.

The Bush regime has sought to revive and sustain the US economy by sticking to the policy of neoliberalism but combining this with military Keynesianism. The occurrence of 9/11 gave the regime the license to whip up war hysteria, to stifle dissent with the USA PATRIOT Act, to make the resources and contracts flow to the military-industrial complex and to unleash wars of aggression against Afghanistan and Iraq with the obvious purpose of seizing major oil sources and supply lines in the Middle East and Central Asia.

The economic formula of Bush has failed. The housing bubble, an additive to the concoction, is in the process of bursting upon the rise of interest rates aimed at attracting more foreign funds. Trade and budgetary deficits are relentlessly widening. The high unemployment rate is camouflaged by taking out of the reckoning those who stop looking for work and by counting in among the employed the part-timers. The Bush regime continues to think it can still use war hysteria and the so-called war on terror to keep its political upperhand in US politics, despite the clear rejection of the US war of aggression in Iraq by the American people.

The US is the No. 1 imperialist power, the No. 1 propagator of terrorism and the No. 1 source of war. Its ongoing atrocities in Iraq and Afghanistan, involving the mass murder of more than 200,000 civilians, are so many times bigger and more barbaric than 9/11 which killed less than 3000 civilians. US monopoly capitalism is an extremely aggressive force as it is being driven by the global capitalist crisis to engage in further acts of aggression.

The US has a track record of extreme violence against the people. It killed 1.5 million Filipinos from the Filipino-America War of 1899-1902 to 1913, 4 million Koreans during the Korean War and 6 million people in the Korean War. It has the despicable distinction of atom bombing the civilian populations of Hiroshima and Nagasaki. Together with its British and Dutch allies, it masterminded the massacre of 1.5 million Indonesians through the instrumentality of the Suharto military fascist regime.

The US colludes with and contends with other imperialist powers in exploiting and oppressing the people of the world, in plundering the natural resources and social wealth created by the people, in employing state terrorism directly and through its puppets to repress the people and in unleashing the worst form of terrorism, which is the war of aggression, against the people and recalcitrant states.

The people's resistance against imperialism

As the crisis of the world capitalist system worsens and the imperialist powers engage in war and plunder, the oppressed peoples and nations are compelled and impelled to resist imperialism and all reaction and to fight for their national and social liberation. They have long engaged in various forms of resistance against the impositions of the imperialist powers directly or through such multilateral agencies as the IMF, World Bank and WTO and through military alliances.

In the long run, the peoples engaged in armed revolution, such as those in Iraq, Turkey, Nepal, India, Tamil Eelam, the Philippines, Colombia and elsewhere, are the most potent in struggling for national and social liberation and realizing just peace against counterrevolution and aggression. They set the example for other peoples to follow. They keep alive the great legacy of armed revolutions that made possible national independence and socialism in many countries in the past century.

The current armed revolutionary parties and movements of the people are achieving their own brilliant victories and are strengthening themselves through hard work and struggle among the oppressed and exploited masses. They are driven by the needs and demands of the people and they rely on the people as the inexhaustible source of strength. But they also know how to take advantage of the contradictions among the local reactionaries, within the imperialist countries, between the imperialist powers and recalcitrant states, and among the imperialist powers.

Revolutionary parties of the proletariat have complemented armed struggle as the main form of struggle with legal forms of struggle and with the united front for armed and legal struggles. The armed revolution spreads faster as the revolutionary party not only relies on the toiling masses of workers and peasants it has organized but also reaches out to the masses that are still under the influence of other entities. It becomes so much easier to organize and mobilize the people as they grasp the general line for national liberation and democracy through the rousing slogans of the united front.

At the moment, revolutionary armed struggles are being waged in countries such as the Philippines, Nepal, India, Turkey and Colombia. At the same time, there are wars of national liberation against imperialist aggression and occupation, such as in Iraq, Palestine and Afghanistan. The social outcome of the politico-military struggles depends on the objective conditions and subjective factors. But whenever there is fierce struggle against imperialism and its puppets in certain countries, the revolutionary party of the proletariat can take advantage of such struggle to optimize the results of the revolutionary struggle.

Some countries steadfastly oppose US imperialism. These include North Korea, Cuba and Venezuela. The persevering struggle of the people and

International Conference Towards a Just and Lasting Peace

government for their national independence and their social system is admirable. It extends support to the revolutionary struggles of the people elsewhere. There are other countries in which the governments are not progressive but which are at loggerheads with the US imperialism for whatever reason. It is good for the revolutionary party of the proletariat to study and utilize the contradictions between the two sides and promote the revolutionary initiative and independence of the revolutionary forces and people.

The great revolutions of Russia and China in the 20th century were successful not only because of the correct revolutionary line set forth by the revolutionary party of the proletariat and followed by the organized masses but also because of the favorable objective conditions provided by the inter-imperialist global wars and the continuing contradictions of the imperialist powers. The line can only be correct and successful as it applies effectively on the concrete conditions.

Within the imperialist countries, the broad masses of the people are in discontent over the exploitative, oppressive and bellicose policies of their governments. They have risen up in gigantic mass actions against anti-worker and anti-people policies, against the ever deteriorating conditions of economic and social life, against all forms of discrimination against the immigrants, the people of color, women and youth, against repression of the people in the name of anti-terrorism and against the US-led wars of aggression in Iraq and elsewhere.

The people fighting for national and social liberation, the countries upholding and defending their national independence against imperialist impositions, and the people struggling in the imperialist countries are all linked by common needs, by a common determination to strengthen their solidarity and mutual support and by common aspirations to overcome their common enemy and achieve a durable and just peace.

How the ILPS can carry forward the peoples' struggle

Since its founding in May 2001, the ILPS has become a major formation and rallying point of the peoples of the world in their struggle for a new and better world of greater freedom, democracy, social justice, all-round progress and peace. Despite its meager resources, it has stood out as one of the most resolute and most militant formations fighting against imperialism and reaction.

By pursuing the correct political line and relying on its constituent organizations and the broad masses of the people, it has successfully spelled out and espoused the most urgent vital issues and confronted the barefaced enemies of the people as well as the reformists and anarchists of various stripes. The worsening crisis of the world capitalist system and the rapidly rising resistance of the people require the constant expansion and consolidation of the ILPS.

The ILPS has assumed the duty of asserting the justness of the peoples' struggle for national liberation, democracy and social liberation and for a just peace against wars of counterrevolution and aggression, promoting the international solidarity of all the forces and people fighting against imperialist war and plunder and encouraging and supporting all forms of struggle by the people.

The ILPS should undertake educational activities such as research, publications, group studies, seminars, forums and conferences in order to propagate its anti-imperialist and democratic line on the 18 concerns and push the development of the study commissions at the national, regional and international levels. The ILPS coordinating committees at all levels should have a resource base for learning sessions and issuing statements on the urgent issues.

The initial participating organizations of the ILPS in any country should attract and invite other organizations to join the ILPS and form the national chapter of the ILPS as a broad alliance along the anti-imperialist and democratic line. Thereafter, national chapters in the same global region can hold its assembly to take up issues and elect its coordinating committee. The International Coordinating Committee is eager to see the national chapters of the United States and Canada to form the coordinating committee for North America.

At any level, the ILPS should always be ready to initiate mass campaigns of information, education, mass actions and raising of resources on important urgent issues, mobilize the participating organizations of the ILPS and engage other organizations, entire communities and individuals to cooperate in the common effort. The ILPS should also be ready to cooperate with other entities that initiate and undertake activities that are compatible with the character and objectives of the ILPS.

On its own account, the ILPS is determined to pursue all possible and necessary forms of legal struggle to uphold, defend and advance the rights and interests of the people. At the same time, it recognizes that the people in any country have the all-important sovereign right to decide and carry out what they consider as the most effective forms of struggle to empower themselves and get rid of those who oppress and exploit them.

Global Trends, Challenges and Opportunities after 9/11
Contribution to the International Solidarity Conference on the Struggle of the People of Nepal for Democracy and Human Rights, Kathmandu, Nepal
September 22, 2006

On behalf of the International League of Peoples' Struggle which is co-sponsoring this conference, I wish to express warmest greetings of solidarity to all delegations from Nepal and other countries, and congratulate the Nepali colleagues for organizing and hosting this conference and all related activities.

I am deeply pleased to be asked to speak on the subject of global trends, challenges and opportunities after 9/11. I shall make a general presentation of these, with the hope that you can relate these further to the struggle of the people of Nepal for national liberation and democracy.

I propose to give a brief background and discuss major socioeconomic and political contradictions within the US and those in the relations of the US with other imperialist powers, with countries and governments that invoke national independence or express anti-imperialist positions, and with the proletariat and peoples of the world.

I shall restate the three fundamental contradictions in the epochal struggle between the proletariat and the bourgeoisie and then point to the four major contradictions that I observe in the current world situation and arrange them according to their current order of strategic importance.

Brief background

The US has enjoyed the position of sole superpower since the disintegration of the Soviet Union and end of the Cold War. It is the No. 1 imperialist power in economic and military terms. It still dictates the policies governing the world capitalist system through the Group of 8, OECD, the IMF, World Bank, WTO, NATO, the UN Security Council, and numerous bilateral and regional treaties and agreements with other countries.

But while the US has apparently become the strongest imperialist power, it has become fundamentally weaker and more vulnerable in a number of definable aspects. It has undermined its own economic, commercial and financial position by expending huge amounts of resources for the military aspect of its anti-communist crusade, and promoting since the late 1940s the reconstruction and growth of the German and Japanese economies and the industrial development of some economies like South Korea and Taiwan since the 1970s.

By providing financial and trade accommodations to the manufactures of the aforesaid countries, the US has been able to maintain and head an all-round imperialist alliance. It has reaped huge benefits from the alliance but in certain important respects it has also paid a heavy price for containing socialist countries, encouraging revisionism to subvert these, and co-opting the newly-independent countries through neocolonialism. It has stunted its production of many types of exportable goods by providing economic and trade accommodations to its allies. It has long assumed the main burden of spending public resources heavily on military production, deployment of US military forces abroad and wars of aggression.

In countering stagflation in the 1970s, the US has blamed so-called wage inflation and social spending by government as the cause of the problem. It has obscured the stagflationary effect of big government spending for military purposes and that of the ever-increasing cost of import-dependent consumerism. Since the end of the 1970s, it has shifted its policy stress from Keynesianism to monetarism and neoliberalism. It has sought to keep up the rate of economic growth through sheer manipulation of interest rates and money flows.

The Reagan regime is known for its policy of providing the giant corporations with tax cuts and other favors, its high-speed high-tech military production, and a high level of consumerism financed by foreign debt. Reaganism eventually made the US the biggest debtor in the world and placed the succeeding regime of the elder Bush in a difficult economic situation that would require the raising of taxes. Basically, the problem of stagflation has remained unsolved and has been covered up by heavy local and foreign borrowing and financial manipulation.

The Clinton regime is known for building a "new economy", supposedly characterized by inflation-free growth due to the US lead in high technology and due to the pressing down of the wage level, loss of regular jobs, erosion of workers' rights and reduction of social spending. Since 2000, the high-tech bubble in the US has burst and a protracted financial meltdown has been going on, exposing the overproduction of high-tech goods in the US and the huge trade deficits due to the heavy importation of other types of goods priorly in overproduction in other countries (basic industrial goods, raw materials and low value-added consumer goods).

Since the collapse of the Soviet Union, the US has become more rapacious and aggressive. Under the policy of "free market globalization", it has accelerated the flow of foreign funds to the US, it has reaped superprofits on certain exports and investments, and has imported cheap the products of other countries. Manifesting the brutal character of imperialism, it has waged wars of aggression against Iraq (twice), Yugoslavia and Afghanistan, and engaged

Global Trends, Challenges and Opportunities after 9/11

in military intervention elsewhere in order to tighten its grip on sources of oil and other natural resources, on markets and fields of investment. It has taken advantage of the weaknesses of the former Soviet bloc countries before Russia can offer any significant kind of economic competition to further cramp the world for imperialist profit taking.

Contradictions within the US

For a while, Bush has been benefited greatly by 9/11. This has given him the chance to stir up war hysteria in order to capture bipartisan support for his role as wartime commander-in-chief, and thus to consolidate his political position against charges of cheating in the elections of 2000 and 2004. Relatedly, he has used the war hysteria and the fear of terrorism to justify bigger government spending for military production and for wars of aggression against Afghanistan and Iraq, and to push state terrorism both within the US and on a global scale.

He has the Reaganite notion of reviving the US economy through heavy government spending for military purposes. He has thus combined military Keynesianism with "free market" globalization. Moreover, he is consciously carrying the "neoconservative" scheme of using a full spectrum of weapons to make the 21st a century of Pax Americana, by undertaking preemptive actions against current adversaries and potential challengers to US hegemony, and consequently spreading "democracy" and the "free market".

It has seemed for a while that military Keynesianism could revive the US economy. But contracts with the military industrial complex for military production in the US and for other war requirements in the field employ only a few people and provide a limited amount of income for US workers and consumers. So, the US economic planners have encouraged the "housing bubble". The rapid appreciation in value of private homes has allowed many people to use these as collateral for further borrowing for the purpose of consumption.

US imperialism has expected to benefit greatly from its invasion and occupation of Iraq by taking over its oil wealth and all kinds of enterprises. But the problem of the US is the resistance of the people of Iraq. The resistance keeps on blowing up the oil facilities and pipelines, and cutting down oil production to a low level. The US budgetary deficit has been ballooning because of the war. And the American people observe that the US easily spends US$ 250 billion for the war but appropriates only US$ 3 billion for the victims of the Katrina disaster and even releases this in driblets.

The "housing bubble" has begun to burst. This is expected to further harm the US economy in a big way. Those who have been encouraged to engage in high consumption will pay dearly. This is the second huge financial disaster for American families in less than a decade. The preceding disaster was the

103

bursting of the "high-tech bubble" and the widescale loss of pension funds in stock market speculation. The extremely high levels of federal, state and household debts can have far-reaching adverse consequences to the US and global economy. Any sharp drop in US consumption can put China and other countries dependent on exports to the US in an economic tailspin.

The American people in their millions have opposed the US war of aggression against Iraq before it even started. Their opposition is fast growing and is fast isolating the Bush regime. The American people denounce Bush for spouting lies to push the war. They cannot accept the heavy casualties suffered by both the American troops and Iraqi people, as well as the huge amounts of resources expended. An increasing number of the American people are offended by the Bush regime's misuse of 9/11 for further misdirecting the US economy and politics, for pushing repressive laws and human rights violations, and for promoting aggressive wars and fascism.

The US has overreached and overextended itself in the world in the vain hope of expanding the scope of its political hegemony and economic territory. The conditions of socioeconomic and political crisis in the US are worsening and are pushing the American working class and the rest of the people to rise in resistance. They have risen up in great number against imperialist war. The millions of migrant workers have also risen up against the criminalization and harsh conditions that they suffer.

There is a high potential for the broad masses of American workers and people to rise up against exploitation and oppression, especially the loss of job tenure, the decrease of jobs, including part-time jobs, the inadequacy of incomes, the lack of pension, health insurance and other social benefits, and the continuing erosion of workers' rights. The US monopoly bourgeoisie and its state are increasingly hard put in devising new ways for deceiving and appeasing the public.

Contradictions between the US and other countries

Following the pattern set during the Cold War, the imperialist powers of the West and Japan have by and large continued to find common interest under the chieftainship of the US against the proletariat and people of the world and against countries that take the line of national independence and anti-imperialism.

In the wake of 9/11, the imperialist powers easily united behind the US to wage a war of aggression against Afghanistan, because the Taliban government was held responsible for coddling al Qaeda. But France, Germany and Russia together with China objected to the war of aggression instigated by the US and United Kingdom against Iraq in 2003. There were clear contradictions between the US and UK on one side and the other imperialist powers on the other, based on differing interests in Iraq. But the US and UK had their way

Global Trends, Challenges and Opportunities after 9/11

and ultimately the other imperialist powers compromised with them within the framework of the UN Security Council.

There are contradictions among the imperialist powers with regards to economic, trade, financial, political and security issues. But the imperialist powers can still make compromises among themselves so long as these can be made at the expense of the proletariat and people of the world and the semi-colonies and dependent countries. The various frameworks for imperialist compromise and agreement are still intact and operative. If for a time no agreement can be arrived at, the imperialist powers simply postpone the resolution of the problem, let the status quo remain, and work around the problem.

But the crisis of the world capitalist system and the crisis in each imperialist country is worsening. The economic and financial crisis is relentlessly driving the imperialist powers to redivide the world and expand their respective sources of materials and cheap labor, markets, fields of investments and spheres of influence. What appear to be constant amicable relations among the imperialist powers can eventually break after a period of imperceptible changes in the balance of strength among the imperialist powers. If they become strong capitalist countries, Russia and China would cramp the world capitalist system and upset its balance. If they become countries of turmoil, they can generate big problems.

The US has overextended itself in outsourcing the production of goods, in over-borrowing from certain countries like Japan and China, and in "staying the course" in the quagmires of Iraq and Afghanistan. In the process, it has aggravated its weaknesses and vulnerabilities in so many ways. Its own imperialist allies can become relatively stronger than before and can move into areas where US attention and strength have thinned out. As a result of its preoccupation with Iraq, the US capability to deal with other regions of the world has lessened.

The European Union has a growing economic interest that is at odds with that of the US in the entire of Europe, Africa and elsewhere in the world. Russia and China have made border agreements with certain Central Asian countries to counter US incursions. China is steadily spreading its interest and influence, mainly in the whole of East Asia, even as Japan banks on its partnership with the US and maintains a prominent imperialist role in the region. North Korea asserts its national independence and continues to defy and oppose US imperialism.

In Latin America, Cuba, Venezuela and Bolivia have anti-US governments and mass movements, and are encouraging other countries to follow suit. Even in the Middle East, the US is far from being able to stop the initiatives of Syria and Iran in cooperation with Russia and China. It has penetrated South Asia in a big way but it has difficulties in gaining complete control over the region.

The imperialist powers can still dictate on most countries. They have been successful in undertaking neocolonialism. But there are countries and governments which are driven by bourgeois nationalist motivations or socialist aspirations and assert national independence in order to fend off the unacceptable impositions and threats of the US and other imperialist powers. We have seen how Iraq of Saddam, Yugoslavia of Milosevich and Afghanistan of the Taliban have come into cross purposes with the US and been at the receiving end of US aggression. We have seen the governments of China, North Korea, Cuba, Venezuela, Iran and Syria invoke and assert national independence against the worst dictates of the US But the US has so far refrained from attacking any of these countries for various reasons.

The sharpest and most dramatic contradictions resulting in war have arisen between the imperialist powers and certain countries whose governments refuse to accept imperialist dictates. It is also in this kind of contradiction, as in the run up to the 2003 US-UK invasion of Iraq, where significant contradictions among the imperialist powers have surfaced. That is because imperialist powers have their own drive to compete for advantages offered by non-imperialist countries. The Saddam government attempted to counter the US-UK combine with concessions to the other imperialist powers.

Under pressure of the crisis of the world capitalist system, imperialist countries can engage in proxy wars among their client states or back different conflicting parties within a client state. Another major potential cause for hostility among imperialist powers would be the rise to power of fascist forces within any or some of them. The severe socioeconomic and political crisis of imperialism and the currency of the so-called global war on terror have laid the ground for fascism and inter-imperialist wars. In fact, the making of so-called anti-terrorist laws in the wake of 9/11 has intensified repression and spawned state terrorism within the US and on a global scale.

The resistance of the proletariat and the people

Throughout the world, the broad masses of the people have engaged on varying scales in protest mass actions and strikes to resist imperialist plunder and aggression. The largest mass mobilizations on an international scale have involved tens of millions of people in hundreds of cities against the US war of aggression in Iraq. In various countries at different times, millions of people have risen up against the exploitative and oppressive policies and practices of their rulers.

In the US, Western Europe and elsewhere, strikes and protest marches have broken out against attacks on the rights of working people, deteriorating working conditions, racial and minority discrimination, the criminalization of migrant workers, and discrimination against the youth in employment. In the former Soviet bloc countries, struggles between the exploiting and exploited classes and between the dominant nationality and the minorities are intensifying. In China, the workers, peasants and the lower petty bourgeoisie are frequently rising in large numbers against the ruling bourgeoisie and their accomplices in private business.

In the imperialist countries, certain factors check the continuous vigorous development of anti-imperialist mass movements. The monopoly bourgeoisie erodes the rights and social benefits of the workers and people but in a gradual or surreptitious way so as not to provoke revolt. The major bourgeois parties, mass media, trade union bureaucracy and schools cloak big bourgeois interests with petty bourgeois rhetoric. There are yet no Marxist-Leninist parties and revolutionary mass movements that are large and strong enough to challenge the monopoly bourgeoisie and its agents.

It will take sometime before the internal crisis of monopoly capitalism and the anti-imperialist resistance of the people in the non-imperialist countries can accelerate the sharpening of the class struggle between the proletariat and the monopoly bourgeoisie in the imperialist countries. In Russia and other former Soviet bloc countries, the proletariat and people should be more inclined to wage armed revolution against the new bourgeoisie that privatized the social assets that they have created for decades. But the revisionists masquerading as communists did their work for decades to undermine and destroy socialism from within. That is also the case in China. However, imperialist plunder and aggression are generating the people's growing armed resistance to imperialism in a number of countries.

The peoples of Iraq, Afghanistan, Palestine, Lebanon and other countries have waged armed resistance against US imperialism and its lackeys. The war of national liberation in Iraq is of great significance and has far reaching consequences in weakening US imperialism. The people's resistance in Afghanistan is growing and is delivering lethal blows to the US and NATO forces. The people of Palestine and Lebanon and other Arab peoples have successfully combated the US-directed and US-supplied Israeli Zionists.

There are many armed conflicts of different types in Asia, Africa and Latin America. There are those between the imperialists or the reactionary state on the one hand, and the revolutionary movements for national liberation and democracy on the other hand, as in Iraq, Palestine, Afghanistan, Nepal, India, Turkey, Peru, Colombia and the Philippines. There are those between the reactionary state and the oppressed minorities fighting for self-determination.

There are also those between reactionary forces who struggle for power by following different imperialist masters and taking advantage of communal, ethnic, religious and racial differences. These armed conflicts have arisen in the wake of economic and social ruin due to depressed prices of raw-material exports and unbearable debt burdens, especially in Africa.

The Marxist-Leninist and Maoist parties that are waging the new democratic revolution through protracted people's war play a signal role in bringing about

107

the world proletarian revolution. They hold high the torch of armed revolution. They illumine the road of revolution for the peoples in the underdeveloped countries, in the retrogressive countries of former socialist countries, and in the imperialist countries. They encourage the formation of Maoist parties where these do not yet exist.

Current major contradictions in the world

In the epochal struggle of the proletariat and the bourgeoisie, the fundamental contradictions to reckon with are those between labor and capital, among the imperialist countries, and between the imperialists and the oppressed peoples and nations. From time to time, the arrangement of these contradictions changes according to concrete conditions.

At this time, these fundamental contradictions may be seen as four major contradictions and may be arranged according to current world reality. These are contradictions between the imperialist powers and the oppressed peoples and nations, between the imperialist powers and countries upholding national independence, among the imperialist powers, and between the proletariat and the monopoly bourgeoisie in imperialist countries.

The contradiction between the imperialist powers and the oppressed peoples and nations ranks first because armed revolutionary movements have arisen within it, even if still few, and the central question of revolution is being answered through the serious endeavor to seize state power. Every day that these armed revolutions for national liberation and democracy exist and develop, they demonstrate that the US and other imperialist powers do not have enough power to suppress them and pacify the entire world. They encourage the people to wage armed revolution. There is high potential for more armed revolutions to arise in Asia, Africa and Latin America because the peoples and nations in these parts of the world are the most oppressed and exploited.

The contradiction between the imperialist powers and countries upholding national independence has in fact resulted in wars that are even more dramatic for a certain time than the revolutionary wars of oppressed peoples and nations. Any government, whether motivated by bourgeois nationalism or socialism, invokes national independence against imperialism to assert its legitimacy and compliance with the sovereign will of the people. We have seen the blitzkriegs launched by the US and its allies against Iraq and Afghanistan. The governments of Saddam and the Taliban have fallen. But the people continue to wage a war of liberation against the occupation and has pushed the US into a quagmire.

Individually, China, North Korea, Cuba, Iran and Syria invoke national independence and take a stand against the dictates of US imperialism on certain outstanding issues, like Taiwan, nuclear research and development, economic sanctions and Israeli Zionism, to cite a few. Politically, economically,

Global Trends, Challenges and Opportunities after 9/11

financially and militarily, there are limits to US imposing itself on any or all of the aforementioned countries. It is already in serious trouble even only in Iraq. Together with its NATO allies, it is increasingly faced with armed resistance in Afghanistan.

The contradiction among the imperialist powers has long been cushioned since the end of World War II by their anti-communist alliance against the socialist countries, the national liberation movements, and the proletariat and people. But it can easily take the No. 1 position when it results in war among the imperialist themselves, as in World War I and World War II. Such a war is always of high significance because it is the most devastating to the people, it is self-destructive to world capitalism in general and gives the people the opportunity to turn the war into a revolutionary civil war for national liberation and socialism. No direct inter-imperialist war has arisen since the end of World War II because the imperialist powers have developed various frameworks for settling their differences at the expense of the proletariat and people.

The contradiction between the proletariat and the monopoly bourgeoisie can be looked at first within the imperialist countries. It can develop rapidly only after the other contradictions develop first. The revolutionary potential of the proletariat can arise from the internal economic and political crisis of imperialist countries. But before the monopoly bourgeoisie resorts to the use of fascism, it uses its superprofits from the rest of the world to counter and delay the rise of a revolutionary movement of the proletariat with the use of reforms and concessions.

We can reckon with the contradiction of the proletariat and the monopoly bourgeoisie on a global scale. The proletariat has a global presence. Outside of the imperialist countries, there are varying degrees of modern industrial development. On the basis of this, the trade union movement and the revolutionary party of the proletariat can arise. As the most advanced political and productive force, the proletariat can amplify its strength by uniting with and leading the peasant masses in the people's democratic revolution in countries like the Philippines and Nepal.

The people's democratic revolutions through people's war on the basis of the worker-peasant alliance and under the leadership of the revolutionary party of the proletariat are very crucial today in keeping alive the hope of the broad masses of the people to defeat imperialism and its lackeys, free themselves from oppression and exploitation, and enjoy a life of freedom, democracy, justice, plenty and progress in socialism.

109

Imperialism in Various Global Regions

ILPS Decries US Hypocrisy on the Russian-Georgian Conflict, Demands US Imperialism and NATO to Get Out of Caucasus
August 19, 2008

The US and its NATO allies have presented a distorted picture of the conflict between Russia and Georgia over South Ossetia and Abkhazia. And the western media have stridently acted as the purveyor of US imperialist propaganda. The hypocrite George W. Bush has spearheaded the propaganda campaign by misrepresenting Russia as the aggressor and violator of the sovereignty and territorial integrity of Georgia in the current Russian-Georgian conflict.

In fact, Georgia unleashed the aggression against South Ossetia and against the Russian peacekeeping force there by raining artillery fire, missiles and bombs on the capital city of Tskhinvali and sending an invasionary armored force against it on August 7 and 8. Hundreds of civilians were killed. Russian peacekeeping troops were also killed and wounded. Only subsequently did the Russian military forces retaliate and take over the Georgian city of Gori.

On the day before the Georgian aggression against South Ossetia, a joint US-Georgian military exercise was completed. It was called "Immediate Response 2008" and involved more than 1,000 US Army, Marine and National Guard troops. The US air force had ferried from Iraq 2,000 Georgian troops. Georgia maintains the third largest contingent of the occupation forces in Iraq.

It is very clear that Georgia would not have gone on its military adventure without backing from the US The US has trained the Georgian army since 1991. It has provided Georgia with more than US$1 billion in "aid" and has been the No. 1 source of foreign direct investments. Soon after the Georgian aggression, the US mobilized more US military forces to go into Georgia under the pretext of humanitarian mission of providing food and other supplies to the country's population.

The US and the European Union within the NATO framework are involved in the armed conflict between Russia and Georgia. Russia has long been alert and sensitive to the expansion of the NATO towards the Russian borders and to the CIA-engineered "Rose revolution" that put the rabid US puppet Mikhail Saakashvili in power. Since the breakup of the Soviet Union, Russia has been alarmed by the fact that countries at its borders become satellites of US imperialism. Through direct and indirect means, the US has spread its hegemony to the Baltic, Caspian and other regions.

Emboldened by US and NATO support and the US promise of NATO membership for Georgia, Saakashvili has long undertaken provocations against Russia and angled for the fortification of Georgia as a base of US military and economic power and as key point for the oil pipelines extending from Central Asia and the Caspian Sea. To stay in power, he has been subservient to and dependent on US imperialism and has frenziedly drummed up Georgian nationalism against other nationalities in South Ossetia and Abkhazia. These were autonomous regions within the Georgia Soviet Socialist Republic in the Soviet era.

When the Soviet Union disintegrated, Georgia became a separate country and annulled South Ossetia's autonomous status. It imposed Georgian as the official language and chauvinist policies on the people. Rebellions broke out in which the Georgian military killed an estimated 1,000 South Ossetians. South Ossetia declared independence and in a referendum conducted in November 2006, ninety-eight percent voted for independence.

Georgia's attack on South Ossetia is aimed at taking back control of the breakaway region. The US backs Georgia on this for its own imperialist interests in the area. Georgia's reactionary nationalism fits well into the hegemonic designs of US imperialism. After the disintegration of the Soviet Union, the danger of war has increased due to a multiplicity of sharpening contradictions at various levels, between the US and NATO on one side and Russia on the other side, between Russia and the surrounding states and between pro-US and pro-Russian forces within these states.

Since the breakup of the Soviet Union and the Eastern bloc and the emergence of the US as the sole superpower, US imperialism has adopted a policy of preventing any prospective rival from challenging its global supremacy. It wants Russia to remain weak and yielding to US demands. It therefore promoted the so-called multi-color revolutions in the small countries in the periphery of Russia, among them Georgia, in order to draw these small states away from Russia and bring them into the US orbit through offers of economic and military aid.

Since Mikhail Saakashvili's assumption of power in 2004 after the US-instigated "Rose revolution", Georgia has turned more and more to the US and the EU to promote Georgia's narrow nationalist interests. He has openly declared his desire for Georgia to join the NATO military alliance. US State Secretary Condoleeza Rice who was in Tsblisi in the first week of July declared that the US supported Georgia's application for NATO membership and that granting NATO Membership Action Plan to Georgia would help resolve the Abkhazian and South Ossetian problems.

It is quite revealing of the puppetry of the Saakashvili regime to US imperialism that Georgia, which is small country with an army of 37,000, could send 2,000 troops running next only to the US and Britain as the largest foreign contingent among the occupation forces in Iraq. But that is the obligation imposed on Georgia in line with its having become a US imperialist outpost at the border of Russia, which the US regards as a rival and potential enemy.

The US has been building military bases and deploying troops in Georgia, Central Asia and other former Soviet Republics. In 2002, it set up a base in Kyrgyzstan which borders China, Tajikistan, Uzbekistan and Kazakhstan. Base agreements have also been concluded with Pakistan and two other former Soviet republics, Tajikistan and Uzbekistan. US warplanes are already deployed at Kandabad air base at Karshi, Uzbekistan, backed by 1,000 US ground troops.

US imperialism knows no bounds in the pursuit of its scheme to prevail as the sole superpower against the trend of multipolarity. The 1992 Defense Policy Guidance paper, authored by the neocons Paul Wolfowitz and Lewis Libby, explicitly declares that the dominant consideration for US strategy is to prevent the emergence of Russia or any other country as a new rival. The policy categorically includes "preemptive war" and the use of nuclear weapons. The sharpening contradictions between the US and Russia as two imperialist powers, with huge nuclear arsenals, are bound to inflame the new world of disorder.

The ILPS decries the hypocritical US preachings about respect for the sovereignty and territorial integrity of countries and about honoring international conventions. US imperialism is the number No. 1 violator of international conventions and norms. It has launched wars of aggression unilaterally ignoring the United Nations and the universally accepted principles and norms in international relations. It lacks any moral standing to preach to others while it continues to flagrantly violate the sovereignty of Iraq and Afghanistan by its invasion and continued occupation of these countries.

We the International League of Peoples' Struggle call on the people of the world to demand that US imperialism get out of the Caucasus and the Balkans, that the US and NATO cease to engage in military intervention and aggression and that the imperialist powers US, European Union and Russia and their puppets cease to generate wars and threaten the people of the world with a nuclear war.

Imperialism in Various Global Regions

ILPS Statement on the Closing of the US Base in Kyrgyzstan
February 19, 2009

The International League of Peoples' Struggle (ILPS) congratulates the parliament of Kyrgyzstan for overwhelmingly voting 78-1 to close down the US base in its territory.

By its decision, the parliament of Kyrgyzstan has exercised its sovereign right to protect the interests of its own people. Its decision is also in accord with the interests of the people of the world who aspire for a peaceful world and oppose the imperialists' wars of aggression and occupation.

The US base in Manas has served as a key supply line for the US and NATO for their war of aggression in Afghanistan. It is an important base that serves as an air hub and refueling and transit point for US and NATO forces. It handles the transit of 15,000 troops and 500 tons of cargo each month to and from Afghanistan.

In an apparent anticipation of the decision, Gen. Petraeus traveled to Uzbekistan last Tuesday to pressure it to reopen the US base in that country which was closed in 2006. The Uzbek government should follow Kyrgyzstan's example and reject US pressure to use its territory as launching pad for aggression against the people in the region.

The US dominates the world with its network of more than 700 overseas military bases in 130 countries in all continents except Antarctica. It deploys over half a million soldiers, spies, technicians and civilian contractors in other nations to maintain its global hegemony. To dominate the oceans and seas of the world the US has deployed 13 naval task forces of aircraft carriers and battleships. It maintains secret bases to monitor what people around the world are saying through the telephone, fax and email.

According to some, it is very difficult to determine the exact number of military installations the US maintains in other countries as the US uses deceptive means to conceal the truth. For instance the Pentagon reports only one military base in Okinawa which has been an American military colony for 63 years now. There are however ten US military bases in Okinawa. One author points to the US$5 billion worth military and espionage facilities based in Britain which are conveniently disguised as Royal Air Force bases.

The International League of Peoples' Struggle has an ongoing campaign to demand the closure of all US bases in foreign territory as these bases are used by the US in launching wars of aggression and occupation, in bullying small nations through gunboat diplomacy and in creating widespread chaos and destruction around the globe. It is in the interest of the people of the world who aspire for peace to struggle for the closure of all US military bases in foreign countries.

Keynote Address to the International Conference on Education, Imperialism and Resistance
Shih Hsin University, Taipei, Taiwan
August 10, 2009

From the International Coordinating Committee and entirety of the International League of Peoples' Struggle (ILPS), I convey warmest greetings of solidarity to all the educators and social activists now gathered. I express high appreciation to the ILPS Working Group on Teachers, Researchers and Other Educational Personnel for organizing this international conference on education, imperialism and resistance and to the International Center for Taiwan Social Studies for hosting it.

Thank you for affording me the honor and privilege of delivering this keynote address. The theme of your conference is urgent and of great importance to the educators, the youth and the people of the world. We need to underscore the decisive importance of education in the service of the people, to criticize and condemn the depredations of imperialism and all reaction and present the anti-imperialist and progressive perspectives of struggle for a new and better world. I keep in mind that the participants of this conference come from advanced industrial economies as well as from underdeveloped ones.

I. The decisive importance of education

The availability of formal education at the basic and higher levels to comparatively larger numbers of people differentiates the modern world of the bourgeoisie and working class from the ancient world of the slave masters and feudal lords. The wider extent of education is made possible by the larger amount of surplus product created by the modern forces of production and is required by the greater need for mass literacy, professional and technical skills to maintain as well as to advance the level of material and cultural development.

Every exploitative ruling class in modern society, be it the monopoly bourgeoisie in imperialist countries or the bourgeoisie in combination with the landlord class in the underdeveloped countries, always puts its class imprint on the character and content of education and lays stress on the preservation of the ruling system and continuing exploitation of the working people. In opposition, the revolutionary forces of the people lay stress on the transformative character and content of education for the purpose of national and social liberation, all-round development and the attainment of socialism.

In large historical terms, capitalism has outlived its progressive character in opposition to feudalism in the industrial capitalist countries. It has reached the stage of monopoly capitalism or modern imperialism since the beginning of the 20th century. It has been responsible for ever worsening levels of economic and financial crisis, state repression, fascism, colonial and neocolonial domination, interimperialist global wars, wars of aggression against independent countries, damage to the environment and the use of the most backward forms of reaction, including racial, religious and gender biases.

Critique of imperialism

You are absolutely correct in declaring that imperialism is at the root of the suffering and misery of billions of people throughout the world. Indeed, imperialist banks and corporations reap superprofits from the exploitation of the working people in both imperialist and underdeveloped countries and do so far more in the latter countries. The gap between rich and poor countries is ever widening. Widespread poverty and unemployment are deliberately maintained in order to keep ever available a large pool of cheap labor for super-exploitation. Concomitantly, environmental destruction proceeds unabated for the same purpose of extracting superprofits.

In recent decades, it has seemed as if capitalism and imperialism were perpetual and as if the cause of national liberation, people's democracy and socialism were hopeless in the face of the betrayal of socialism by the revisionists, the full-scale restoration of capitalism in revisionist-ruled countries and the imposition of "neoliberal globalization" on the world by the imperialist powers and their local puppets. With Russia having shifted from social-imperialism to rejoin the ranks of the traditional imperialist powers and with China aiming and trying hard to be a major imperialist power, the contradictions within the world capitalist system have intensified, such as those between the imperialist powers and the people of the world, among the imperialist powers themselves and between the bourgeoisie and the working class in the imperialist countries.

The slogan of "free market" or "neoliberal globalization" stands for the systematic attack by the monopoly bourgeoisie on the working class and the rest of the people. It blames supposed wage inflation and social spending by government for the stagflation that surfaced in the imperialist countries in the 1970s and manifested the crisis of overproduction and the financial crisis in the imperialist economy. Since then, the imperialist countries headed by the US have gone on a rampage of pressing down the real wage level, cutting back on social spending for education, health and other social services and curtailing the rights and hard-earned social benefits of the working people.

The imperialist powers have pushed the underdeveloped countries to denationalize their economies, liberalize investments and trade in favor of the

Keynote Address to the International Conference on Education

foreign monopolies, privatize state assets and social services and deregulate all previous restrictions on foreign monopoly capital and on the exploitation of the working people, women, children, migrants and the environment. The essence of the policy of "neoliberal globalization" is gobble-ization of the world by the monopoly banks and corporations. It unleashes the insatiable greed of the monopoly bourgeoisie.

Such monstrous policy has degraded and devastated education. Government spending for public education has been reduced. Teachers, researchers, and other education personnel suffer the consequences of stagnant and decreasing real salaries as these do not keep up with the rising costs of living. Large numbers of education personnel are laid off as governments close down schools and universities. As the academic and non-academic employees and the student masses become restive, they are subjected to repression by state authorities.

II. The imperialist powers keep on tightening their grip on education on a global scale

They use the WTO General Agreement on Trade in Services (GATS) to treat education as a commodity for profit-making in the so-called free market and to push the privatization of public schools at all levels. The purpose, content and conduct of teaching and research are made to serve the interests of the imperialist powers and local reactionaries. These factors of miseducation design and produce the curricula, study materials, education and research programs and institutional structures. They use the combination of schools, mass media and other means of information and education as tools of imperialist domination in the cultural field as well as in the socioeconomic and political fields.

The adoption of higher technology in combination with the pushing down of the incomes of the working people in order to maximize corporate profits have engendered a series of worsening crises of overproduction under the policy of "neoliberal globalization". Every rise of production has been accompanied by the reduction of wage incomes and the shrinkage of the market. The attempt of monopoly capitalism to override the crisis of overproduction and the tendency of the profit rate to fall through massive doses of debt financing, the creation of financial bubbles and the financialization of the economy have served to aggravate the crisis.

We are now faced with the worst financial and economic crisis of the world capitalist system since the Great Depression. If we look at the drastic fall of economic growth, unemployment and trade on the global scale since the second half of 2007, we can say that the current crisis follows a trajectory which is already worse than the Great Depression. But the officials and propagandists of the US obfuscate the severity of the crisis by calling it euphemistically as

119

the Great Recession and merely focusing on some temporary effects of the huge bank bailouts in the US

The downward trend of the US economy continues. It is most evident in the rise of unemployment and the concomitant decline in consumption. The Obama regime continues the neoliberal bias of the Bush regime for bailing out the banks and feeding the greed of the finance oligarchy. The funds that are supposed to stimulate the economy are channeled to certain monopoly corporations that use them to make profits rather than to expand production, create jobs and revive consumer demand. The US will continue to generate crisis in the world capitalist system, worsen the conditions of the working people and even the middle social strata, cause political turmoil within the ruling systems and incite the people to wage all forms of resistance.

The worsening crisis of the world capitalist system leads to the escalation of state terrorism and wars of aggression. The imperialist powers continue to band together to shift the burden of the crisis to the working people and the underdeveloped countries. But the broad masses of the people are bound to fight back for national and social liberation. The imperialist powers become ever more driven by greed as the financial and economic crisis constrains their profit-making. Their struggle for a redivision of the world is bound to intensify as they scramble for the sources of cheap labor and raw materials, markets, fields of investment and spheres of influence. The worsening crisis, the rise of fascism and the imperialist propensity for war are driving the workers and the rest of the people to fight back and move for a radical change of social system in various countries.

Struggle for a new and better world

To be able to fight for a new and better world, the people need to be aroused, organized and mobilized by the revolutionary party and progressive alliances in every country. In this regard, the revolutionary party analyses the global and domestic situation and sets forth the general program of action and the strategy and tactics. The people must be aroused through information and education work. They must be organized on the basis of class or sectoral affinity as well as on the basis of major social issues. They must be mobilized through mass campaigns and through sectoral and multisectoral alliances.

The teachers and researchers play a crucial role in the struggle of the people for a new and better world. They must develop and utilize knowledge and research against the imperialist domination of these and for the liberation of the people from national and class oppression, for the realization of democracy, for all-rounded development in the service of the people, for world peace and the protection of the environment. They must promote and realize a new type of education and culture that is anti-imperialist, scientific and pro-people.

Keynote Address to the International Conference on Education

It is of urgent necessity that the teachers and researchers put forward a critique of imperialist ideology. Such a critique is an important instrument for defining the targets and tasks in the struggle for a radical transformation of society. We must be able to confront imperialist globalization and its terrorist complement of state repression and wars of aggression. In this regard, we must be able to build ever stronger the solidarity of the people of the world and advance their struggle to defend their rights and welfare, including the people's right to education, and advance in stages the struggle for a new and better world of greater freedom, justice, development and peace.

I am pleased to know that participants in this conference are urged to contribute to the critique of any aspect of imperialism and education and are encouraged to make interdisciplinary approaches to such concerns as access to education, the so-called neoliberal reforms in the education sector, the right to education and livelihood, the political economy of education, the politics and theories of knowledge, production and research, the impact of privatization and liberalization on educators and students and adverse effects of neoliberal reforms in education on societies.

The organizers of this conference guide well all the participants by setting forth certain tracks of discussion and calling for papers under each track. I look forward to the publication of the papers on education and imperialism, dealing with historical perspectives, the relation of imperialist globalization to the basic and higher levels of education and the relation of debt and so-called aid to education; to the papers on education and markets, dealing with the relations of education with industry and imperialist globalization, free trade agreements and transnational education; and to the papers on education, oppression and resistance, dealing with the relations of education to social movements, the cause of national liberation, the issues of race, ethnicity and gender and the rights and welfare of educators and related personnel.

The direction, scope and content of your conference are comprehensive and take up the most important issues and concerns. I wish you the utmost success. I am confident that your conference will be very successful not only in interpreting the world but also in proposing how to change it. Thank you.

Imperialism in Various Global Regions

Capitalist Crisis Makes Socialism Necessary
Statement on the 20th Anniversary of
the Fall of the Berlin Wall
November 9, 2009

Since the fall of the Berlin wall on November 9, 1989, the world capitalist system has sunk deeper into crisis. It is now undergoing its most severe crisis since the Great Depression of the 1930s, with some commentators calling the present crisis "the Greater Depression" in terms of its effects on the jobs and livelihood of the workers and peoples of the world.

After emerging as the world's sole superpower in the wake of the collapse of the former Soviet Union, the US itself is wracked by a severe crisis and is further plunging the world with it. The imperialists and their propagandists perorate on how value and value-creation in the economies of the socialist states and then the modern revisionist regimes were distorted by the state bureaucracy.

Now all the countries of the world in varying degrees are reeling from a crisis driven by unbridled private greed under the slogan of "free market globalization" involving the fantastic accumulation of immense wealth by the financial oligarchy and monopoly capitalists through unrelenting super-exploitation of the working people, financial manipulation and the berserk generation of fictitious capital.

Since the fall of the Berlin Wall, the social conditions of the workers and peoples of Eastern Europe and the former Soviet Union have plummeted under the conditions of unbridled capitalist exploitation, oppression and violence. Poverty levels have risen due to massive unemployment and depressed incomes. Inflation has been cutting down the value of wages, pensions and savings.

State investment in production and job creation has been significantly reduced. Public allotment to education and other social services has plummeted. The educated have difficulties finding work and illiteracy is spreading. The workers' and peoples' health have taken a beating, causing severe malnutrition, stunting growth among the youth and shortening the average life span of people.

The number of children living in the streets and left to fend for themselves in these very cold countries has multiplied. The suicide rate has grown among them by significant percentages. The situation of the street children and society at large is being further aggravated by the current financial and economic crisis.

The anger and discontent of the workers and peoples of Eastern Europe and the former Soviet Union are becoming manifest in different ways. Parties of the Left are becoming popular and are gaining strength in national elections. The workers and people are speaking out against the accelerated escalation of exploitation, oppression and violence of the big bourgeoisie.

Survey after survey shows that the people feel they are plunging deeper into poverty and that they are increasingly disillusioned and angry with capitalism and its unfulfilled promises. With the onslaught of the current economic and financial crisis, there is rising interest in and study of Marxist and progressive writings. The imperialists and the local ruling classes are responding to this by deflecting the workers and peoples from the class struggle and anti-imperialist solidarity by promoting divisions and hatred based on chauvinism, racism, ethnocentrism and religious bigotry.

The Comecon is gone. But all the former revisionist-ruled countries are now in the tight grip of the US-controlled world capitalist system and are caught up in the turmoil of the gravest economic crisis since the Great Depression. The crisis is whipping up fascism and aggressive wars. The room for interimperialist competition has become more cramped and more intense, with Russia and China joining in as big power players.

The Warsaw Pact is gone. But the NATO has been expanded as to include the former revisionist-ruled countries in Eastern Europe, reaching the borders of Russia. Most of the former revisionist-ruled countries are potential hotbeds of fascist repression and wars of aggression as already indicated by the violent disintegration of Yugoslavia by a series of wars instigated by the imperialists and by wars involving Chechnya and Georgia. Mercenary forces from the former revisionist-ruled countries have been deployed by the NATO to distant lands like Iraq and Afghanistan.

The crisis of monopoly capitalism has brought ever-greater suffering among the workers and peoples of the world. The imperialist-controlled multilateral agencies underestimate world hunger when they report that only 1 billion people go hungry out of the more than six billion human population. They say that this is the largest number of people going hungry in history, and the same number of people suffer from malnutrition.

This situation is bound to get worse, as world economic output is predicted to decrease this year, the first time since World War II. The contraction of employment is estimated to last for another eight years. The number of people living on less than US$2 per day will increase by hundreds of millions. Decreasing demand for consumer goods, semi manufactures and raw materials impacts heavily on millions of workers and peasants in neocolonial economies.

The workers and peoples of the world are waging various legal and illegal forms of organized action to protest the anti-people policies of imperialism. International gatherings of the monopoly capitalists, the finance oligarchy,

Capitalist Crisis Makes Socialism Necessary

and heads of imperialist states have become occasions for mass protests by indignant workers and peoples in the meeting areas and in various countries. Countries assertive of national independence are exposing and lambasting the dictates and impositions of imperialism.

Armed revolutions for national liberation and democracy are continuing and gaining strength in the Philippines, Colombia, India, Peru and Turkey. The peoples of Iraq and Afghanistan are waging armed resistance against the US occupation and colonization of their countries. The armed forms of struggle are bound to grow in strength and advance as a result of the intensification of the crisis of monopoly capitalism.

Since the fall of the Berlin Wall, the workers and peoples of Eastern Europe, the former Soviet Union and the world have undergone ever worsening economic and social conditions. They see monopoly capitalism as an evil and bankrupt system that is destroying the world's productive forces and is inflicting immense suffering on the people.

Monopoly capitalism is igniting the people's desire for socialism. So long as imperialist oppression and exploitation persist, the people fight for national and social liberation. It is farthest from the truth that monopoly capitalism is the end of history. The utter bankruptcy of monopoly capitalism and its descent to ever more barbarous forms of plunder and aggression drive the people to fight for their rights and for a bright socialist future. The workers and peoples of the world are called upon to persevere in the struggle for genuine socialism and against monopoly capitalism that is now in the throes of its worst crisis since the Great Depression of the 1930s. The crisis of the world capitalist system makes socialism necessary for humankind.

Contrary to the claims of the imperialists and their propagandists that socialism fell in 1989, the fall of the Berlin Wall has actually meant the collapse of the modern revisionist regimes in the former Soviet Union and Eastern Europe and the completion of the restoration of capitalism. It is the end result of the revisionist betrayal of socialism started by Khrushchev in 1956 and completed by Gorbachov in the years of 1989-91.

The history of socialist countries from the Bolshevik victory of 1917 up to 1956, and from the founding of the People's Republic of China up to 1976 shows great leaps in the advancement of the social, economic, political, cultural and defense situations of the workers and peoples of those countries. The poverty, hunger, joblessness, and the cruelties of exploitation and oppression before the victory of the socialist revolution were overcome. The great victories in socialist construction and revolution were achieved despite imperialist wars of aggression and economic and military blockades and subversion.

The rise of modern revisionism in socialist countries and elsewhere reversed all the great achievements of socialism. Advances in the situation of the workers and peoples were slowly but surely eroded, and prerevolutionary forms of exploitation, oppression and violence were restored. Together with criminal syndicates in the so-called free market, the modern revisionist big bourgeoisie grew fat on bureaucratic corruption and enjoyed the lifestyles of the rich and famous, while the workers and peoples suffered from the decrease in food, jobs, savings and social services.

As workers and peoples grew restive and began clamoring for reforms, the ruling revisionist regimes imposed severe political repression. In Eastern Europe, and in East Germany especially, this condition fueled the mass protests that brought about the fall of the Berlin Wall in 1989. The revisionist regimes in Eastern Europe and the former Soviet Union peacefully gave up power and gave way to the legalization of their bureaucratic loot, the barefaced restoration of capitalism and the blatant privatization of state assets.

Since Nikita Khrushchov's reign in the Soviet Union, genuine proletarian revolutionaries the world over have called the ruling regimes in the Soviet Union and its satellite states in Eastern Europe as modern revisionists, who mouth socialism but practice capitalism. They have predicted that it will not take long before capitalism reveals itself barefaced in these countries.

The fall of the Wall has shown how accurate are their predictions. The modern revisionists in these countries have since exposed themselves as pseudocommunists and anti-communists. It is modern revisionism, not socialism, which fell with the Berlin Wall and delivered the workers and peoples of the former Soviet Union and Eastern Europe into the even more predatory and violent rule of barefaced capitalism. The revisionists had earlier undermined, eroded and destroyed socialism.

Since 1989 until the present, imperialism and its well-paid propagandists in the mass media and academe have tirelessly repeated their line on the fall of the Berlin Wall. They have misrepresented the revisionist regimes as socialist and boasted that their fall meant the futility of socialism and the end of history with capitalism and liberal democracy.

They have touted the jump from the frying pan of revisionist-ruled state monopoly capitalism to the flames of barefaced capitalism as the beginning of development and democracy. But the imperialist powers are incomparable in discrediting monopoly capitalism through their unbridled plunder and wars of aggression and the recurrent and increasingly severe crisis.

The workers and peoples of the world are subjected to ever- increasing exploitation, oppression and violence and are impelled to wage resistance, seek national and social liberation and aim for the attainment of socialism. The present crisis, which has been generated by the US-directed policy of neoliberal "globalization" in the last three decades, incites the people to struggle for socialism.

The world capitalist system continues to sink deeper into crisis. It is devastating jobs and livelihood of the workers and peoples of the world. The profuse use of public funds to bail out the big banks and corporations in the military industrial complex is building bigger bubbles than ever before. These are bound to burst and cause a steeper fall in the crisis.

Capitalist Crisis Makes Socialism Necessary

The US and its imperialist allies have generated the global financial and economic crisis, have plunged the world into a state of economic depression and have aggravated and deepened the conditions for state terrorism and aggressive wars.

The combination of state monopoly capitalism and monopoly capitalism in imperialist countries is responsible for the unprecedentedly greatest devastation of productive forces through the most rapacious forms of private profit-taking and private accumulation, including the wanton creation of fictitious capital.

We are in the era of modern imperialism and proletarian revolution. Further economic crisis, social disorder, state terrorism and imperialist wars of aggression are in prospect. These are the objective conditions for the rise of revolutionary movements for national and social liberation led by the working class.

Imperialism in Various Global Regions

Intensify the Struggles of the Proletariat and Peoples against Imperialism and Reaction
May 1, 2010

On this glorious day of the international proletariat, we, the International League of Peoples' Struggle, join the workers and peoples of the world in celebrating their struggles, sacrifices and victories. It is of the greatest importance to raise the banner of proletarian unity and struggle against exploitation and oppression by imperialism and all reaction. Once again, we renew our resolve to dismantle the monopoly capitalist system and replace it with a just, democratic and peaceful new world in which socialism prevails.

Crisis of global capitalism continues to worsen

The enemies of the working class and the oppressed peoples do not cease to demonstrate their contempt for the masses with their lies and their violence. The mouthpieces of the monopoly bourgeoisie are busy proclaiming the end of the global economic and financial crisis, and celebrating the so-called beginnings of recovery. Not only is this claim of recovery patently false, it actually signals a heightened offensive against the workers and peoples of the world.

Bourgeois economists are prating about rising GDP figures, rallies in the stock market, the "stabilization" of the financial system, increasing bank profits and more business activity. In reality, the so-called recovery is artificial and temporary as it is solely reliant on trillions of dollars handed out by the state to the biggest banks and failing conglomerates as bailout money. This is the largest-ever simultaneous raid of public treasuries by the wealthiest stratum of the capitalist class which uses the money to rake in more profits from speculative investments.

Conditions in the real economy remain grim, especially in terms of rising unemployment and the dismal living conditions of the working masses. Tens of millions have lost their jobs or livelihoods since 2008 when the worst crisis since the Great Depression of the 1930s erupted in the heartland of the global capitalist system. Millions more have been kept employed but on a part-time basis, with lower wages and ready to be axed at the bosses' say so. In the US alone, millions of families are set to lose their homes in the coming year. The monopoly bourgeoisie is seizing on mass unemployment and profound social insecurity to cut costs, take back hard-won workers' benefits and boost profits.

In the underdeveloped countries, the social consequences have been more devastating to those economies most deeply penetrated by international monopoly capital as foreign investments, credit, so-called aid, export revenues and remittances have fallen along with the economies of the advanced capitalist countries. Chronic economic depression is compounded by the multiple crises generated by the monopoly capitalist system including the food, water and ecological crises.

While the masses face a bleak future, the managers of finance oligarchy responsible for the crisis continue to raise their share of the loot. The top 25 managers of US hedge funds took home a record US$25.33 billion in 2009 — greater than the GDP of about 100 nations combined. They "earned" these obscene sums not from production but from mere speculation, specifically by correctly betting that the US government under Obama would shore up Wall Street at virtually any cost.

Obama certainly did not disappoint his financiers. Not only has he continued to funnel trillions to the finance sector, his administration has also scuttled any attempt to apply restraints on the predatory operations of finance capital, despite calls even from reform-minded bourgeois economists. He is generating the biggest kind of bubble in the form of public debt and is engaged in deficit spending that promotes monopoly profit-taking but not employment and economic recovery.

He has also indulged the military-industrial complex with the biggest war budget in US history since World War II, even adjusted for inflation. The US is building more bases and upgrading its military facilities all over the world to secure its control over strategic resources (such as oil and gas in West and Central Asia, and West and Central Africa); encircle potential rival powers, particularly China and Russia; and attack or intervene in regions where US interests are being challenged (such as in Latin America, Pakistan, Iran, and Korea.). It is also paying out billions to US monopoly firms to supply and service US bases overseas and "reconstruct" the civilian infrastructure destroyed by US invasions in Iraq and Afghanistan.

All this generosity to the most parasitic and brutal fraction of the big bourgeoisie has resulted in the rapid increase in public deficits and debts in all the major economies. The Bank for International Settlements estimates that the debt-to-GDP ratios of the G-7 countries are likely to shoot up to between 150 and 300 percent within the next decade. Hence the executives of the monopoly bourgeoisie are preparing a new assault on the working masses in their own countries and against Third World peoples in order to squeeze out more surplus value.

The Obama administration has for instance frozen discretionary social spending, laid off thousands of teachers and public sector employees, and is getting ready to further whittle down Medicare and Social Security. Leaders of the Group of 20 are now talking about "deficit containment" and "returning to a normal policy stance" even amidst an ocean of unemployed and dispossessed masses. By this they mean withdrawing stimulus measures, imposing fiscal

Intensify the Struggles of the Proletariat and Peoples against Imperialism

austerity and new taxes in order to raise revenues needed to cover the bailouts handed over to the finance oligarchy. This translates to wholesale job cuts particularly in the public sector, and slashing education, health, housing and other social and welfare programs. This is what all this talk of "recovery" means for the working masses.

The International Monetary Fund is again stepping in to impose devastating austerity measures and wage cuts not just in debt-stricken Third World countries in Asia, Africa and Latin America but now also in Eastern Europe and the less advanced capitalist countries such as Greece. In countries that have managed to steer clear of the IMF by relying on private capital markets, international finance capital still issues decrees through ratings agencies such as Moody's and Standard and Poor. Countries that refuse to reduce their fiscal deficits through cutbacks in social services, layoffs and more regressive taxes are punished by poor ratings and higher interest rates.

Even then, there remains the threat of widespread defaults and financial meltdown in the near future. In fact, these are inevitable because the response of the ruling class to the crisis — intensified exploitation of the working masses, over-accumulation of capital, debt-driven spending, and financialization — actually aggravates the basic conditions which lead to crises. The expected bursting of the public debt bubble will have far worse consequences than the bursting of previous bubbles.

While continuing to rave about the free market masquerade of monopoly capitalism, the US is now desperately carrying out a protectionist policy and trying to reduce its external deficits through cutting imports and more aggressive export promotion. Obama recently launched the National Export Initiative which aims to double US exports in five years. The US can therefore be expected to become even more aggressive in prying open foreign markets, enforcing its "property rights" overseas while restricting the entry of imports. This is sure to exacerbate trade frictions between the US and its commercial competitors as well as intensify inter-imperialist rivalry for plundering the Third World.

In the face of the economic crisis and challenges to its hegemony, US imperialism is escalating militarism, state terrorism and wars of aggression. The biggest armed conflicts and greatest instability are happening in regions where US intervention is most extensive – West, Central and South Asia, and West and Central Africa. These are also the regions with the greatest concentration of strategic resources, foremost of which is oil, the control of which is an explicit aim of US military policy since the 1950s.

The US occupation of Iraq has entered its seventh year with no end in sight, contrary to Obama's promise to end US combat mission in Iraq by Aug. 31, 2010. The US is ramping up its war in Afghanistan by sending 30,000 additional troops plus tens of thousands of private contractors, using the country as a laboratory for new US weaponry and combat tactics, such as the use of drone attacks. It has entered into a new nuclear agreement with India to support the latter's military upgrading and keep the Pakistan-China alliance in check.

The US continues to use the US-Zionist alliance to terrorize the entire Middle East and to seize the oil and other natural resources. US support for Israeli aggression against the Palestinian people has resulted in the most atrocious war crimes and human rights violations by Israeli Zionism and in the humanitarian crisis such as that in Gaza.

In Africa, the US has fortified its military presence by creating the African Command or Africom, and has increased arms sales, military aid and training provided to a number of African countries, particularly in the oil and mineral-rich countries.

The US has also recently sealed a deal to use seven military bases in Colombia for 10 years to use as its staging ground for intervention within the country and expand its "expeditionary warfare capability" throughout the region, particularly against "anti-US governments" identified by the Pentagon such as Venezuela, Cuba and Bolivia. In Honduras, the US-inspired coup d'etat that deposed elected President Manuel Zelaya will mark its one-year anniversary on June 28, 2010 as rumors of other possible coups spread in Ecuador, Paraguay, Venezuela (and possibly in other countries that have rejected the increasingly discredited Washington Consensus). Hugo Chavez, in particular, is the object of vitriolic propaganda in the monopoly capitalist media – which is possibly a precursor to and justification for destabilization or even direct aggression against Venezuela. Even the recent humanitarian disaster in Haiti is used by the US to extend direct military control over the Haitian people and their economy.

In the whole East Asia, the US continues to apply on China a policy of engagement and containment and is increasingly exerting economic and political pressures. It is exerting more of such pressures on Democratic People's Republic of Korea. In the Philippines, the continued presence of US troops and military facilities and the continued supply of military aid underwrite the government's vicious counterinsurgency program which targets both armed and unarmed civilians alike and props up the corrupt and fascist puppet Arroyo government.

US military aggression and intervention throughout the world is resulting in massive civilian deaths, destruction of vital infrastructure, trampling of national cultures, pillaging of natural resources, massive displacement and other gross human rights violations, spread of hunger and disease.

The proletariat and peoples of world resist

The worsening conditions of global economic and financial crisis and the escalation of imperialist plunder and wars of aggression are inciting the proletariat and peoples of the world to wage various forms of struggle.

Intensify the Struggles of the Proletariat and Peoples against Imperialism

Workers of the world are confronted not only by individual capitalist bosses extracting surplus value in particular workplaces. The monopoly bourgeoisie is attacking the working masses by using the entire coercive apparatus of the state in the imperialist countries and in the imperialist-dominated countries. The workers and peoples of the world are aware that they cannot simply bargain for higher wages and benefits. They are desirous of wresting political power from their oppressors and use state power to uphold their rights and interests.

In various countries, large-scale protests mainly against governments' responses to the crisis are breaking out and catching international attention. Greece was recently rocked and brought to a standstill by strikes and other forms of actions that oppose government plans to cut down on social spending and raise taxes to address foreign debt and mounting deficit. Farmers' tractors were used to block roads; ferries were left tied up at the ports; hospitals, schools and other public services were shut down; and even news broadcasts were suspended as hundreds of thousands joined militant protests. The workers and people of Greece are saying "no" to government efforts to make them pay for decades of misuse of government funds for political patronage, corruption and consumption through debt financing.

In France, hundreds of thousands also joined protests against the Sarkozy regime's plan to overhaul the national pension system by cutting pension and raising the retirement age in an attempt to solve the country's deficit. Organizers of the protests also raised demands for job security, better working conditions and higher wages. In all countries of Europe, especially in Portugal, Ireland, Iceland, Greece and Spain, the level of social discontent and protest is rising because of the increasing rate of unemployment, the erosion of social benefits and the deterioration of living conditions.

In the US, the workers and immigrants undertook strikes and protest rallies. Hundreds of thousands of students and faculty launched protests against cuts in the education budget and increases in tuition. They were expressing outrage at the Obama regime's policy of bailing out banks and huge corporations and of pouring money into the war in Iraq and Afghanistan to the detriment of education and other social services.

Despite US imperialism's sabotage attempts, the governments of Cuba, Venezuela, Bolivia, and North Korea are vocal in asserting national sovereignty and opposing imperialism's dictates to their countries and the world. Their popular leaders declare that their countries are waging revolution for socialism. Their governments have been able to cushion the worst effects of the current crisis on the workers and peoples, and have even improved the standard of living in their respective countries. They are now mobilizing workers and peoples to change the socioeconomic structures. Cuba, Venezuela, Bolivia are active in encouraging their fellow Latin American countries to enhance economic cooperation in that region.

133

Imperialism in Various Global Regions

In Iraq and Afghanistan, the armed resistance of the workers and peoples against direct US colonial rule and for national liberation are dealing severe military and political blows on the military might of US imperialism. The imposition by force of US-backed puppet governments in these countries has only intensified the workers and peoples' anger at US imperialism.

The armed resistance in these countries is encouraging the American workers and peoples' condemnation of their government's continuing war of aggression. It is also showing to the workers and peoples of the world that US military might can be resisted and put to shame, and that direct US occupation and colonial rule must be opposed at all costs.

There are proletarian parties in Asia, Latin America and Asia that are waging or are preparing to wage revolutionary armed struggle. The workers and peoples of the Philippines, India, Turkey, Congo, Niger Delta, Peru and Colombia are waging people's wars for national liberation and democracy. They are persevering in the face of various campaigns of suppression by regimes that are supported by US imperialism under the pretext of the latter's so-called "global war on terror." In the Philippines, the revolutionary movement is aiming for a qualitative leap from strategic defensive to strategic stalemate in five years, by taking advantage of the intensifying global and national crises and building on current strengths and experiences.

In India and Nepal, revolutionary armed movements led by proletarian revolutionary parties continue to advance with the support of the workers and peoples in these countries. The revolutionary movement in India is steadily gaining strength, forcing the prime minister to say that "We are losing the war with the Maoists". After overthrowing the monarchy and achieving great successes in the legal militant struggles and elections, the revolutionary movement in Nepal is now gearing for the seizure of state power to defend national independence and build socialism.

After two decades of blabbering about the "end of history," the imperialists and their paid propagandists are being put to shame by the perseverance of ordinary workers and people in revolutionary struggle in order to collectively and militantly make history, and to put an end to such a backward and moribund system as imperialism.

All the struggles of the workers and peoples against imperialism and reaction are contributory to the relentless advance towards a new and better world of national independence, democracy, development, social justice and peace. We call on the workers and peoples of the world to intensify their struggles against imperialist plunder and wars of aggression and open the way to socialism.

134

Intensify the Struggle against Imperialist Exploitation and Plunder to Attain Development and End Poverty
September 20, 2010

From September 20-22, 2010, the United Nations is hosting the largest gathering of heads of state since the Millennium Summit in the year 2000 when 189 world leaders made pious pledges to reaffirm the principles and values of the UN for the new millennium and declared that the central challenge for the moment was "to ensure that globalization becomes a positive force for all the world's people."

In this connection, the UN promulgated eight Millennium Development Goals (MDGs), targeted for fulfilment by 2015. With barely five years left before the deadline and in the midst of the first global depression of the 21st century, world leaders are convening in New York to proclaim their continued commitment to pursue the MDGs while diverting people's attention away from the real roots of the problems that these goals are supposed to solve.

The MDGs were adopted ostensibly to marshal the efforts of governments towards "doable" and "measurable" targets. The real intent was to legitimize "neoliberalism" and make pretenses that the world capitalist system was humane even as the rapacity of imperialist exploitation and plunder remains the reality. The goals were deliberately chosen—principally by bureaucrats and spin-doctors from the OECD, IMF and WB—to deal superficially only with the most obvious symptoms of poverty and oppression which riled even the imperialist-funded NGOs and some rock stars.

They obscured the necessity of overcoming colonial and neocolonial domination and monopoly capitalist exploitation which have shackled the majority of the world's population to chronic poverty and dehumanizing privations. They brushed aside the longstanding demands of underdeveloped countries within the UN system to redress the unequal relations between countries and to respect national sovereignty and mutual benefit in international relations. They dismissed the demands for social justice and structural transformation voiced by people's movements in all continents.

Indeed, the Millennium Declaration and the MDGs were essentially propaganda offensives to push back the advance of the progressive forces against imperialist globalization. During the last decade of the previous millennium, such forces had been mounting increasingly militant actions in connection with the People's Conference against Imperialist Globalization in Manila in 1996, the People's Caravan Against APEC in 1997, and the Battle of Seattle in 1999.

Since their 2000 launch, the MDGs have been used to sugarcoat the bitter overdosages of "neoliberal" policy that the imperialist financial institutions have been shoving down the throats of people in the impoverished and bankrupt countries. The MDGs, thus, have served to perpetrate the exploitative relations between the imperialist powers and the client countries. The first goal, "eradicate extreme poverty and hunger," is farther from realization than ever, with the number of hungry people worldwide increasing from 842 million in 1990 to over 1 billion last year.

The aggravation of hunger is due to the tightened monopoly capitalist control of the global food system—from production inputs, to credit, to marketing and distribution. This has deepened the longstanding crisis of agriculture and food production in underdeveloped countries. This is also rooted in the legacy of feudal land monopoly and compounded by governments that would rather support foreign agribusiness, mining and logging interests and landed elite interests than uplift the condition of the peasantry and poor consumers.

The UN claims that the MDG target of halving the number people living in extreme poverty is well on the way to being met. But that target is based on the puffing up of the aggregate figures with the reported rise in household incomes of a narrow section of the Chinese population. Concealed are the decline of employment and incomes among the workers and peasants and the reduction of social incomes in the form of public goods and services as a consequence of capitalist restructuring and the worsening global economic crisis.

In 2005, there were still supposedly about 1.4 billion people living below US$1.25 per day, down from 1.8 billion in 1990. Without China, to which most of the reduction is ascribed, the number actually increased by 36 million. Rising food prices and the global economic crisis that erupted in 2008 is pushing millions more into absolute poverty. The share of the poor in the world's income is also declining. In 1990, the ratio of the per capita income in the richest 20 countries to that in the poorest 20 was US$42 to one dollar; in 2005, it was US$59 to one dollar.

The UN claims that universal primary education is on its way to being achieved. But nearly half of all secondary school-age children in developing countries are known to be out of school, especially those from impoverished families in remote rural areas where public schools, teachers and other basic social services are not provided by governments due to fiscal tightening or austerity imposed by imperialist financial institutions. Monopoly capitalists are also pushing for the privatization and commercialization of education in order to profit from building schools, charging fees and churning out students adapted to the needs of multinational corporations.

The UN admits to making little headway in redressing gender discrimination, whether this be in the realm of education, employment, incomes and most especially in terms of maternal health. As of 2005, a woman in the third world

Intensify the Struggle against Imperialist Exploitation and Plunder

dies of complications related to pregnancy every minute while more than one million infants are left motherless every year. Some 8.8 million children under the age of five die every year—13 times more likely in poor countries compared to advanced capitalist countries.

Malnutrition and preventable diseases due to lack of access to health care, water and sanitation are the primary causes. As in the case of education, the priority given to servicing foreign debts and privatization has eroded most third world government's capacities to provide these basic services and deploy health personnel where they are needed most. Monopoly control of giant pharmaceutical companies over medicines, medical technologies and medical research, reinforced by so-called intellectual property rights protection provided to them by governments and the WTO, also undermine efforts at combating HIV/AIDS, malaria and other diseases that are rampant in poor countries, particularly in sub-Saharan Africa.

While the MDGs include environmental sustainability in the wish list, the anarchic, wasteful and destructive capitalist production for profit has now pulled our world close to the brink of ecological disaster. The massive dumping of greenhouse gases (GHG) in the atmosphere by the operations of monopoly capitalist firms in the energy industries, manufacturing, transportation, industrial agriculture, mining, construction, etc., is now generating climatic changes that are causing massive devastation and loss of human lives around the world.

The relentless extraction of mineral ores and wanton destruction of forests by multinational mining corporations persist in the underdeveloped countries that are rich with natural resources. Massive environmental destruction and pollution, widespread landlessness and displacement, loss of livelihood, distortion of local culture, and rampant human rights violations are left in their wake.

Central to the MDG schema is the avowed obligation of the advanced capitalist countries to provide more development aid, debt relief, access to markets, medicines and new technology for the underdeveloped countries in the name of "global partnerships for development." But in fact, these are the very same instruments by which imperialists exploit and keep backward countries dependent. Debt relief and aid granted to the most indebted countries are a mere fraction of the resources siphoned off by monopoly capitalists from underdeveloped countries in the form of debt payments, unequal trade, profit remittances, tax evasion, capital flight, and resource plunder.

According to UN estimates, the underdeveloped countries are transferring resources to the industrialized countries at an average rate of nearly US$500 billion per year since 2000, reaching a peak of US$891 billion in 2008. Moreover, so-called development assistance remains attached to policy conditionalities such as liberalization, privatization and deregulation that favor monopoly capitalist interests over the requirements of real national development.

The MDGs are a grand and expensive distraction from the real effort to address the structural roots of poverty, injustice, oppression and underdevelopment—the struggle against imperialist exploitation and plunder through painstaking education, organizing and mobilization of the masses. This is the only path to national and social liberation and all-rounded development.

Notes on the International Situation
For BAYAN-USA in New York and New Jersey
October 2010

1. Prolongation of financial and economic crisis

The financial and economic crisis, which has sharpened since 2008 and has become the worst since the Great Depression, has become prolonged, especially because the policy makers of the imperialist countries persist in the dogmatic rut of neoliberalism. Public money has been used to bail out the big banks and certain favored corporations. It has been used merely produce profits in balance sheets and stimulate the financial markets.

Even that part of the bailout money that is supposed to stimulate production by the favored corporations in the military industrial complex is used to generate profits on paper and is subject to labor cost-cutting. Due to the neoliberal mania for reducing the wage fund, the so-called stimulus packages for infrastructure, car production, health services and green projects have not resulted in the expansion of production and unemployment. Joblessness, homelessness, deterioration of social services and other maladies continue to mount.

2. Austerity measures in imperialist countries

Public deficits and public debts have soared because of the bailouts given to the banks and corporations, the tax cuts given to the corporations and the wealthy families, the mounting debt service and rising expenditures for the military and intelligence services. But the financial oligarchy and the entire monopoly bourgeoisie continue to cover up their criminal culpability for the crisis and for the growth of the public debt bubble.

They simplistically blame government spending and obfuscate the fact that the public money has been used for their corporate welfare rather than for social relief and the stimulation of production and expansion of employment. They proceed to shift further the burden of crisis to the working people through austerity measures which include pushing down wages, eroding social relief and pension benefits, increasing the premium on health insurance, raising the fees for social services and so on.

3. Further plunder of the underdeveloped countries

Under the US-directed policy of neoliberal globalization, the underdeveloped countries have run into huge amounts of public deficits and public debts. The further growth of these has further accelerated during the current stage of the crisis even as terms of foreign borrowing have become more onerous. The types of goods exported by the underdeveloped countries to the imperialist countries like raw materials and semi-manufactures are afflicted by less demand and lower prices.

The underdeveloped countries are hard pressed to adopt austerity measures, far harsher than in the imperialist countries. They are vulnerable to the inflow of extremely exploitative investments aimed at grabbing the land and natural resources. The dire conditions of economic depression result in the further loss of economic sovereignty and accelerated plunder by the foreign multinational corporations. The people of the underdeveloped countries suffer the main brunt of the global economic crisis.

4. Interimperialist contradictions

Among the imperialist powers, there are growing contradictions regarding economic, financial, trade and security policies. The most conspicuous of these involves the competition for sources of energy and other raw materials, fields of investments, for markets and spheres of influence. There is resentment by certain imperialist and nonimperialist countries over the incresing use of military intervention and aggression by the US in order to maintain hegemony and preempt the rise of its rivals.

However, there are yet no conditions driving the imperialist powers to divide into violently conflicting groups as on the eve of the last two world wars in the 20th century. The imperialist powers still manage to be united in drawing up common policies within the G-8 and the G-20 and using the IMF, World Bank, WTO, the US Security Council, NATO and certain bilateral and multilateral treaties at the expense of the oppressed peoples and nations.

5. Scapegoating China

China has been the main partner of the US in carrying out the policy of neoliberal globalization and is at the head of the so-called emergent markets, departing from previous economies with state-owned enterprises in a commanding position. It has been integrated in the world capitalist system as the producer of cheap consumer goods for the imperialist countries. US and other multinational firms own most of the sweatshop operations in China.

By producing and exporting cheap consumer goods, China has accumulated a huge amount of export surpluses and has used a great part of these to buy US treasury bonds and certain private US securities. Thus, the US has become heavily indebted to China. It now bashes China as responsible for the economic and financial crisis of the US and the world by keeping low the value of its currency, restraining imports and driving up its exports.

140

Notes on the International Situation

6. The US global war of terror

The Obama regime has continued the Bush policy of using 9/11 as the pretext for waging a global war of terror against the peoples that wage revolution, nations that fight for liberation and countries that assert independence. It whips up the terrorism scare in order to, suppress democratic rights, promote war production, maintain 800 military bases overseas and unleash military intervention and wars of aggression.

Under the direction of the US, the fascist current is running high in both imperialist and underdeveloped countries. It involves chauvinism, racism, xenophobia and religious bigotry. It is used to cover up the roots of the crisis in both the imperialist and underdeveloped countries and to counter the rise of progressive popular movements and the revolutionary forces for national and social liberation.

7. Anti-Imperialist forces

Due to past revolutionary struggles and current mass movements there are countries like China, DPRK, Cuba, Venezuela, Bolivia, Iran and Sudan that are invoking national independence and even socialism in opposing the worst imperialist policies.

Legal anti-imperialist mass movements are surging on a global scale. In varying degrees, they are effective in putting forward the demands of the people in influencing the policies of governments and in shaping the character of the government.

Revolutionary armed struggles for national and social liberation persevere in the Philippines, India, Colombia, Peru, Kurdistan and elsewhere. As the crisis is worsening, they are gaining strength and are likely to spread.

8. Prospects

There is no end of the crisis of the world capitalist system in sight. Legal anti-imperialist mass movements will continue to expand and intensify. So will the revolutionary armed struggles. More governments in underdeveloped countries that assert national independence can arise as a result of the legal anti-imperialist mass movements and the revolutionary armed struggles.

In the imperialist countries, the current of fascism is becoming stronger. But the progressive forces of the proletariat and the people are resurgent. In the underdeveloped countries, the mass movements are paving the way for national and social liberation.

As a result of the worsening crisis of the world capitalist system, we can look forward to the rise of the revolutionary forces and a bright future of greater

141

freedom, democracy, social justice, development, peace and international solidarity.

We Unite to Fight Imperialism

We Unite to Fight Imperialism
Message of solidarity to the
3rd Anti-Imperialist Conference in Dhaka
November 27, 2011

We of the International League of Peoples' Struggle (ILPS) are deeply pleased and highly honored by the invitation to participate in the 3rd International Anti-imperialist Conference, jointly convened by the International Anti-imperialist and People's Solidarity Coordinating Committee (IAPSCC) and the Socialist Party of Bangladesh in Dhaka, from November 27 to 29, 2011.

We are in solidarity with all the anti-imperialist fighters attending the conference. We consider this conference a major opportunity for raising the level of consciousness and militancy against imperialism. In this connection, we have authorized our Vice Chairperson for External Relations Comrade Bill Doares to represent the ILPS. He carries full mandate to express our determination to unite with you against imperialism and to take active part in the Conference.

The conference is of urgent importance in view of the brutal imperialist attacks on Iraq, Afghanistan, Palestine and Libya, the threats of regime change in Syria and Iran and the blockades against Cuba and North Korea. The theme is keenly appropriate: "Imperialist Attack: Economic, Political, Cultural and Military Aggression and Occupation, with special reference to imperialist attack and aggression in Latin America, Middle East, Afghanistan, Cuba and DPRK."

We agree with the purposes of the conference: to discuss the economic, political, cultural and military aspects of imperialist aggression, to exchange experiences of struggle, to clarify the ways and means of building a global movement against imperialism and to heighten solidarity among the various anti-imperialist forces of the people. We look forward to the formulation of a comprehensive declaration against imperialism.

The imperialist powers headed by the US are stubbornly clinging to the neoliberal policy of so-called free market globalization, which has led from one serious crisis to another and more serious crisis. They continue to aggravate the chronic crisis of overproduction by pressing down wages and cutting back on hard-won social benefits in order to help the monopoly bourgeoisie maximize profits and accelerate the accumulation of capital. However, as the profit rate tends to fall in the real economy, the monopoly capitalists have abused finance capital to generate profits and financial bubbles through debts and derivatives.

The result is an economic and financial crisis comparable to the Great Depression and worse in certain respects. Public funds have been used to

143

bail out the big banks and corporations in order to improve their financial statements and induce temporary spikes in the financial markets but not to stimulate production and employment. Now, the imperialist powers and their client states are confronted with a far bigger financial crisis in the form of public debt bubbles bursting and about to burst.

Their reaction is to impose austerity measures on the people and further shift to them the burden of crisis. The toiling masses of workers and peasants are subjected to higher rates of unemployment, lower incomes and soaring prices of basic goods and services. They are made to suffer worse forms of exploitation to enable the monopoly bourgeoisie, especially the finance oligarchy, to obtain their superprofits. The global depression is protracting, worsening and deepening.

Year after year the summits of the G8 and G20 and the conferences of the IMF, World Bank and WTO have failed to come up with any solution or relief from the global economic and financial crisis. The imperialist powers are increasingly engaged in a struggle for a redivision of the world in seeking to expand their respective economic territory in a constricted global market. They are scrambling for cheap sources of labor, oil and other raw materials, for markets, fields of investment and spheres of influence. The integration of Russia and China into the world capitalist system has further crammed the space for mutual accommodation among the imperialist powers.

As a result of the ever-worsening crisis of the world capitalist system, all major contradictions are intensifying: those between the imperialist powers and the oppressed peoples and nations; those between the imperialist powers and certain states that assert national independence and democratic rights and invoke socialist aspirations, those between capital and labor; and those among the imperialist powers themselves. The imperialist powers continue trying to override their differences, maintain their alliance and assert their joint and separate ultranational interests against the oppressed peoples and nations in the underdeveloped countries. They continue to control as semicolonies most of those countries that have ceased to be outright colonies as a result of struggles for national independence. The preferred neocolonial means of control are economic and financial.

But the imperialist powers and their local puppets are ever ready to use military means to suppress revolutionary movements for national liberation, such as in India, the Philippines and Colombia as well as against the states assertive of national independence, such as Iraq of Saddam, Yugoslavia of Milosevic and Libya of Gaddafi. For extended periods of time, they use a wide spectrum of military and non-military means, blockades, sanctions and threats against states that assert national independence, such as the Democratic People's Republic of Korea, Cuba, Venezuela and others.

After the end of the Cold War, the imperialist powers have so far avoided direct military confrontation with each other. They have pre- erred to use proxy wars by backing different sides in local and regional wars. They have taken different positions on whether or not to take unilateral or joint military actions within or outside the purview of the UN Security Council. So far, no rival imperialist powers or blocs of imperialist powers have threatened to use hightech weapons of mass destruction against one another.

For more than three decades under the neoliberal economic policy, the monopoly bourgeoisie has one-sidedly waged an intense and relentless class war against the working classes by pressing down wages, and social spending by government and suppressing trade union and other democratic rights, while the corporations and wealthy enjoy tax cuts and the benefits of trade and investment liberalization, privatization of public assets and deregulation. Now that the workers and the rest of the people are steadily fighting back, the monopoly bourgeoisie is unleashing all kinds of reactionary currents, including chauvinism, racial discrimination, religious bigotry, fascism and war- mongering in a vain attempt to obfuscate the roots of the crisis and distract the people.

Long before 9/11, the US and its imperialist partners laid the legal, ideological and political justification for state terrorism and wars of aggression. Thus, when 9/11 occurred, the PATRIOT ACT USA and the war plans could be instantly promulgated and put into effect. The monopoly bourgeoisie orchestrates the think tanks, academic departments, special committees of the executive and legislative branches, the political parties, nongovernmental organizations, the churches and most important of all the corporate mass media to drum up and spread the most specious arguments and schemes for state terrorism and wars of aggression.

The imperialist powers headed by the US have extremely powerful hightech weapons of mass distraction and mass destruction in order to realize imperialist objectives. The weapons of mass distraction can be used to impose overnight a police state on any of the imperialist countries, as indicated by the swiftness of the Bush regime in generating abroad both state terrorism and wars of aggression consequent to 9/11. At the same time, the hightech weapons of mass destruction have distinctively made wars of aggression look as easy as playing video games.

The ever-worsening crisis of the world capitalist system has generated a strong tendency towards fascism and bellicosity in the imperialist countries. The monopoly bourgeoisie, particularly the military-industrial complex, has stepped up war production and has used war hysteria and actual wars of aggression for the purpose. They consider these as effective means for stimulating the economy and expanding economic territory abroad. They unleash wars of conquest against countries that are ruled by nationalist regimes and have rich natural resources, especially oil and mineral ores of strategic value.

Imperialism in Various Global Regions

But these wars of aggression have their downside even for the imperialist powers. They are costly, with expenditures running into trillions of dollars and aggravating the public debt crisis. They inflict large casualties on the people of the victim countries and destroy their private properties and the social infrastructure. They arouse deep- seated hatred for the aggressors and result in wars of national liberation. The imperialist powers get bogged down in certain countries and cannot give attention to other countries. They become fundamentally weaker by being overextended.

Under the neoliberal economic policy, the US has developed close economic relations with China but US policymakers now openly regard it as the rising main US rival and are trying to use the so-called Trans-Pacific Partnership to perpetuate US hegemony in East Asia. However, the US and its NATO partners are still bogged down by wars in such areas as Central Asia, South Asia, West Asia and Africa. The US and NATO war of aggression against Libya and the growing threats against Syria and Iran show that the US has difficulties in shifting the focus of its aggressions to East Asia, particularly against China and the Democratic People's Republic of Korea. In the meantime, China has the opportunity to strengthen its own defense capabilities and develop the Shanghai Cooperation Organization even as the US maintains the deployment of large military forces in East Asia and the Pacific.

The imperialist powers headed by the US cannot do their evil work without meeting the resistance of the people. National liberation movements have arisen and are growing in countries that have suffered wars of aggression and extreme forms of oppression and exploitation. Revolutionary armed struggles have a high potential for spreading against imperialism and puppet states. Mass uprisings have spread in entire countries and continents, such as in the Middle East, North Africa, South Asia and Latin America.

The broad masses of the people are rising up against the crisis of the world capitalist system and its consequences, including high rates of unemployment, austerity measures and other impositions. Millions of people have risen in mass protests in major capitalist countries. Right at the center of global capitalism, the occupy movement has expanded and intensified and the US authorities are now brazenly carrying out repressive measures.

Our representative Bill Doares can explain further our brief description of the world capitalist system, the scourge of imperialist plunder and war and the people's resistance. He can share with you the results of the Fourth International Assembly of the ILPS, especially the General Declaration and resolutions on 17 concerns in the global anti-imperialist and global struggle of the people. The point is to raise the level of common understanding between the ILPS and the IAPSCC and to enhance practical cooperation between them.

We of the ILPS are of the view that the international united front against imperialism and reaction includes a wide range of progressive and democratic

We Unite to Fight Imperialism

forces and is ever expanding because of the growth and advance of the people's struggle. We are always receptive to mass organizations that wish to become our member-organizations in accordance with the ILPS Charter. But we are also always ready to forge strong links of militant solidarity with other international formations and to cooperate with them in undertaking definite campaigns and activities against imperialism and reaction. By all means, let us unite in the anti-imperialist and democratic struggle and aim for greater freedom, democracy, social justice, development and world peace.

Imperialism in Various Global Regions

A Review of Ray O. Light's Book: "US Democracy": the US Empire's Indispensable Myth
Read at the book launch at the ABC Tree house in Amsterdam, February 25, 2012

Dear colleagues and friends, Ray O. Light speaks from the vantage of a proletarian revolutionary, a long-time trade union leader in the US and a firm proletarian internationalist. In his book, he succeeds in exposing so-called US democracy as a fraud and as an indispensable myth enabling the US monopoly bourgeoisie to deceive, exploit and oppress the American proletariat and people of various nationalities as well as the world's people in a vast empire.

He debunks the notion that US monopoly capitalism is a democratic exception to the teachings of Lenin on the economic features and political character of imperialism. His articles compiled in the book, which cover the period of 2000 to the present , provide us with accurate insights and analysis of the workings of the two-party US political system and the resulting policies which serve the unified interests of US monopoly capitalism.

In looking at US elections, Ray O. Light is guided well by his lead quotation from Lenin: "Nothing can be done in our times (by the imperialists) without elections; nothing can be done without the masses, And in this era of printing and parliamentarianism it is impossible to gain the following of the masses without a widely ramified, systematically managed, well-equipped system of flattery, lies, fraud, juggling with fashionable and popular catchwords, and promising all manner of reforms and blessings to the workers right and left— as long as they renounce the revolutionary struggle for the overthrow of the bourgeoisie."

So-called US democracy and periodic elections

Ray O Light demonstrates that the periodic elections in the US and the debates between the Republican and Democratic parties before, during and after the elections are meant to conjure the illusion of democracy, obfuscate the anti-democratic class dictatorship of the monopoly bourgeoisie, preempt the center stage of US politics, preclude the voice of the proletariat and people and confine the masses to a superficial choice between two brands of the same kind of product, like Coca Cola and Pepsi Cola.

In a US presidential election like the one in 2008, the Democratic Party candidate Obama glibly passed himself off as better than the Republican Party candidate McCain, who was very much burdened by the disasters brought about by Bush. But even during the electoral campaign, the two presidential candidates competed to trumpet their loyalty to monopoly capitalism and the bankrupt neoliberal policy and agreed to bail out the big banks and corporations from the economic and financial crisis that these had made. While never denouncing the US wars of aggression, Obama sought to underscore some of his differences with Bush regarding Iraq and Afghanistan and certain issues of human rights.

But since he became president, Obama has continued the Bush policy of aggression on the pretext of combating terrorism and the policy of bailing out the financial oligarchy. Thus, he has failed to revive production and employment. He has gone into a series of compromises with the Republican Party regarding economic policy, domestic repression and the war budget.. He has expanded the overseas deployment of US military forces for intervention and aggression. He has extended the USA PATRIOT Act and has signed into law the authority of the US military to detain Americans indefinitely without due process.

No US president can escape the confines and dictates of the ruling system of the monopoly bourgeoisie and the financial oligarchy. The Democratic and Republican parties engage in debates to conjure the illusion of democracy. They do so not only to compete for votes among the electorate but more importantly to win campaign money, media support and other favors from the monopoly bourgeoisie. Directly and through various instrumentalities inside and outside of the US government, the US monopoly bourgeoisie can compel bipartisan agreements and shape what amounts to a Republican rule in the name of national interest and national security.

The US monopoly bourgeoisie misrepresents its interests as the golden mean or the moderate middle between the extremes of Left and Right and likewise between the Democratic and Republic parties which in fact compete in clinging tightly to such malevolent kind of middle. Concurrent with its rise and persistence as No. 1 imperialist power, US monopoly capitalism has relentlessly pushed the Republican and Democratic parties more than ever before towards the Right even as the myth of US democracy is used against the cause and forces of proletarian revolution and national liberation.

Ray O. Light exposes how Browderite revisionism and the continuance of such mode of thinking have assisted US imperialism in perpetuating the myth of US democracy, As leader of the Communist Party of the USA, Earl Browder touted US monopoly capitalism as exceptional for being supposedly democratic and as early as 1940 used this claim as ground for bringing the CPUSA out of the Third Internationale. He eventually blared out the call for peace and democracy under the auspices of the US and decided to liquidate the CPUSA and replace it with the Communist Political Association, with an open aversion to the revolutionary objective of overthrowing the monopoly bourgeoisie.

150

A Review of Ray O. Light's Book: "US Democracy"

Violence behind the democratic facade

Behind the democratic facade of electoral struggles between the Republican and Democratic parties is the long chain of violence to violate the rights of the American proletariat and people and make them submit to capitalist exploitation. The US acquired and expanded its territory by using brute force to grab land from the native American tribes and the northern third of Mexico. It subjected the African-Americans to slavery for a long period of time and even after the Civil War continued to regard them as three-fifths human and deprived them of civil rights, including the right to vote, until the civil rights movement won victories in the late 1960s.

The US provoked the outbreak of the Spanish-American War in order to grab Puerto Rico, Cuba and the Philippines from a decrepit colonial power. This was one of the three major wars signaling and defining the emergence of monopoly capitalism as modern imperialism at the close of the 19th century and beginning of the 20th century. Since then, US imperialism has intensified its exploitation of the American working class, including the African-Americans, Latinos and Asians and has acquired colonies, semi-colonies , dependent countries and spheres of influence.

The US collaborated mainly with British imperialism in expanding economic territory for exploitation in Latin America and Asia. It made profits from war production before entering late World Wars I and II and collected the lion's share of the spoils of war. It took over colonies from its imperialist allies and promoted neocolonialism in Asia, Africa and Latin America. It became the No. 1 imperialist power and spearheaded the Cold War against the socialist countries. It stepped up war production and deployed US military forces on a global scale. It carried out wars of aggression, as in Korea and Indochina, and instigated massacres as in Indonesia.

US propaganda about so-called US democracy has been so effective that US imperialism has so far succeeded to evade full accountability for such colossal crimes as the following: the murder and maiming of millions of people in US wars of aggression and massacres as in he Philippines, Korea, Vietnam and Indonesia; the extreme exploitation and oppression of people under the dominance of the US in one form or another; and the ceaseless extraction of profits from the American working class.

Let me say a bit more about US democracy so-called in the Philippines. US imperialism murdered 1.2 million Filipinos from the start of the Filipino-American War in 1899 to 1914. And it coopted the liberal bourgeoisie that had drawn inspiration from the French Revolution and led the old democratic revolution in the Philippines. It did so by embellishing the US colonial rule with the language of Jeffersonian democracy and by undertaking a few reforms to shift the economy from a feudal to a semi-feudal one.

The US misrepresented its colonial rule as a period of tutelage in democracy and further Christianization. Since after the US granted nominal independence to the Philippines in 1946, turning it into a semi-colony, the Filipino puppet politicians have patterned their concept and practice of sham democracy after the US model. The electoral contests conjure the illusion of democratic choice for the people, even as the reactionary politicians of various parties serve the interests of the US and the local exploiting classes of big compradors and landlords.

In the last three decades, the US monopoly bourgeoisie and its political agents in the Republican and Democratic parties have been guided by the neoliberal economic policy. They have blamed the stagflation of the 1970s on wage inflation and big social spending by government and have pressed down the wage level and cut back on social spending but stepped up military spending and every way, like liberalization, privatization and deregulation, to aid the monopoly bourgeoisie to make bigger profits and accumulate productive and financial capital.

The crisis of overproduction has recurred more frequently and more severely. Every attempt to override it through debt financing at the levels of the state, corporations and consumers and through one kind of financial bubble to another have only led to a worse economic and financial crisis. A severe and increasingly worse public debt crisis has come about due to the bailout of the banks and corporations and profligate government spending to benefit the financial oligarchy, the military-industrial complex and the high bureaucracy.

The inane reaction to the rising public deficits and public debt is austerity measures at the further expense of the people, thus aggravating the economic decline and the high rate of unemployment. The most reactionary forces in the US undertake something like the Tea Party movement in order to obscure monopoly capitalism as the root cause of the crisis, scapegoat the African-Americans, the immigrants and other people and push the Obama regime towards actions that aggravate the crisis. But the widespread social discontent is bursting out and developing into a resolute and militant resistance of the people at the very center of global capitalism. The Occupy Movement has burst out and can lead to larger and more militant actions of the proletariat and the people.

Global crisis and the need for resistance

A global depression is now wreaking havoc on the lives of the people in both the imperialist and dominated countries. For quite sometime already, the imperialist powers have failed to solve the economic and financial crisis, because of their blindness to the internal laws of motion of capitalism and their dogmatic adherence to the neoliberal economic policy. The crisis is now engendering fascism and aggressive wars. On the surface, these appear

A Review of Ray O. Light's Book: "US Democracy"

as directed against recalcitrant countries of the third world and the long-oppressed peoples but they are part of the interimperialist struggle for a division of the world.

The rapidly worsening crisis of the world capitalist system is inflicting grave hardships and suffering on the people of the world. At the same time, it is compelling the people to resist. There is an urgent need for intensifying the anti-imperialist and democratic struggle of the people on a global scale. There is at the same time, as emphatically pointed out in his book by Ray O. Light, the urgent need for the leading role of the revolutionary party of the proletariat in the revolutionary mass struggles in various countries and for the strengthening of the international communist movement.

Imperialism in Various Global Regions

Note on the Occupy Movement
April 12, 2012

The initiators of the Occupy Wall Street Movement have proclaimed themselves as anarchists since the beginning. They espouse the direct action of small groups to ignite the masses, the so-called leaderless movement and the supposed revolution that does not aim to replace the incumbent oppressive state with a new democratic or socialist state.

They draw inspiration currently from the writings of Prof. Gene Sharp of the Albert Einstein Institute. He is the author of From Dictatorship to Democracy, which is being used by anarchists as a kind of manual for non-violent resistance. The book conceives of dictatorship as merely the authoritarianism of an individual or a ruling clique and ignores the bourgeois state as a class dictatorship.

The most notorious purveyors of the notions of Gene Sharp are trainees of the Serbia-based Centre for Applied Non-Violent Action and Strategies (CANVAS), a consulting and training firm funded by the US New Endowment for Democracy. It was set up in 2003 by OTPOR (Resistance), a CIA-funded Serbian organization which opposed Slovodan Milosevic and helped cause his downfall consequent to the NATO bombing of Yugoslavia in 1999. The OTPOR logo with a white fist on a black circle as background is conspicuous in group actions of the Occupy movement.

The International League of Peoples' Struggle has endorsed the Occupy Wall Street Movement and its subsequent spread to many US cities insofar as they use the political tactic of occupying public places for indefinite periods and denouncing the imperialist system and its policies. The ILPS is appreciative of the Occupy Movement for having occupied the park in Wall Street to denounce the finance oligarchy and the imperialist system. It has flexibly initiated or joined in several cities mass actions acclaimed as part of the Occupy Movement.

But the ILPS has never endorsed the comprehensive anarchist ideas, outlook and method of struggle of the initiators of the Occupy Wall Street movement. Up to a certain point, the actions of the anarchists can be positively imaginative and can help to arouse the people to rebel but cannot be sustained until the overthrow of the bourgeois state. The anarchists are ultimately reactionary because they allow the bourgeois state to remain intact, notwithstanding the anti-statist and individualist or anarchist propositions.

The researchers of the ILPS and Michel Chossudovsky of Global Research have closely studied the shady character and activities of the Occupy initiators and their exaggerated claims of .having masterminded the so-called color revolutions of Eastern Europe in the recent past and the so-called Arab spring. Of course, the US avails of special agents like those in CANVAS but it relies in the first place on its main line operatives and collaborators.

"Bringing Back the State to the Revolution" by Salud Sakdal and Benedicto Algabre critiques the Occupy Movement at the historical, philosophical and political planes comprehensively and profoundly. It takes up the question of state as a real unavoidable factor on both sides of revolution and counterrevolution. The article is excellent in dealing with its main point that the revolutionary process must overthrow the bourgeois state and install the new democratic or socialist state, notwithstanding the anti-Stalinist scare kicked up by the anarchists and Trotskyites.

It is gratifying that the article gives high appreciation for Amado Guerrero's Philippine Society and Revolution and generously compares it with the Communist Manifesto with regard to the essence and requirements of the revolution led by the proletariat.

On the Growing Violent Conflict in Egypt
September 6, 2013

Before the so-called Arab spring of 2011 seemingly swept into Egypt from Tunisia, Egyptian workers and their trade unions had manifested their grievances and demands against the worsening economic and social conditions in Egypt as a result of the bankruptcy and crisis of the world capitalist system and the Egyptian ruling system, under the US-dictated neoliberal economic policy.

The social and economic crisis was the underlying factor why the broad masses of the people in their millions joined the mass actions. They denounced the high rate of unemployment, the soaring prices of basic commodities, the corruption and repressiveness of the authoritarian Mubarak regime. They demanded democracy and better living conditions. The forces of the Left and liberal democracy, especially among the workers and the youth, stood out in the mass struggle. But the Muslim Brotherhood also participated in the mass actions and was in fact the biggest organized force against the Mubarak regime.

When the military bourgeoisie could no longer stop the huge mass actions which began on January 25, 2011, it followed the US instruction to sacrifice Mubarak and made him step down on February 12, 2011. Subsequently, the Muslim Brotherhood formed the Freedom and Justice Party and won all national votes since 2011, including the election of Mohamed Morsi as president in 2012. For a while, the US thought that it had enough handle on the Muslim Brotherhood directly and through certain Gulf states which had Wahabi affinity with the brotherhood and could offer financial help to the ailing Egyptian economy.

But the military bourgeoisie, built up for decades as the most powerful part of the ruling class by the US with huge military assistance since Camp David when Sadat shifted from Soviet to US support, became wary of the moves of the Muslim Brotherhood to apply the strict Sharia law, retool the army and police and maintain close relations with Hamas. It regained its composure from the turmoil of the Arab spring and maneuvered to forge an alliance with the forces of the Left and the liberal democracy on the ground of maintaining a secular democratic state.

The military bourgeoisie secured US permission for the ouster of Morsi and the formation of an interim presidency under military control. The defense minister General Abdel Fatteh el-Sisi orchestrated the coup d'etat on July 3, 2013 in the name of democracy and a secular state by using a temporary alliance with the forces of the pro-US liberal bourgeoisie. The US and its puppets disregarded the popular election of Morsi as president and considered as far more important the maintenance of servility of the Egyptian state to the US and Israel.

The Muslim Brotherhood opposed the military coup, invoked the democratic prerogative to rule by virtue of elections and launched massive demonstrations on a nationwide scale. The military reacted by massacring demonstrators, thus discrediting its claims to democracy. The liberal bourgeoisie was embarrassed and its best known representative Mohamed El Baradei resigned from the interim government. The military bourgeoisie has used state terrorism to suppress the Muslim Brotherhood. Mubarak henchmen are prominently in the councils of state and military and are hellbent on exculpating and releasing Mubarak from prison.

The elections have provided the Muslim Brotherhood the justification to rule Egypt as a matter of democratic right, to condemn the military bourgeoisie for the coup and the massacres and to carry out all forms of struggle, including the legal mass protests and armed struggle. The military bourgeoisie and the Muslim Brotherhood are now absorbed in a process of spiraling violence, similar to what happened in Algeria some decades ago when the Islamic party was prevented from taking power after winning the elections.

While the US favors the military bourgeoisie and calculates that Saudi Arabia and the emirates can provide support in this regard, the Muslim Brotherhood has its autonomy and is favored by the rise of the Salafi and other Islamic forces, including the Al Qaida, in nearby countries. For a long time to come, the US and other imperialist powers will face an increasingly unwieldy situation in Egypt and in North Africa. Uncle Sam is talking through his hat when he speaks of pivoting to East Asia on the presumption that he has lessened his problems elsewhere.

It is necessary for the ILPS to understand the historical and current complexity of the character, changing alliances and antagonisms of major political forces in Eqypt (the military bourgeoisie, the Muslim Brotherhood and the advocates of the secular and democratic state) and how the US tries to get a handle on each of said forces and manipulate all of them in favor of the US-Israeli power tandem. But of course we must make allowance for the broad masses of the people and the still relatively small revolutionary forces of the Left to take advantage of the turbulent situation and strengthen themselves against US imperialism and all forms of reaction in the long run.

In 1952 the "Free Officers" organization overthrew the royal regime, adopted the republican system and liberated Egypt from British colonialism. It included those from the Muslim Brotherhood, Communists, bourgeois liberals and those who constituted the military ruling elite. They were bound by a sense of national unity against colonialism and the monarchy. In 1954, Gamal Abdel Nasser led the military elite to seize political power after the failed assassination attempt against him and the resignation of President Mohammed Naguib.

On the Growing Violent Conflict in Egypt

The military elite stood aloof and even tended to offend the Muslim Brotherhood and the Left and liberal bourgeois organizations. But consequent to Nasser's anti-imperialist position and nationalization of the Suez Canal in 1956, the Left organizations allied themselves with him, despite his pronounced aversion to communists. In 1965 the Muslim Brotherhood tried to overthrow the military clique and failed. Members of the brotherhood were imprisoned.

In 1968 big mass demonstrations of the youth broke out and demanded democracy and fierce struggle against Israel. Left organizations allied themselves with the Muslim Brotherhood. They continued to support mass protests in 1972 against the Sadat regime and called for the liberation of the areas seized and occupied by Israel in previous wars. In 1972 Sadat succeeded in forging an alliance with the religious organizations against the Left organizations.

In 1977, the Left organizations undertook massive protests because of soaring prices of basic commodities. In 1981, a section of the Muslim Brotherhood assassinated Sadat. Mubarak reacted by waging a campaign of suppression against the Muslim Brotherhood and certain religious groups considered as violent. In the 1980s and 1990s, he tried to mollify the major Islamic organizations by appointing them to government positions as well as the Left organizations by allowing them limited representation through parliamentary elections.

Imperialism in Various Global Regions

No to US Bases, Intervention and Plunder! Fight the US Imperialist Agenda in Asia-Pacific Region
October 10, 2013

The International League of Peoples' Struggle calls attention to the strategic scheme and maneuvers of US imperialism to strengthen US military bases and escalate US military intervention and plunder in the Asian-Pacific region and calls on all the oppressed peoples in the region to fight US imperialism in every way possible and necessary. The US imperialist agenda has been highlighted by US pronouncements an actuations in multilateral meetings and side meetings and in country visits by US top officials. The multilateral meetings include the annual Asia-Pacific Economic Cooperation (APEC) Leaders' Summit in Bali, Indonesia, the 8th East Asia and 23rd ASEAN summits in Brunei and negotiations on the Trans-Pacific Partnership Agreement. The frenzied country visits by top US officials underscore the efforts of US imperialism to advance its economic, political and military interests in the region despite its domestic budgetary problems and its worsening troubles on a global scale. The US imperialist agenda pursues its "strategic pivot" to Asia, which involves not only the further deployment of military forces but a broad-spectrum offensive that includes, among other objectives, forging the Trans-Pacific Partnership Agreement, a mega-free trade agreement favorable to the US-led imperialist alliance, and consolidating its strategic alliances especially with ASEAN countries.

Imperialist chieftain Barack Obama was originally scheduled for a Southeast Asian trip, which would have included the APEC Summit in Bali, the 8th East Asian Summit followed by a US-ASEAN meeting in Brunei, along with stops in Malaysia and the Philippines. He was forced to cancel his trip at the last minute because of the ongoing deadlock between Democrats and Republicans in Congress on how to deal with the US fiscal crisis.

The deadlock on the budget has resulted in the shutdown of the Federal government and the forced leave of some 800,000 federal workers. It has arisen from the erosion of the US tax base by the tax cuts for the corporations and the wealthy, the decline of the real economy and massive unemployment. While military expenditures are ever rising, there is scrimping for social services and the Obamacare in particular. The US has long abused quantitative easing (printing of money without the corresponding support from civil production) to cover its budgetary and trade deficits. Now, the abuse has made the debt ceiling a crucial issue amidst conflicting demands of the Republicans and Democrats.

In lieu of Obama, US Secretary of State John Kerry is now leading the US delegation and personally pushing the US imperialist agenda in the meetings and visits. Kerry, the chief agent of US foreign policy, has recently heightened his hawkish profile by acting in recent months as the lead warmonger in the US plan to attack Syria.

Despite its fiscal crisis, which has resulted in partial shutdown of Federal government services, the US ironically continues to push for the massive deployment of troops and ships towards East Asia as a means to advance US economic, geopolitical, and military interests and to keep rival China in check. US imperialism apparently ignores the fiscal crisis and growing antiwar sentiments among the American people as it threatens bombing and war on Syria and undertakes military actions in Somalia and Libya.

Since late 2011, the US has pursued its strategic pivot towards Asia, with the goal of deploying 60 percent of its naval forces to the region. The US is aggressively seeking or renewing basing opportunities, access agreements, mutual defense pacts, and bilateral and multilateral military exercises in the region. US treaty allies such as Japan, South Korea, the Philippines and Australia are being called on to host an increasing number of US troops and ships on a so-called "rotational" but effectively permanent basis.

The US also wants its treaty allies to shoulder the increasing cost of hosting US military forces, imposing on host countries the burden of paying for bases construction and maintenance, accommodation of troops, environmental degradation, and other social costs. In South Korea, the US is preparing to use the military base being constructed by the Korean government in Jeju Island near China. Similarly, in the Philippines, it is expected to use a naval base now being constructed by the Philippine government in Oyster Bay near the disputed Spratly group of islands.

In Australia, some 200 to 250 US troops are being rotated and are considered de facto based in Darwin Airbase. By 2014, the US expects to have 1,150 troops in Australia; the number is further expected to increase to 2,500 by 2016. Also in the Philippines, the US is negotiating a framework agreement that will allow increased rotational US troops, access to Philippine facilities, and prepositioning of weapons. The visit by Obama was seen as an incentive for the Philippines to fast track the signing of the de facto basing agreement, despite repeated strong objections by constitutionalist and patriotic groups that the new arrangement violates a constitutional ban on foreign troops and weapons of mass destruction and expands the already questionable premises of the current US-Philippine Visiting Forces Agreement.

The move to "rebalance" towards Asia is both to escalate US military intervention and to secure US economic interests as stated in Sustaining US Global Leadership, Priorities for 21st Century Defense, a Department of Defense strategic guidance document. The US seeks to dominate strategic sea lanes, control the source and flow of strategic resources, and force countries in this vast global region to accede to neoliberal economic dictates.

No to US Bases, Intervention and Plunder!

On the sidelines of the APEC Summit, US negotiators were busy hammering out multilateral consensus on the Trans-Pacific Partnership Agreement (TPPA), which Obama wants to seal with 11 other countries by the end of the year. The proposed TPPA under the US baton would encompass 40 percent of the global economy and would include countries such as Australia, New Zealand, Japan, Singapore, Malaysia, Brunei, Vietnam, Chile, Canada, Mexico and Peru.

The trade pact's details have largely been kept secret from the public, but main provisions are expected to require member-countries to remove any remaining barriers to investments, to strictly enforce intellectual property laws that would raise pharmaceutical costs and stifle digital innovation and freedom of expression, and to allow private corporations to sue states before an international tribunal—thus in effect obliging member-countries to surrender big chunks of their national sovereignty to the imperialist masterminds of the TPPA.

The current and persistent conditions of global depression have made the US more desperate in its efforts to rebalance towards Asia even as it desperately clutches to maintain control in other global regions. However, the Obama government is also bogged down by the crisis in its own backyard, as the still-unfolding impacts of the unresolved budgetary deadlock and shutdown have shown. The American people are also more vigilant and vocal than ever in opposing US military interventionist actions and increased spending for war while the people suffer the burden of the crisis.

The people of the world demand an end to US imperialism and oppose its desperate efforts to dig its claws deeper into Asia-Pacific and other global regions. Countries want to assert their national sovereignty, with a wide range of patriotic forces calling to oust US bases and troops from their shores, and to resist the plunder of their resources and work force by transnational corporations. As elsewhere in the world, national and social liberation is the only alternative to the US imperialist agenda in the Asia-Pacific.

Imperialism in Various Global Regions

ILPS Condemns US for Instigating Coup Scheme, Demands Respect for the Sovereignty of Venezuela
February 19, 2014

The International League of Peoples' Struggle condemns the US and its puppets in Venezuela for causing artificial shortages of certain basic goods and inflation and inciting crimes and sham protests aimed at destabilizing the Bolivarian government of President Nicolas Maduro.

The malicious scheme of the US and its puppets headed by Leopoldo Lopez is to fabricate conditions for a military coup against the government which was duly elected last April. President Maduro is justified in taking the necessary steps against the US and local malefactors in the coup scheme.

The interventionist remarks of US Secretary of State John Kerry against the Maduro government are an attack on the national sovereignty and independence of Venezuela and exposes the dirty hand of the US in causing shortages and inflation and emboldening criminal gangs to attack government buildings and personnel, Bolivarian activists and ordinary citizens.

The same kind of ultra-rightist stooges of the US like Leopoldo Lopez who launched a failed coup against Hugo Chavez in 2002 are again at work in a conspiracy to destabilize and overthrow the Maduro government.

They have been openly funded by US congressional appropriations amounting to hundreds of millions of US dollars in the last 15 years. In the 2014 US federal budget, US$5 million is openly appropriated for supporting the activities of the anti-Bolivarian opposition. Covert funds for covert activities are far bigger.

The cause of the street violence in Venezuela is not the Maduro government but the US and its puppets. The entire scheme of destabilization and regime change is masterminded by the US and violates the national sovereignty and independence of Venezuela and the democratic will of the people of Venezuela.

We fully and unconditionally support the national sovereignty and independence of Venezuela and the democratic will of the Venezuelan people who have risen up to defend the Maduro government. We demand that the US and its puppets to stop causing shortages and inflation and committing crimes.

We call on all our member-organizations and allies in all countries to stand and act in solidarity with the people of Venezuela, Latin America and the whole world in defending the Maduro government and opposing US imperialism and its puppets.

Imperialism in Various Global Regions

On Obama's Visit to East Asia
April 22, 2014

The International League of Peoples' Struggle views the upcoming visits of United States President Barack Obama to Japan, South Korea, Malaysia and the Philippines from April 23 to 29 as part of the US imperialist objective of further entrenching its hegemony and imposing its neoliberal agenda while undermining the sovereignty and coveting the patrimony of countries in the region, in line with its avowed "strategic pivot" to Asia.

The US "pivot to Asia" is a multipronged offensive that includes the further deployment or "rebalancing" of US military forces and military bases into the region, the drive to forge a long-sought Trans-Pacific Partnership Agreement (TPPA), and the consolidation and expansion of its strategic alliances with selected countries in the region. These objectives are part of the long-term efforts of US imperialism to advance its economic, political and military interests and reassert its preeminent power in the region.

The renewed US focus on Asia, highlighted since late 2011 by a series of policy statements and positions in various summits and country visits by top US officials and considered a cornerstone of current US foreign policy, will be further pushed by Obama in his upcoming four-country visit. He is expected to advance or finalize a number of multilateral agreements when he visits Japan from April 23 to 24, South Korea from April 25 to 26, Malaysia from April 26 to 28, and the Philippines from April 28 to 29.

Obama's Asian swing has particular urgency especially in light of China's steady rise as a major regional capitalist power while the US has had its hands full elsewhere. He had canceled scheduled trips to Asia twice already, once in 2010 and more recently in October 2013 due to the US fiscal crisis. The US imperialist chieftain is determined this time to erase any doubt about the seriousness of the US pivot to Asia despite its growing problems on the domestic front and its worsening troubles on a global scale, especially in the Middle East and the Eurasian belt.

US military 'rebalancing'

The ILPS reiterates the urgency of exposing and opposing the strategic scheme and maneuvers of US imperialism to strengthen its military bases, escalate its military intervention, and consolidate its geopolitical alliances in East Asia under the flag of "rebalance" or "pivot" to Asia. The US is currently building new military bases in Japan, South Korea and Guam, pushing to deploy an increasing number of troops as well as preposition war materiel in

Australia and the Philippines, and plans to move 60 percent of its warships to Asia by 2020.

To this end, the US is aggressively seeking or renewing basing opportunities, access agreements, mutual defense pacts, and bilateral and multilateral military exercises in the region. It is pushing its treaty allies such as Japan, South Korea, the Philippines, and Australia to host an increasing number of US troops as well as naval and air force assets on a so-called "rotational" but effectively permanent basis.

Faced with its own fiscal crisis aggravated by huge military expenditures due to its self-appointed role as global cop, the US now wants host countries not only to provide land for new bases and access to existing bases, but also to impose on them the burden of paying for base construction and maintenance, accommodation of troops, environmental degradation, and other social costs. These other costs that typically come with foreign bases and foreign troops include worsened prostitution of women and children, drug trafficking, other vices in the name of troop "rest and recreation," abandoned Amerasian children, and violent crimes including rape and murder.

The strategic military, political, and economic objectives of the US pivot to Asia are stated in Sustaining US Global Leadership: Priorities for 21st Century Defense, a Department of Defense strategic guidance document. The US seeks to dominate strategic sea lanes and control the sources and flow of strategic resources such as oil in this vast global region. At the same time, it wants to use this tremendous clout to force countries to accede to neoliberal economic dictates, and to impose a virtual embargo on countries that may resist such dictates and assert their own national interests.

The US is desperate to finalize as soon as possible a multilateral consensus with 11 other countries on the Trans-Pacific Partnership Agreement (TPPA), if only to mitigate its own imperialist economic and financial crisis. As designed and dominated by the US, this comprehensive trade agreement would encompass 40 percent of the world's GDP and would include countries such as Australia, New Zealand, Japan, Singapore, Malaysia, Brunei, Vietnam, Chile, Canada, Mexico and Peru. Notably, the TPP talks have excluded China for now although Obama's national security advisor Susan Rice recently said the US will "welcome any nation" to join the pact.

While the trade pact's details have largely been kept secret from the public, a recent draft revealed by Wikileaks has triggered controversies even among some Western policymakers and US allies, who question clauses that favor US monopoly control and undermine governmental processes. The TPPA's main provisions are expected to require member-countries to remove any remaining barriers to investments, to strictly enforce intellectual property laws that would raise pharmaceutical costs and stifle digital innovation and freedom of expression, and to allow private corporations to sue states before an international tribunal. In effect, countries joining the TPPA will have to surrender big chunks of their national sovereignty to the trade pact's imperialist masterminds.

US-China relations as key issue

China has become the single biggest factor in the US imperialist agenda in East Asia. Despite its own internal problems, China is fast rising as a regional power, with a growing capacity to project its power in the rest of Asia and beyond. While the US eyes China as a potential long-term rival, the two capitalist powers remain in an uneasy partnership, comprising trade and investment ties, on top of some US$1.28 trillion in US debt to China. The collusion and contention of the US and China operates not just in East Asia but throughout the world. The BRICS, in which China is a stalwart, provides a counterpoint to the US in certain respects, but it also promotes the US-instigated neoliberal policy in many other respects.

Obama's forthcoming trip to Asia does not include a visit to China. However, a basic premise of the US agenda is to further contain China's ambitions as a regional power, pressure it to keep within the present limits of the US-China partnership, and more strictly hew to the neoliberal framework. The US imperialists are further pushing China to further dismantle its state enterprises so that Western multinationals can more freely exploit its vast market and cheap labor.

The US is wary of China's inclusion of the South China Sea as among its "core interests"; its fast-rising military capability to project its own "String of Pearls" maritime strategy in the Asia-Pacific and South Asia-Indian Ocean; its use of "soft power" and various diplomatic initiatives in its expansion of trade, investment and aid in and outside the region; and its growing alliance with Russia at the core of the Shanghai Cooperation Organization (SCO). These moves, directly or indirectly, pose a counterpoint to the US strategic pivot to Asia.

Despite China's territorial disputes with neighboring countries over islands islets, reefs and rocks in the East China Sea and South China Sea, it maintains a good leverage including strong bilateral ties with Cambodia, Laos, and Sri Lanka; a standing offer of "joint exploitation of the South China Sea for mutual benefit" directed at the Philippines and Vietnam; and the potential for a China-ASEAN FTA and a China-South Korea-Japan FTA as its counter-balance against the US-led TPPA.

The US exploits territorial disputes involving China and its neighbors such as Japan, South Korea, and some ASEAN countries. It pretends to help these countries against China as a pretext in expanding US military forces and operating military bases in these countries. But the US interest is not in supporting territorial claims in the South China Sea, but in gaining control of the sea lanes. The US would not risk open war with China in the near future as the US has far greater economic interests there compared to countries like the Philippines or Vietnam.

Russia, Japan, and China also view the vast territories covering the East China Sea and South China Sea as strategic in terms of natural resources, shipping, and military access. For now, all the big powers collude and compete for a bigger share of the Asia-Pacific pie without resort to war, although they beat their war drums to signal a readiness to escalate conflict whenever it fits their strategic plans.

On April 23, Obama is scheduled to attend the Japan-US summit to affirm the two countries' military and economic alliance. Even as it has been in the economic and political doldrums in recent decades, Japan hosts a wide range of US military bases, serves as its second largest trade and investment partner, and has long been the main US ally in the post-war Asia-Pacific. The Obama visit intends to enhance the US-Japan military and economic alliance.

A few days before Obama lands, on April 20, a new US military installation will be inaugurated in Ukawa district, Kyotango City, Kyoto. An X-band radar facility will be installed as an essential part of the US Missile Defense network in East Asia, in connivance with the Japanese government.

Despite the transfer of a big US Marine contingent to Guam and the unresolved relocation of the sprawling Futenma Marine Corps Air Station from a heavily populated part of Okinawa to Nago City, the US continues to enjoy strategic basing rights in Japan. Some 49,000 US troops are deployed in Japan-hosted bases, through which the US is able to project its imperialist power in East Asia, encircle China, and threaten the Democratic People's Republic of Korea (North Korea).

The TPPA is also on the agenda of the Japan-US summit. The US wants Japan to join the trade pact as a crucial member, but it must convince Japanese big business that the TPPA has more advantages for them compared to a more localized trade pact such as a China-Korea-Japan FTA. The US also wants Japan to settle its disputes with South Korea.

In Seoul, Obama is expected to meet with South Korean President Park Geun Hye, affirm the US military alliance with South Korea, and review the continuing US-led program of economic, political, and military pressure against the Democratic People's Republic of Korea (North Korea). Despite calls from both sides to move towards peaceful reunification, the US has refused to defuse tensions by continuing to maintain a heavy military presence of 30,000 troops in the peninsula (including nuclear and other weapons of mass destruction), instigate repeated armed provocations along the so-called demilitarized zone and through offshore naval exercises, and seek to isolate North Korea by focusing on the DPRK's nuclear program and imposing sanctions.

Despite strong opposition from the Korean people, the US is preparing to use a military base being constructed by the Korean government in Jeju Island near its border with China.

170

Next, Obama will visit Malaysia as the first US president to do so in the past half-century, to make another pitch for the TPPA. Past Malaysian governments, with strong Islamic influence especially during the premiership of Mahathir Mohammad, had been critical of US foreign policy, opposed US wars in the Middle East, and supported the setting up of a Palestinian state. Obama intends to sweeten US-Malaysia bilateral ties by offering economic advantages to the Najib Razak government in exchange for keeping to a moderate and pro-US Islamic position.

Obama's last stop will be the Philippines, a former US colony that hosted a major US Air Force base in Clark and a major US Navy station in Subic, and a long-time postwar ally under successive pro-US regimes. He is expected to meet with President Benigno Aquino III and sign a de facto basing pact disguised as an "Enhanced Defense Cooperation Agreement" (EDCA).

The Filipino people had successfully driven away these US bases in 1991, but pro-US regimes continued to allow US ships, troops, armaments, drones, and electronic espionage facilities on the excuse of "nonpermanent" presence as covered by the US-Philippine Visiting Forces Agreement (VFA).

Nevertheless, the EDCA that may be signed during the Obama-Aquino meeting would further expand the questionable premises of the VFA. This would allow the US practically unhindered access to Philippine facilities in order to station its troops and equipment, to even set up its own exclusive military facilities within Philippine bases or virtual "bases within bases," and for its troops to operate in any part of the country in the guise of joint military exercises or humanitarian missions. Like the US-RP VFA, the US-RP EDCA would be in brazen violation of the country's 1987 constitution that bans foreign troops and weapons of mass destruction on Philippine soil.

The US imperialists and their local puppets have been hyping the Philippine-China maritime dispute over the exclusive economic zone and extended continental shelf of the Philippines under the UNCLOS, and terrorist scares as well in the southern islands bordering Malaysia and Indonesia, in order to justify the urgent signing of the EDCA and the entry of more US armed forces. Alarmingly, they are pushing the Philippine government to construct or renovate more bases, such as in Oyster Bay near the disputed Spratly islands, supposedly to counterbalance the Chinese presence in the area. They also rode on super typhoon Haiyan's disastrous impact by calling on the US Seventh Fleet to play the high-profile role of "savior," suggesting it can do more humanitarian good if only it is allowed unhampered operations within the country.

Obama is also expected to quietly urge Manila to remove any remaining constitutional restrictions to foreign investments, including land ownership, and thus pave the way for the Philippines joining the TPPA.

171

Call for broader struggle vs US imperialism in East Asia

In the face of the current global crisis, the US wants to rush its military rebalancing act in the Asia-Pacific even as it is harried by major troubles in other global regions and in its own backyard. But the people in all countries of East Asia will not allow this imperialist scheme to ride roughshod over their national sovereignty. The International League of Peoples' Struggle and a broad range of patriotic and progressive forces in the region are calling to oust US bases and troops from their shores, and to resist the intensified imperialist plunder of the region's human and natural resources through the TPPA.

The ILPS calls on all the oppressed peoples in the region, as elsewhere in the world, to resist the US imperialist agenda and to fight for national and social liberation in all possible realms of struggle. We support the East Asian peoples' broad opposition to the US bases, military buildup, and aggressive actions in their respective countries and throughout the region as a whole. We support their equally broad opposition to the neoliberal economic agenda in all its despicable aspects, including the US-dictated TPPA. We support their aspirations and demands for peace, genuine development, and social justice.

We reiterate our full support for the Japanese people's protest actions against the new US base in Kyoto, and stand in solidarity with the AWC-Kyoto, the Kyoto Coalition, and the Kinki Coalition that are in the forefront of the anti-bases protest. We likewise express our support for the Okinawa people in opposing the plan to relocate the Futenma US base to Nago City, and hope that their struggle leads to the full ousting of all US bases from the Okinawa islands.

We again express our solidarity with the Korean people on both halves of the Korean peninsula in their long-aspired-for peaceful reunification, against the heavy US military presence in the south and US-instigated provocations against the north, and against the planned construction of a US naval base in Jeju. We call on the Malaysian people to resist the sugarcoated pills being offered by the US through the Obama visit, with the intent of pulling their country deeper into the neoliberal trap of the TPPA. We are confident that anti-US imperialist groups in Malaysia will join hands and launch common protest actions to confront Obama and local pro-US reactionaries.

We salute the Filipino people in their century-old struggle against US imperialism. We commend Bagong Alyansang Makabayan (BAYAN) and other ILPS member-organizations in the Philippines for exposing and opposing the so-called US-RP Enhanced Defense Cooperation Agreement, for their planned week-long protest in time for the Obama visit, and for linking up with other anti-bases and anti-imperialist organizations in the United States, Japan, South Korea, China, and elsewhere.

We extend our solidarity to the people of the United States, who are as victimized by US imperialism as the rest of the world. We welcome the

On Obama's Visit to East Asia

increasing ranks and growing militancy of anti-war, anti-globalization, and anti-imperialist organizations in the US, especially in opposing domestic repression, military adventures overseas, and increased spending for war while the American people suffer the burden of the crisis.

All over the world, as in East Asia, countries and peoples are resisting US imperialism's desperate efforts to extend its talons and dig its claws deeper as it continues on a path of long-term decline. The ILPS is one with them in the struggle until victory.

No to US bases, and imperialist wars and intervention!

US troops, out of East Asia!

Resist neoliberal economic dictates!

Fight the TPPA!

Down with US imperialism and its domestic puppets in East Asia!

Long live the people of East Asia!

Long live international solidarity!

Imperialism in Various Global Regions

Foundations and Motivations of Imperialist Aggression and Most Important Tasks of the People in the Struggle
Keynote Address to the Symposium: Demanding Justice for Imperialist Crimes against Humanity De Karaganda, Utrecht February 21, 2015

On behalf of the International League of Peoples' Struggle, I thank the Filipino Refugees in the Netherlands and the Netherlands chapter of the ILPS for inviting me to deliver the keynote address. It is an an honor and privilege to be among the distinguished speakers, the members of the ILPS International Coordinating Committee, and all other participants in this symposium on demanding justice for imperialist crimes against humanity. I am deeply pleased that representatives of revolutionary movements in Palestine, Kurdistan, Philippines, Ireland, Belgium and other countries are here.

It is my assignment this afternoon to try setting the context and tone for the presentations and discussions by describing the foundations and motivations of imperialist aggression and pointing to the most important tasks of the people in struggling against imperialism and achieving revolutionary objectives.

I. Foundations and motivations of imperialism

Adam Smith and his successors have pontificated that the supposed invisible hand of self-interest in the capitalist market has produced the social good through the ever dynamic balance of supply and demand. Indeed, capitalism is founded on greed and exploitation. And to keep the system of exploitation going, there is the concomitant system of oppression. The bourgeois state or the class dictatorship of the bourgeoisie consists of the instruments of coercion, such as the army, policemen, the courts and prisons, to enforce the law of the oppressor class against the working classes of workers and peasants.

The bourgeoisie used the most vicious methods of exploitation and oppression in the primitive accumulation of capital. Workers, including women and children, were forced to work extremely long hours, 14 to 16 hours a day for six days a week, and accept extremely low wages. The enclosure movement or similar actions of the bourgeoisie deprived the peasants of the land in order to proletarianize them in the course of making capitalist farms, force the dispossessed peasants to take factory jobs and make a reserve army of unemployed manpower to press down the wage level. Colonialism and slavery were major components of the primitive accumulation. Forced labor was used and natural resources were plundered in the colonies. Men and women were abducted in Africa and traded as slaves.

Marx and Engels explained how new economic values are created by labor power by using the equipment and raw materials in the process of production, and how the owners of capital take away a greater amount of surplus value by pressing down the wages paid to the workers. The crisis of overproduction arises because the capitalist exploiters keep on increasing profits and accumulating capital by pressing down wages. As a result, the market slumps because the workers cannot afford to buy the very goods they produce for their consumption.

The use of finance capital to override the economic crisis with the ever growing private and public debt, and likewise to override the tendency of the profit rate to fall, has resulted in financial bubbles and financial crises. The recurrent bouts of economic and financial crisis result not only in worse conditions of the working class but also in the intensified competition of capitalist firms, leading to the bankruptcy of weaker capitalist firms and the ultimate growth of the winning capitalist firms into monopolies. Thus, towards the end of the 19th century, the era of free competition led to monopoly capitalism or modern imperialism.

Lenin described the features that characterize the imperialist countries. Monopoly capitalism has become dominant over society. Industrial capital and bank capital have merged, thus creating a financial oligarchy. The export of surplus capital has gained importance over the export of surplus commodities. Monopoly capitalist firms based in various countries engage in combinations like syndicates and cartels in order to compete with and prevail over their competitors. The competition for economic territory and the struggle for a redivision of the world intensify among the monopoly capitalist powers, which form blocs against each other.

Towards the beginning of the 20th century, there was no longer any part of the world, outside of the imperialist countries, which was not somehow covered by the earlier colonial powers as colony, semicolony or dependent country and as a source of cheap labor and cheap raw materials, as a market, as a field of investment or as spheres of influence. To join the colonial game in order to gain economic and political advantage over other countries, the new players jointly and separately took a collision course with the old players.

Thus, a series of wars occurred from 1898 to the eve of World War I (the Spanish-American War of 1898, the Anglo-Boer War of 1899-1902 and the Russo-Japanese War of 1904-05) to signal the arrival of the era of modern imperialism and manifest the extremely violent and aggressive character of monopoly capitalism. State monopoly capitalism arose to bring the domestic crisis under control and to ensure preparedness for wars of aggression. It emerged overtly in the form of state monopoly companies or, as in the US,

Foundations and Motivations of Imperialist Aggression

through private companies favored by state subsidies and contracts to produce war equipment.

The first full-scale global inter-imperialist war between two imperialist powers, the Allied Powers and the Central Powers, broke out in 1914. It signified the inability of the imperialist countries to peacefully solve their domestic economic and social crisis and the general crisis of capitalism. World War I cost the lives of more than 23 million people. It proved beyond doubt the moribund and aggressive character of monopoly capitalism. Far more telling was the victory of socialist revolution over one-sixth of the surface of the earth in the October Revolution of 1917.

The Bolsheviks and the Soviet Union showed how a new social system could arise and develop through the exercise of proletarian class dictatorship against the bourgeoisie, the growth of socialist industry and collectivization of agriculture through a series of five-year economic plans, and the promotion of a socialist culture ennobling the working people and inspiring them to achieve greater revolutionary victories. They established the Third International to cause the establishment of the revolutionary parties of the proletariat and encourage the advance of movements for national liberation and socialism.

The Soviet Union was flourishing when the world capitalist system was again wracked by a general crisis (the Great Depression) and the rise of fascism, while two blocs of imperialist powers were threatening each other. In due time, World War II broke out between the Allied and Axis Powers. It was essentially an interimperialist war. But this time, the Allied Powers could not have won if not for the immense Soviet war effort, leading to the decisive defeat of Nazi Germany at Stalingrad and the subsequent Soviet counteroffensive which liberated Eastern Europe and the eastern part of Germany. The war cost the lives of more than 50 million people, including those of 27 million Soviet people.

The communists excelled in fighting the fascist powers. As a result, people's democracies and socialism came to power in several countries. The colonial system weakened. One third of humanity were in countries under the leadership of communist and worker's parties up to the time Khrushchov and modern revisionism came to power in the Soviet Union in 1956. China won power in 1949 and became one giant bulwark of anti-imperialism and socialism. National liberation movements continued to grow in strength in Asia, Africa and Latin America.

Among the imperialist powers, the US emerged as the No. 1 economic and military power. It spearheaded the establishment of the United Nations and the Bretton Woods Agreement. It declared the Cold War against the socialist countries and carried out wars of aggression against peoples in the third world. In 1951, the Korean people defeated the US war of aggression and its scheme of occupying the entire Korean peninsula. The Vietnamese and other Indochinese people defeated the US war of aggression in an even more resounding way in the middle of the 1970s.

177

Modern revisionism turned the Soviet Union into a monopoly bureaucrat, social fascist and social imperialist power. The US and the Soviet Union competed in the practice of neocolonialism. China stood for the cause of national independence and socialist revolution and construction. Under the leadership of Mao Zedong, the Chinese Communist Party stood for Marxism-Leninism and for the proletarian revolution, combated modern revisionism, imperialism and reaction and carried out the Great Proletarian Cultural Revolution from 1966 to 1976. But the Dengist capitalist counterrevolution categorically defeated socialism in 1978.

By 1975, the US was already crisis-stricken and in a process of decline because of stagflation brought about by its high military spending and wars of aggression, and the competition offered by Germany and Japan. In 1980, it began to carry out its economic policy of neoliberalism, imposed it on the entire capitalist system, and used it to engage both the Soviet Union and China by extending loan and trade accommodations. By 1989, the US was in a far worse position than in 1975. It had accelerated its military spending, it had become the biggest debtor country in the world and its manufacturing base had been significantly undermined. Japan was also on the eve of beginning its decades-long stagnation.

But the crisis of the US and world capitalist system was obscured by the events of 1989 to 1991 that were interpreted as the final fall and death of socialism. These included the outbreak of mass protests against corruption and inflation in some 80 cities of China and the Tiananmen protests which led to the Dengist massacre in 1989, the breakdown of the Soviet bloc revisionist regimes, the full scale privatization of public assets in an undisguised restoration of capitalism, and the collapse of the Soviet Union in 1991. The bourgeois ideologues and publicists trumpeted that history could no longer go beyond capitalism and liberal democracy, and that peace dividends would come from the end of the Cold War and from the acclamation of US imperialism as the sole superpower.

Since the end of the Cold War, however, the US has freely imposed its neoliberal economy on the whole world and has unleashed a series of aggressive wars to break up Yugoslavia, to destroy the Saddam government in Iraq, to oust the Taliban government in Afghanistan, to overthrow the Qaddafi government in Libya, and now to seek the overthrow of the Assad government in Syria. The bankruptcy of the neoliberal economic policy has been thoroughly proven. It has resulted in a series of economic and financial crises, which are increasingly worse and which have led to the current crisis that started in 2008. This is comparable to the Great Depression that led to World War II.

The US imperialists, their allies and puppets have been boasting that the full restoration of capitalism in China and Russia has killed the revolutionary cause of national liberation and socialism once and for all time. But the

178

integration of Russia and China into the world capitalist system has in fact led to the intensification of inter-imperialist contradictions. The BRICS Bloc has emerged as a foil to the US hegemony over the global economy. The Shanghai Cooperation Organization is also a foil to the aggressiveness of the US-NATO combine.

All major contradictions in the world are sharpening: between the imperialists and the oppressed peoples and nations; between the imperialist powers and the self-respecting independent states; among the imperialist powers themselves; and between labor and capital in the imperialist countries. The conditions are favorable for the rise and spread of armed revolutionary movements for national and social liberation, for independent states to become more assertive, for the peoples of the world to take advantage of the inter-imperialist contradictions; and for the proletariat in imperialist countries to wage fiercer class struggle against the big bourgeoisie.

II. Most important tasks in the anti-imperialist struggle

The most important tasks in the anti-imperialist struggle include the following: building the revolutionary party of the proletariat that leads the anti-imperialist struggle; waging the anti-imperialist and democratic mass struggles in the imperialist countries and in the dominated countries; bringing the anti-imperialist and democratic struggles to the level of social revolution; and promoting and strengthening proletarian internationalism and international anti-imperialist solidarity of peoples.

Since the rise of modern imperialism as the dominant force in the world, the class struggle of the bourgeoisie and the proletariat has intensified and become the most crucial dynamic in the process of social revolution. The necessity of proletarian-socialist revolution is most discernible in the industrial capitalist countries even as the struggle for democracy must be waged against repression and the threat of fascism. The socialist revolution is definitely prepared by a new type of democratic revolution led by the proletariat in the underdeveloped countries.

The era of modern imperialism and proletarian revolution has been validated without any doubt by the emergence of socialist countries as a result of capitalist crisis and inter-imperialist wars. Although modern imperialism has dealt a major blow to the cause of socialism and has effected its strategic retreat, the class struggle between the bourgeoisie and the proletariat has persisted and has intensified as a result of the severe economic and political crisis generated by neoliberal economic policy and the recurrent wars of aggression.

At this stage of world history, the proletariat is the most advanced productive and political force. It is capable of emancipating itself and other exploited classes. And it is capable of bringing about socialism after seizing political power from the bourgeoisie. It must have for its advanced detachment a revolutionary party. This must be built in order to lead the proletariat in the class struggle against the bourgeoisie and achieve the overthrow of the bourgeois dictatorship and the establishment of the proletarian dictatorship. In the process, it must lead the broad masses of the people in order to defeat imperialism.

The revolutionary party of the proletariat must build itself ideologically by educating its cadres and members on the basic principles of Marxism-Leninism-Maoism in philosophy, political economy and social science, and training them to apply materialist dialectics in analyzing history and current circumstances. They must understand materialist and historical materialism, political economy from capitalism to socialism, the strategy and tactics of proletarian revolution, and the ever continuing process of socialist revolution and construction towards the threshold of communism. They must combat subjectivism and rise to the level of understanding how to fight and defeat revisionism.

The revolutionary party of the proletariat must build itself by adopting and implementing the general line of political struggle based on the concrete social conditions, and by arousing, organizing and mobilizing the people accordingly. There are two very distinct types of societies in the world today: the industrial capitalist societies and the underdeveloped pre-industrial societies. In the industrial capitalist countries, the general line of socialist revolution applies, but the struggle for democracy must be taken into account because the monopoly bourgeoisie is bound to use state terrorism or fascism to prevent socialist revolution. In the underdeveloped pre-industrial societies, the general line of people's democratic revolution based on the worker-peasant alliance is a necessary preparation for the consequent socialist revolution.

If truly revolutionary, the proletarian party in any country must seriously study the Marxist-Leninist theory of the state and revolution and the historical experience of the working class in applying the theory. No exploiting ruling class is ever willing to give up its power voluntarily. And it is the central task of the oppressed and exploited people to develop the process of armed revolution in order to forcibly seize power from the exploiting ruling classes.

In the underdeveloped pre-industrial countries, the chronic crises and extreme conditions of exploitation and oppression allow the proletarian revolutionary party to organize the people's war. But even in the industrial capitalist countries, it is possible to organize armed self-defense groups against criminality and state repression, or even just sports gun clubs. Such groups can transform themselves into revolutionary combat units against intolerable oppression or in the course of transforming an imperialist war to a civil war.

But arms are of no use for a possible revolution if in the first place there is no revolutionary mass movement. There must be mass organizations

Foundations and Motivations of Imperialist Aggression

of the workers, peasants, women, youth, minority nationalities, and other exploited and oppressed people, and these must be engaged in developing mass movements that uphold, defend and promote the political, civil, economic, social and cultural rights of the oppressed and exploited. These mass organizations can develop their groups for self-defense. And the mass movements must become so strong as to create influence and following even within the counterrevolutionary apparatuses of the state, especially among the personnel recruited from the exploited classes and who continue to suffer oppression and exploitation by the system and by their corrupt and bullying officers.

When the revolutionary party of the proletariat is successful at educating and organizing the revolutionary mass organizations, it can also be successful at mobilizing not only their mass following but also the masses which are not organized or who belong to other organizations. Being successful at arousing, organizing and mobilizing the masses, the revolutionary party of the proletariat can engage in alliances with other parties, organizations and personages who agree to a united front against imperialism and reaction on particular issues or a whole range of issues. In having its own mass base and allies, the party can easily build its self-defense groups or even an entire people's army.

The membership of the revolutionary party can increase only on the basis of an increasing mass base. The mass organizations are the recruiting ground for the party. The party makes it a point to recruit as its candidate members those mass activists who come from the ranks of the toiling masses of workers and peasants and the urban petty bourgeoisie, and those who have shown resoluteness, militancy and willingness to join the revolutionary party of the proletariat, to study, and to work harder for the advance of the revolution.

The revolutionary party of the proletariat must build itself organizationally on the basis of the mass organizations and ensure that it is deeply rooted among the toiling masses and has a national scale. It must follow the principle of democratic centralism. Decisionmaking is based on democracy and is guided by centralized leadership. At every level of the organization, the majority prevails over the minority vote. The higher organs prevail over the lower organs. The Central Committee is responsible for centralized leadership in accordance with the Constitution and Program and the decisions of the Congress.

In each country, the revolutionary party of the proletariat wages all forms of struggle to fight and defeat imperialism, its allies and puppets. The most decisive form of struggle is the armed struggle because it is the most effective way for ending the class dictatorship or state of the bourgeoisie, and installing either a socialist state or a people's democracy under the leadership of the working class within certain national boundaries. At the same time, the proletariat and people of the entire world must unite and fight to defeat imperialism and allies because these are an international force exploiting and oppressing the entire humankind.

The working class and the rest of the people who are in the belly of the beast in the imperialist countries have a special duty in defeating imperialism in its own home ground. The metaphor should be well understood. If you are in the belly, you can hit the heart and other vital organs of the beast, especially when it brings to you one catastrophe after another. In the other parts of the world, the overextended body, arms and legs of imperialism are vulnerable to the people's counteroffensives and can also make the beast bleed to death.

It is important for the revolutionary parties of the proletariat as well as the mass organizations and mass movements of the exploited and oppressed to hold their respective international gatherings to share ideas and experiences and learn from each other on how to fight imperialism most effectively and how to take advantage of the economic, social and political crisis and the interimperialist contradictions.

The world proletariat and the revolutionary parties of the proletariat must raise high the Red banner of proletarian internationalism against the imperialist powers. The peoples of the world must further strengthen their international anti-imperialist solidarity. The respective international gatherings of proletarian revolutionary parties and of the people's organizations can initiate and carry out international campaigns against imperialism on the issues of oppression, exploitation and environmental destruction.

As a global alliance of mass organizations and mass movements, the International League of Peoples' Struggle has successfully launched anti-imperialist and democratic campaigns of mass work and political action on the following major concerns: the cause of national liberation, democracy and social liberation; socioeconomic development and social justice; human rights in the civil, political, economic, social and cultural fields; the cause of just peace; independent trade union and workers' and toilers' rights and reduction of working hours at full pay against mass unemployment and decreasing wage levels; agrarian reform and rights of peasants, farm workers and fisherfolk; the cause of women's rights and liberation; rights of the youth to education and employment; children's rights against child labor, sexual abuse and other forms of exploitation; rights of indigenous peoples, oppressed nations and nationalities against chauvinism and racism; the rights of teachers, researchers and other educational personnel; the right of the people to health care and the rights of health workers; science and technology for the people and development, and environmental protection; arts and culture and free flow of information in the service of the people; justice and indemnification for the victims of illegal arrest and detention; rights and welfare of displaced homeless persons, refugees and migrant workers; and rights of gays, lesbians, bisexuals and transgendered.

As Chairperson of the International Coordinating Committee of the International League of Peoples' Struggle, I am happy to announce that we have just concluded a meeting of the aforesaid committee to review the work

Foundations and Motivations of Imperialist Aggression

of the ILPS and to prepare for the Fifth International Assembly of the ILPS in Manila in November this year. Your mass organizations and mass movements are invited to participate. We hope to work harder and achieve greater victories in the anti-imperialist and democratic struggle. Thank you.

Imperialism in Various Global Regions

Strengthen the Unity of the Peoples of Asia and Africa against US-Led Neocolonialism: Fight for National Sovereignty
Keynote Speech at the People's Conference to Celebrate the 60th Anniversary of the Bandung Conference
Auditorium of Padjajaran University, Bandung
April 23, 2015

I am highly honored to be invited as keynote speaker of the People's Conference to celebrate the 60th anniversary of the Asian African Conference of 1955 in Bandung and to unify the people for a joint declaration of struggle against imperialism and for national sovereignty. I congratulate the Indonesian Chapter of the ILPS and the Front Perdjuangan Rakyat (People's Struggle Front) for realizing this conference.

I am deeply pleased that this conference is a crucial part of the campaign with the theme:

Strengthen the unity of the peoples of Asia and Africa against US-led neocolonialism: fight for national sovereignty. Yours is the celebration worthy of the spirit of the Bandung Conference which clearly opposed colonialism and neocolonialism, in contrast to the official commemoration which shall pay lip service to the Bandung Conference but will condone and even promote neocolonialism and neoliberalism.

The Asian African Conference of 1955 arose upon the initiative of newly independent countries that were concerned about upholding and strengthening their national sovereignty and independence in the face of the persistent attempts of the imperialist powers headed by the US to preserve colonialism wherever still possible, to impose neocolonialism on the newly-independent countries and to divide and rule over the newly-independent countries.

The US and other imperialist powers deemed neocolonialism as a clever and effective method for controlling the newly-independent countries, without having to pay for the costs and risks of outright colonial domination, especially in the face of the rise of national liberation movements and several socialist countries in the aftermath of World War II. Neocolonialism involves the persistence of imperialist economic and financial interests and privileges within a previously colonized country and the continued subservience of the local exploiting classes to foreign monopoly capitalism. Unequal treaties are forged in the economic, trade, financial and military spheres in order to bind the neocolonies or semicolonies.

The organizers of the Bandung Conference were the states of Indonesia, Burma, Pakistan, Sri Lanka (then still known as Ceylon) and India. Twenty nine countries, with more than one half of the world's population, were represented in the conference. The newly-established states were a mixture of those that acquired national independence through armed revolution, through grants of independence by the previous colonial ruler or through a combination of both. They were able to make a consensus in forging the 10-point Declaration which reiterated principles from the UN Charter and integrated those principles of peaceful coexistence governing the relations of states.

The principles of the Declaration are as follows: 1) Respect for fundamental human rights and for the purposes and principles of the charter of the United Nations; 2) Respect for the sovereignty and territorial integrity of all nations; 3) Recognition of the equality of all races and of the equality of all nations large and small; 4) Abstention from intervention or interference in the internal affairs of another country; 5) Respect for the right of each nation to defend itself, singly or collectively, in conformity with the charter of the United Nations; 6) (a) Abstention from the use of arrangements of collective defence to serve any particular interests of the big powers (b) Abstention by any country from exerting pressures on other countries; 7) Refraining from acts or threats of aggression or the use of force against the territorial integrity or political independence of any country; 8) Settlement of all international disputes by peaceful means, such as negotiation, conciliation, arbitration or judicial settlement as well as other peaceful means of the parties own choice, in conformity with the charter of the United Nations; 9) Promotion of mutual interests and cooperation; 10) Respect for justice and international obligations.

The Five Principles of Peaceful Co-Existence, which were previously codified in a treaty between China and India in 1954, are as follows: 1) Mutual respect for each other's territorial integrity and sovereignty; 2) Mutual nonaggression; 3) Mutual noninterference in each other's internal affairs; 4) Equality and cooperation for mutual benefit; and 5) Peaceful coexistence.

The US and other imperialist powers took a negative position towards the above principles and interpreted them not as a guide to the harmonious relations of all countries but as an attack on colonial and imperialist hegemony. They were hostile to the Bandung Conference. and they made every attempt to prevent the holding of the next Asian African Conference. They considered it as an instrument of the most assertive newly-independent countries for opposing neocolonialism, colonialism and imperialism, supporting the peoples still fighting for national liberation in Asia and Africa and for cooperating with the socialist countries.

The Bandung Conference was followed by the Afro-Asian People's Solidarity Conference in Cairo in 1957. And the Belgrade Conference of the 1961 led to the establishment of the Non-Aligned Movement (NAM).

The imperialist powers succeeded in preventing the holding of the Second Asia African Conference in Algiers in 1965 by emboldening a coup against the Ben Bella government. The Non-Aligned Movement appeared to be the

Strengthen the Unity of the Peoples of Asia and Africa

extension and expanded version of the Bandung Conference, especially in upholding the Five Principles of Peaceful Coexistence and overriding the Cold War between the US and the Soviet Union. However, the imperialist powers headed by the US could sow intrigues and manipulate some member-states against others to render NAM less effective as an instrument for defending national independence and promoting genuine development. The US feverishly unleashed political and economic sanctions, subversion and overthrow of governments that opposed imperialism, colonialism and neocolonialism in the course of the Cold War.

After the turmoil in revisionist-ruled countries, the fall of revisionist ruling cliques and the collapse of the Soviet Union, the US and its imperialist allies have been able to impose neocolonialism and neoliberalism on other countries more freely than ever before and unleash state terrorism and wars of aggression with impunity more than ever before. Oblivious of these catastrophes, the summits of Asian-African states in 2005 and 2015 to commemorate the Bandung Conference are mere passing rituals. The so-called New Asian-African Strategic Partnership invokes the Bandung Conference in vain as it accepts and promotes the framework of neocolonialism and neoliberalism in claiming to stand on such generalities as political solidarity, economic cooperation and sociocultural relations.

It is important and relevant to recall how extremely the US hated the Indonesian leader Sukarno for championing the Bandung Conference and the "new emerging forces" against neocolonialism, colonialism and imperialism. The US masterminded and provided logistics to the regional and sectarian rebellions against the Sukarno government. It became even more vicious when the Indonesian government relied on the support of the NASAKOM united front. It prepared for the 1965 massacre of 1 to 3 million people, by indoctrinating and training a number of officers in the Indonesian Army, and collecting in advance the intelligence for the massacre of those classified as communists or sympathizers (those in mass organizations). The massacre ultimately made impossible the continuance of the Asian-African organizations based in Indonesia.

The Indonesian government under Sukarno gained high prestige by co-initiating and hosting the Asian African Conference. But the 1965 massacre of communists and a far bigger number of noncommunists with impunity and the subsequent fascist dictatorship of Suharto which lasted for more than three decades brought ignominy to Indonesia. To this day, the people of Indonesia and the world are outraged that no justice has been rendered for the victims of the massacre and for the entire Indonesian nation subjected to the most brutal forms of oppression and exploitation by foreign monopoly capitalism and the local reactionaries headed by the military fascist regime of Suharto.

Under the Suharto fascist dictatorship, neocolonialism prevailed at the expense of the Indonesian people and for the benefit of the multinational firms and banks and the local reactionaries who collaborated with them in plundering the country as big compradors, landlords and bureaucrat capitalists. It was also in the time of Suharto rule that neoliberalism came to aggravate neocolonialism from the early 1980s onwards. Neoliberalism has meant the unrestricted liberalization of investments and trade, privatization of public assets, deregulation of social and environmental restrictions and full denationalization of the Indonesian economy.

To this day, neocolonialism and neoliberalism are policies dictated by the imperialists and implemented by the local reactionaries in order to ensure the extraction of superprofits through the plunder of the natural and human resources, the foreign monopoly control of trade and investments and the practice of international usury in Indonesia, in the countries of Asia and Africa and in the whole world. Like the exploited and oppressed peoples of Asia and Africa, the Indonesian people suffer a high rate of real unemployment, low income and dispossession of independent means of livelihood, the lack or inadequacy of social services and the deterioration of infrastructure and public utilities. These are the result of the extreme methods of extracting superprofits under neocolonialism and neoliberalism.

The rampant poverty and social suffering in Indonesia and in most countries of Asia and Africa are the consequence of the lack of genuine national independence, people's democracy, social justice, a well-balanced industrial development, a patriotic and progressive culture and a policy of international solidarity for peace and development against imperialism and reaction. In the joint declaration that your conference intends to issue, you must take the standpoint of the people, describe their situation and make all the necessary demands to build an Indonesia and countries of Asia, Africa and Latin America that are truly independent , democratic, socially just, developed in all basic respects and in concert with the people's of Asia and Africa and the whole world.

By way of celebrating the Bandung Conference, you must give special attention to strengthening the unity of the peoples of Asia and Africa against imperialism, neocolonialism and neoliberalism and renew the call to fight for national sovereignty and independence.

You must expose and oppose not only the cruel economic methods of plunder by neocolonialism and neoliberalism but also the use of state terrorism against the working people and the wars of aggression that the US and NATO have wantonly unleashed to violate and destroy the national sovereignty and independence of countries and their peoples.

We, the International League of Peoples' Struggle, resolutely and militantly support all your efforts the uphold the spirit and principles of the Bandung Conference and to strengthen the unity of the people in the struggle for national liberation and democracy against imperialism and its puppets and their policies and acts along the line of neocolonialism, neoliberalism, state terrorism and aggression.

On China's Expansion and the US Pivot to East Asia
Interview by Jan Victor Ayson
June 6, 2015

I have some complex questions on the issue of Chinese expansion and the US pivot to East Asia.

1. People are wondering about the stand of the mass movement and the revolutionary movement, as well as yours on the issue of Chinese aggression in the Kalayaan group of islands and Bajo de Masinloc in the West Philippine Sea. Kindly state your personal analysis on this issue and your personal stand.

JMS: I resolutely and vigorously oppose the aggressive acts of China, especially the occupation of the Bajo de Masinloc and the ongoing reclamations being made in the Kalayaan group of islands. I have published my position in several articles and interviews.

I agree with the revolutionary underground forces and the open legal forces of the national democratic movement that have expressed their position against China's acts of aggression, which seek to grab 100 percent of the ECS and 80 percent of the EEZ of the Philippines.

There is a new broad alliance called PINAS which oppose the US and China for violating Philippine national sovereignty and territorial integrity. PINAS will be launched on June 8 and will spearhead the mass actions against the US and China for committing such violations.

2. The Aquino regime and its military and political underlings have repeatedly begged for US military assistance in the Filipino nation's territorial claims. Is it possible that US intervention would sustain this nation's territorial claims?

JMS: The US has expressed a neutral position on the maritime dispute between the Philippines and China and speaks only for freedom of navigation in the South China Sea. But it has expressed support for Japan's invalid claim on Diaoyu islands on the basis of previous imperialist aggression of Japan.

It has its spy satellites always in operation. It has known about China's reclamations in the West Philippine Sea since the beginning. But it has not made any timely opposition. It is mainly and essentially interested in making its own violations of Philippine national sovereignty and territorial integrity in collaboration with its Filipino puppets. It allows China's acts of aggression and yet cites them to further entrench itself in the Philippines and reestablish US military bases under the Enhanced Defense Cooperation Agreement (EDCA).

3. China's emerging economic power is the presumed target of the US "pivot" (another English word for rebalance) from the Middle East to East Asia. Kindly state your observations on the rebalance of American military forces on East Asia as a political scientist and an international situation observer.

JMS: The US pivot to East Asia or rebalance towards deploying 60 percent of its naval assets and 50 percent of its ground and air assets is meant to influence China's economic, social, political, military and cultural policies and affairs in the direction of favoring a pro-US big bourgeoisie within China and restraining the trend of Sino-Russian collaboration. At the same time, the US is unwittingly pushing China to strengthen its relations with Russia. US is using Japan as a pawn to pressure China.

4. What can the Filipino people do in spite of the Filipino nation's economic underdevelopment/maldevelopment, absence of military modernization for the defense of Philippine waters (lack of planes, ships and missiles), the shameless treason of the Philippine government's highest officials, and the Chinese expansion, the US pivot to East Asia, and current international events?

JMS: The Filipino people can become more resolute and militant in carrying out the people's revolution and realize full national sovereignty, the nationalization of the economy, the development of the economy through national industrialization and land reform, boycott against the hostile powers and disable or dismantle their enterprises on Philippine territory.

There are many people already proposing that mass organizations and the people's army can take offensive actions against the enterprises of hostile powers. They say that they can disable or even dismantle such enterprises, like mines, plantations, logging, power plants, warehouses, real estate businesses, towers, commercial and financial enterprises, and so on.

Many people say that they only need to have a patriotic will, a lighter or match box and cans of petrol to disable or even destroy any unwanted enterprise. They are outraged by China's reclamations and by the basic condonation of these by the US. They oppose the US and China trying to divide and dominate the Philippines for their respective imperialist benefit.

Because of the ever-worsening crisis of the world capitalist system, the contradictions among the imperialist powers will continue to intensify and will result in opportunities for revolutionary advances. The global crisis, depression and the imperialist wars of aggression inflict terrible suffering on the people. Thus, the people are bound to rise up and take their destiny into their own hands. The movements for national liberation, democracy and socialism will resurge to a new and higher level.

US Uses Japan to Strengthen its Hegemony in Asia
June 16, 2015

The International League of Peoples' Struggle (ILPS) views with alarm a series of developments involving Japan that have the clear intent and potential to strengthen the hegemony of US imperialism in Asia in the short run and increase the factors for war in the region in the long run. These developments are in the context of intensified interimperialist contradictions, ever worsening conditions of crisis and plunder and the spread of wars instigated mainly by the US imperialism.

On April 27, 2015, the US and Japan released the newly revised Guidelines for US-Japan Defense Cooperation, containing major new commitments to their 50-year formal alliance as defined in the 1960 US-Japan Treaty of Mutual Cooperation and Security. The importance of these new guidelines was underscored by Shinzo Abe's speech three days later before the joint session of the US Congress—a historic first for a Japanese prime minister visiting the US.

Ostensibly, the guidelines and its "Alliance Coordination Mechanism" are focused on military cooperation between the two powers in case of a military attack against Japan by a third power (presumably China). However, such cooperation is clearly framed by much broader security concerns of the US and Japan, which span the entirety of Asia-Pacific and even beyond. (In the words of the US-Japan guidelines: "Such situations cannot be defined geographically.")

In his speech before the US Congress, Abe also emphasized Japan's full support for the US strategic pivot to Asia, at the same time promising to enact all Diet legislation needed by Japan's military commitments "by this coming summer." These so-called defense reforms alarmingly include the fascist strong-arm tactics to disembowel Article 9 of Japan's postwar Constitution, in order to free its Self-Defense Forces to undertake offensive military actions beyond Japan's territory, even joining US-led military aggression elsewhere in the world.

The conservative government of Shinzo Abe and his Liberal Democratic Party/New Komeito coalition has been gung-ho in reviving Japanese militarism and other extreme right-wing trends such as those represented by Shigeru Ishiba and Gen Nakatani, who want to revive the prewar ambitions of imperial Japan. The Abe government takes pains to ensure that resurgent Japanese militarism remains within the ambit of the US-Japan global alliance.

In recent years, the US has strengthened its ties with Japan as its main post-World War II ally in the Asia-Pacific not only as its second largest trade and investment partner, but as a military ally that hosts huge and strategic US military bases, and that could pose additional pressure points against China, North Korea, and Russia's own eastern borders and Asian interests.

The US-Japan alliance has been playing up the threats to Asia of a China-Russia military alliance in order to further inveigle the people of Asia, especially those of Japan and South Korea with their strong anti-war, anti-foreign bases, and anti-nuclear sentiments, to tolerate and even welcome the US pivot, the growing reach of Japanese "Self-Defense" Forces, and the more frequent US-Japan war games in the region.

Long before Obama's declared strategic rebalance to Asia, the US has already been maintaining a huge military presence in East Asia, with strategic bases and nuclear arms in Japan in the front line. Of the US bases in Japan, 75 percent are in the Okinawa islands, which until now remain under US military control despite the islands' reversion to Japan's sovereignty in 1972. The Abe government has aggressively pushed for the construction of a new US military base on Oura Bay in Henoko while fudging on the early closure of the US Marine Air Station in nearby Futenma.

Despite the lawful claim of China over the Diaoyu islands in the East China Sea, the US has openly sided with Japan in its dispute with China over the said islands, citing its commitment in the 1960 US-Japan treaty. Japan's claims are based on its having seized the islands from China during the 1894-95 Sino-Japanese war, while China insists that the ceded islands should be returned to it—like the other territories seized by Japan from other countries in World War II were returned to their rightful owners in 1945. In contrast, the US has expressed neutrality over China's unlawful claims over the exclusive economic zone and extended continental shelf of the Philippines under the UN Convention on the Law of the Sea.

The US has used the South China Sea dispute between China and several ASEAN countries in order to justify its strategic-pivot plan to increase the movement and "visiting rights" of its forces in Southeast Asia and establish bases in the Philippines not only for US military forces but also for Japan's SDF. Ominously, Japan and the Philippines have announced on June 5 that the two countries would soon start talks on a Visiting Forces Agreement that would allow Japan SDF access to Philippine military facilities—as the US and Australia had achieved in earlier agreements with the Philippines.

Philippine defense secretary Voltaire Gazmin has in fact announced that the US and Japan are welcome to establish military bases in the Philippines and supply weapons to the Philippine puppet forces. In support of the US pivot to Asia and in line with its own militarist big-power ambitions, Japan has pursued closer military links with key Asia-Pacific states such as Australia, ASEAN, India, and South Korea. Japan is also highlighting its various "peacekeeping" operations around the world.

Under the Abe government, Japan has been quietly rearming itself with offensive weaponry, including fifth-generation F-35 fighters equipped with US-developed smart bombs, AAV7 amphibious assault vehicles, V-22 Osprey combat aircraft, and a Mitsubishi-initiated fighter project using US Stealth technology. For fiscal year 2015, Japan has approved a US\$ 45-billion defense budget—its largest military budget in 70 years. In 2014, Japan started selling military hardware to other countries—a move unprecedented since World War II.

The US efforts to use Japan to strengthen its hegemony in Asia are further manifested in the US inveigling Japan to join the talks on the Trans-Pacific Partnership Agreement. The TPPA is a core component of the US pivot-to-Asia strategy and campaign to contain and pressure China to stay within the ambit of US hegemony or else suffer isolation. In the pursuit of its own national and ultra-national interests, China is using its growing collaboration with Russia to strengthen the Shanghai Cooperation Organization and the BRICS economic bloc and to undertake infrastructure projects to link Asia and Europe as a form of capital expansion.

However, the Abe government sees the TPPA as the prior and more convenient means of jump starting the long-stagnant Japanese economy and is going over the top to support Obama's TPPA agenda in getting US Congress' approval, notwithstanding the strong anti-TPPA public sentiment in Japan, and misgivings among some Japanese business sectors that appear more interested in a China-Korea-Japan FTA or a China-led Regional Comprehensive Economic Partnership (RCEP). Even among the Japanese ruling class, there have been rumblings about Japan's groveling subservience to the US, acting like a geisha that dutifully serves America's every need.

In many Asian countries, the people have not forgotten the war crimes and other atrocities of Fascist Japan under its slogan of the East Asia Co-Prosperity Sphere from 1937 to 1945. Their detestation of Japanese imperialism may have been dampened by Japan's resounding defeat in World War II, the renunciation of war under the postwar constitution, and the overweening dominance of US imperial- ism in maintaining military bases and a nuclear umbrella throughout Japan.

However, from the 1960s onwards, the resurgence of Japanese zaibatsu monopolies, its financial control of the Asian Development Bank (ADB), militarist agitation, and brazen cultural imperialism have rekindled distrust of Japan—even if its long recession, the persistence of the emergent markets in Asia, and the rise of China as a new imperialist power have overshadowed the reality and danger of Japanese imperialism. The renewed use of Japan as the fugleman of US imperialism is alarming.

The International League of Peoples' Struggle (ILPS) reiterates its call on the peoples of Asia to uphold their national sovereignty and independence, see through the growing complexity of inter-imperialist contradictions and resist every scheme of US imperialism to use Japanese militarism as its junior partner in Asia and to contend and collaborate with China in maintaining inter-imperialist balance at the expense of the oppressed and exploited people and the underdeveloped countries.

Everywhere in the Asia-Pacific region, the people's movement must revitalize and further strengthen their anti-imperialist and democratic campaigns. They must oppose and defeat the scheme of the US to make Japan its adjutant in the making of military bases and visiting forces agreements, warmongering and the TPPA even as the people of Southeast Asia must stand against acts of aggression by China. We support the people of Japan in their multi-sided mass struggles to reject the US bases in Okinawa and elsewhere and to oppose Japanese militarism and its collaboration with US imperialism.

On the International Situation
Presentation to the 5th International Assembly of BAYAN USA on its 10th Anniversary Celebration in Washington, DC July 18, 2015

First let me thank you for inviting me to make a presentation of the international situation. I congratulate BAYAN USA for waging anti-imperialist and democratic struggles and winning victories in the national and democratic interest of the Filipino people in the Philippines and abroad and in solidarity with other peoples in the US and elsewhere in the world. I join you in celebrating the last ten years of the life, struggles and victories of BAYAN USA.

It is of crucial importance that the Filipino people and BAYAN USA know the international situation. In the world era of monopoly capitalism or modern imperialism, the US is the most powerful force exploiting and oppressing the Filipino people and has the most effective ways of doing so. You are inside the belly of the imperialist beast that is responsible for the violent suppression of the Filipino people's national sovereignty, the underdevelopment of the Philippine economy, the widespread poverty and diaspora of more than 10 percent of the Philippine population or 20 percent of the work force.

On the status of the US in the world

The US is still the strongest imperialist power. It imposes the neoliberal policy of imperialist globalization on the entire capitalist world. It uses the Bretton Woods agreement, the Washington Consensus and supremacy of the US dollar in investments and trade. It continues to extract superprofits as it avails of higher technology and plunders the human and natural resources of the world. It uses the high-tech weapons of mass indoctrination and propaganda, surveillance and state terrorism and wars of aggression to suppress the revolutionary movements of the people and to isolate and topple states that assert national independence.

However, the US is already on a long-term track of general decline, which was first signaled by the problems of stagflation, excessive military spending and defeat of the US war of aggression in Indochina in the 1970s. For a while, such a decline was overshadowed by the turmoil in the revisionist-ruled countries, the collapse of the Soviet Union, the US self-proclaimed winner in the Cold War and sole superpower, the accelerated US-instigated wars of aggression against Iraq, Afghanistan and Yugoslavia and the rapid growth of capitalist China as the main US partner in pushing neoliberal globalization.

But a series of economic and financial crises have beset the US and the capitalist world. The worst of them, which started in 2008 with the mortgage meltdown in the US, has protracted and worsened. It has hastened the decline of the US economy and has generated socioeconomic and political turmoil in the US and throughout the world. You know better than I do how much life has deteriorated for the working class and people of color in the US because of unemployment, reduced real incomes, rising costs of basic necessities, homelessness, racial discrimination, religious bigotry, state terrorism and wars of aggression.

Despite the high cost of aggressive and proxy wars, at the expense the people in the targeted countries as well as the American people themselves, the US has continued to unleash such wars in the Middle East, recently against Libya and Syria; and has continued to threaten and make war provocations against Iran and the Democratic People's Republic of Korea for an extended period of time.

Growing US aggressiveness is a direct consequence of the worsening crisis of US monopoly capitalism and the desperate attempt to control the human and natural resources of the world. In a vain attempt to perpetuate or even expand US hegemony in the 21st century, the US is implementing the neoconservative line of using full-spectrum dominance (especially high-tech military superiority). The danger of further wars still exists because of the aggressive nature of imperialism, despite current improvements of US relations with Cuba and Iran.

The US is still preoccupied with quagmires of its own making in the Middle East and Africa. It has made the motions of reducing its forces in these regions, negotiating with Iran and the Taliban and has gone to the extent of training, arming and using the Islamic state or Daesh to wreak havoc on and destabilize states seen as threats to the US-Zionist-NATO dominance and to the Saudi model of subservience to the US and the US oil companies. And yet with overweening arrogance, the US engages in subversion, terrorism and military intervention in so many regions and is generating turmoil on a global scale.

The US has pushed the expansion of the NATO to the borders of Russia and has instigated and assisted so-called color revolutions to pressure Russia towards further subordination and to undermine the growing economic cooperation between Russia and Germany. Most recently, it has emboldened, funded and armed the neofascist forces in Ukraine in order to seize power and launch a war against the Russian-speaking people there. But the people in Novorassiya and Crimea have fought back and established people's republics. The people of Crimea have reintegrated themselves with Russia.

The US and its European allies, including a reluctant Germany, with its interest in the energy supply from Russia, have gone further by imposing sanctions on Russia and suspending Russia from the G-8. Russia has defied the sanctions and declared its own counter sanctions. It has strengthened its back-to-back economic and security relations with China. It supplies China with energy and some equipment and China supplies it with manufactures and food products. The two countries have vowed to cooperate in building the new Silk Road from China to Germany.

Previously, the US was offended by the establishment of the Shanghai Cooperation Organization as a security alliance to counter the US-NATO alliance as well as the establishment of the BRICS economic bloc to counter the worst economic, trade and financial impositions of the US. It has become even more offended by the establishment of the BRICS Development Bank and the Asian Infrastructure Investment Bank. It regards all these as challenges to the US-controlled global financial system.

Despite having grown economically in collaboration with the US, China has espoused multipolarity in world affairs and has become wary of the detrimental consequences of the crisis within the US and the world capitalist system. Thus, it has adopted measures in its national self-interest. The US maintains its dual policy of engagement and containment towards China but in recent years it has engaged in more containment measures in order to further strengthen the pro- US big bourgeoisie within China. Thus, despite the annual US-China Strategic and Economic Dialogue, the US has pushed the Trans Pacific Partnership Agreement and the strategic pivot to East Asia.

At the time that the revisionist regimes gave way to undisguised full restoration of capitalism and the Soviet Union collapsed, the US and other imperialist powers were delirious with joy and boasted that socialism is a hopeless cause and that history cannot go beyond capitalism. Since then, the economic and financial crisis of global capitalism has become more frequent and worse at each recurrence. The addition of Russia and China to the circle of imperialist powers has become problematic to the US and has caused the intensification of inter-imperialist contradictions.

Oppression and exploitation of the people

Since the full restoration of capitalism in China, Russia and Eastern Europe, the exploitation and oppression of the people have escalated in these areas and in the whole world. The imperialist powers, the developed countries and a few so-called emergent markets try to override the recurrent and worsening economic and financial crisis by expanding the money supply and credit.

But these merely feed the financial markets and do not revive production, employment and demand. The capitalist states cannot stop the next more serious crisis from coming because of their growing debt and their policy of shifting the burden of crisis to the lower levels of the bureaucracy and to the broad masses of the people through austerity measures.

After the end of World War II, the imperialist powers avoided direct wars among themselves and united against the socialist countries and national liberation movements. They avoided interimperialist wars by always passing the burden of crisis to the peoples of the world. They adopted the policy and measures of neocolonialism to keep on controlling the underdeveloped countries through economic and financial means. But they did not hesitate to unleash military intervention and aggression against the peoples and states that assert national independence. Eventually, since 1979, the US has aggravated the policy of neocolonialism with the policy of neoliberalism.

In the absence of any formidable socialist country like the Soviet Union before 1956 and China before 1978, the oppressed peoples and nations of the world find themselves under conditions similar to those in the decades before World War I when there were yet no such countries as bulwarks of proletarian revolution and socialism. Indeed, there are now no formidable socialist countries that can effectively challenge and keep the imperialist powers at bay and can serve as the rallying points for peoples and states assertive of national independence.

The situation now is complex. We can cheer China and Russia in being the stalwarts of the SCO and BRICS and in standing up to the intolerable policies and actions of the US. We can stand up with China against the US strategic pivot to East Asia and support China's sovereign rights on Diaoyu islands in the East Sea against the contrary claims of Japan based on its previous imperialist aggression. But we certainly oppose China in grabbing 90 percent of the South China Sea and in particular 100 percent of the extended continental shelf and 80 percent of the exclusive economic zone of the Philippines in accordance with the UN Convention on the Law of the Sea.

Resistance of the proletariat and peoples

Under current circumstances, the proletariat and oppressed nations and peoples of the world have to struggle more resolutely, more militantly and self-reliantly than ever before within their respective national borders for greater freedom, democracy and socialism against the imperialist powers and the local reactionary forces. The escalating plunder and wars unleashed by the imperialist powers inflict terrible suffering on the people but at the same time incite and drive them to resist and engage in revolutionary struggles to overthrow the unjust system and establish the just system.

The broad masses detest and want to change the system in which the imperialist powers and their agents engage in unbridled exploitation under the policies of neocolonialism and neoliberalism, in state terrorism and all forms of oppression, in counterrevolutionary wars and aggression, in the use of weapons of mass destruction, in threats of nuclear war and in the relentless destruction of the environment. The social degradation of the working people

On the International Situation

and the political turmoil cannot go on without the growing resistance of the people. The unbridled attacks on the people and the people's seeming helplessness are but the prelude to their revolutionary rising.

The revolutionary parties of the proletariat and the revolutionary mass movement of workers, peasants, youth, women, professionals, cultural activists keep on developing in both the industrial capitalist countries and in the underdeveloped countries. Among these revolutionary forces, those in the Philippines are demonstrating that they can preserve themselves and further gain strength in waging a protracted people's war in an archipelagic country that has long been a stronghold of US imperialism and its big comprador-landlord agents.

Even as the revolutionary forces and people of the world must struggle more resolutely than ever before within their respective national borders, they must continue to communicate with each other, learn from each other, hold meetings bilaterally and multilaterally and reach agreements of unity, cooperation and coordination.

The imperialist powers are ultra-national and global forces of exploitation, oppression and war. It is therefore necessary to strengthen further the international workers' movement and the anti-imperialist and democratic solidarity of the peoples of the world. This international solidarity is being developed by the International League of Peoples' Struggle.

Long live BAYAN USA!

Long live the Filipino people and the Philippine revolution!

Long live the anti-imperialist and democratic solidarity of the peoples!

Imperialism in Various Global Regions

ILPS Statement on US Imperialism's Drive to Annihilate the DPRK
September 5, 2017

US imperialism is once again pushing the world to the brink of nuclear war with its provocative war maneuvers, illegitimate sanctions and malicious disinformation campaign directed against the Democratic People's Republic of Korea (DPRK).

From August 21 through August 31, 2017, the US Combined Forces Command and the south Korean military conducted their annual "Ulchi Freedom Guardian exercise" with approximately 17,500 US. troops participating joined by south Korean military personnel from all services, as well participants from seven other allies of the US, including Australia, Canada, Columbia, Denmark, New Zealand, the Netherlands and the United Kingdom. This is the second of two annual war games conducted by the US and its puppet south Korea designed to simulate a "preemptive" nuclear strike against the DPRK as well as an invasion and decapitation of its leadership. Just last week, US fighter jets and bombers conducted military operations over a training range east of Seoul. These included B-1B bombers capable of releasing nuclear payloads.

The DPRK has repeatedly asked the US to end these provocative and reckless military exercises held right at its doorstep–in exchange for a moratorium on the DPRK's missile testing–but the US has stubbornly refused.

Instead US imperialism has been escalating its warmongering against the DPRK with Trump famously threatening to unleash "fire and fury like the world has never seen" if the DPRK ever endangers the US. His Defense Secretary, James "Mad Dog" Mattis echoed this by stating recently that "Any threat to the United States or its territories including Guam or our allies will be met with a massive military response, a response both effective and overwhelming." South Korea's puppet Defense Minister followed suit by calling for the redeployment of US tactical nuclear weapons in the Korean Peninsula.

Western media is presenting this shrill sabre-rattling as the justifiable response to the DPRK's recent missile tests. The DPRK has made significant advances in its weapons development program this year, successfully testing an intercontinental ballistic missile (ICBM) that can potentially reach US bases in Guam or Alaska; a hydrogen bomb with an estimated yield of up to 100 kilotons, which can be loaded onto an ICBM; solid-fueled missiles that reduce launch times from hours to minutes; and fortified missile batteries that could be hidden in forests, underneath cliff overhangs, under bridges, or positioned in other launch sites not easily tracked by enemy satellites.

The DPRK's weapons development program is part of its deterrence strategy against the long-running US policy of aggression towards North Korea. US

Imperialism in Various Global Regions

bombs killed 20 percent of the population and leveled more cities in North Korea between 1950-53 than they did in Japan and Germany during World War II. US imperialism and its puppet south Korea has never signed a peace treaty with the DPRK. The US has never recognized the DPRK diplomatically and has threatened it with annihilation ever since it was founded in 1948. It has positioned tens of thousands of US troops and maintains 15 bases in south Korea as a constant threat to the DPRK's existence.

Its latest ploy is to pressure China and Russia to join the US and its allies in cutting off all economic relations with the DPRK. Trump is threatening to cut US trade with any country that conducts any economic activity with DPRK–in order to trigger the latter's collapse. These threats are accompanied by a major military build-up on the Korean Peninsula in preparation for outright war.

The ILPS condemns in the strongest terms US imperialist aggression, war provocation and blackmail directed against the DPRK. We hold US imperialism and its south Korean puppets responsible for creating the extremely volatile situation in the Korean Peninsula at present.

The ILPS calls on all our global regional committees, national chapters and member-organizations to carry out a campaign of information and mass protest in order to expose, condemn and oppose the war provocations and military buildup of US imperialism and its south Korean puppets in the Korean Peninsula and the Asia-Pacific region.

The ILPS firmly stands in solidarity with and vigorously supports the DPRK and the Korean people in upholding and defending their national sovereignty and in seeking unity, justice and peace.

We Salute and Support the DPRK and the Korean People Stand against US Nuclear Threats, Sanctions and Provocations
September 6, 2017

We, the International League of Peoples' Struggle, admire and salute the Workers' Party of Korea, the Democratic People's Republic of Korea (DPRK) and the Korean people for asserting national sovereignty, self-reliantly pursuing socialist development and strengthening the capacity for nuclear deterrence and self-defense. US imperialism merely exposes its aggressive character and the futility of its attempts to intimidate the people of Korea and the world with threats of nuclear war, provocative war maneuvers, illegitimate sanctions and malicious disinformation campaign directed against the DPRK.

From August 21 to August 31, 2017, the US Combined Forces Command and the South Korean military conducted their annual "Ulchi Freedom Guardian exercise" with approximately 17,500 US troops participating joined by South Korean military personnel from all services, as well participants from seven other allies of the US, including Australia, Canada, Columbia, Denmark, New Zealand, the Netherlands and the United Kingdom. This is the second of two annual war games conducted by the US and its puppet South Korea designed to simulate a "preemptive" nuclear strike against the DPRK as well as an invasion and decapitation of its leadership.

Just last week, US fighter jets and bombers conducted military operations over a training range east of Seoul. These included B-1B bombers capable of releasing nuclear payloads. The DPRK has repeatedly asked the US to end these provocative and reckless military exercises held right at its doorstep in exchange for a moratorium on the DPRK's missile testing but the US has stubbornly refused. Instead US imperialism has been escalating its warmongering against the DPRK with Trump brazenly threatening to unleash "fire and fury like the world has never seen" if the DPRK ever endangers the US. His Defense Secretary, James "Mad Dog" Mattis echoed this by stating recently that "Any threat to the United States or its territories including Guam or our allies will be met with a massive military response, a response both effective and overwhelming." South Korea's puppet Defense Minister followed suit by calling for the further deployment of US tactical nuclear weapons in the Korean Peninsula.

Western media is presenting this shrill saber-rattling as the justifiable response to the DPRK's recent missile and nuclear tests. The DPRK has made significant advances in its weapons development program this year, successfully testing an intercontinental ballistic missile (ICBM) that can

Imperialism in Various Global Regions

potentially reach US bases in Guam or Alaska; a hydrogen bomb with an estimated yield of up to 100 kilotons, which can be loaded onto an ICBM; solid-fueled missiles that reduce launch times from hours to minutes; and fortified missile batteries that could be hidden in forests, underneath cliff overhangs, under bridges, or positioned in other launch sites not easily tracked by enemy satellites.

The DPRK's nuclear weapons development program is part of its deterrence and self-defense strategy against the long-running US policy of hostility towards the DPRK. US bombs killed 20 percent of the population and leveled more cities in North Korea between 1950 and 1953 than they had done in Japan and Germany during World War II. Without its development of nuclear weapons and missile delivery systems, the DPRK would have become the easy target of high intensity aggression like Iraq, Libya and Syria.

US imperialism and its puppet South Korea have never signed a peace treaty with the DPRK since the armistice in 1953. The US has never recognized the DPRK diplomatically and has threatened it with annihilation ever since it was founded in 1948. It has positioned tens of thousands of US troops, missile systems, nuclear and other weapons of mass destruction in 15 bases in South Korea as a constant threat to the DPRK's existence. And yet the US has never solved the problem of offending China and Russia by unleashing all-out aggression or nuclear war against the DPRK.

But the US persists in its scheme of pressuring China and Russia to join the US and its allies in cutting off all economic relations with the DPRK. Trump is threatening to cut US trade with any country that conducts any economic activity with North Korea in order to trigger the latter's collapse. The US threats of further sanctions are accompanied by a major military build-up on the Korean Peninsula and the THAAD deployment in preparation for outright war, rapid invasion and the strategy of instantly decapitating the DPRK leadership.

The ILPS condemns in the strongest terms the long and continuing record of US imperialist aggression, economic blockade, war provocations and nuclear blackmail directed against the DPRK. We hold US imperialism and its South Korean puppets responsible for creating the extremely volatile situation in the Korean Peninsula at present. We encourage the Korean people of north and south to aim and work for peaceful reunification and defeat all divisive schemes of US imperialism.

The ILPS firmly stands in solidarity with and vigorously supports the Workers' Party of Korea, DPRK and the Korean people in upholding and defending their national sovereignty, developing their socialist economy self-reliantly, building their capacity for self-defense, seeking the peaceful reunification of north and south Korea, replacing the armistice agreement with a peace treaty and fostering global conditions of greater freedom, cooperation, peace and development against US imperialism and all reaction.

204

We Salute and Support the DPRK and the Korean People

The ILPS calls on all our global regional committees, national chapters and member-organizations to carry out a campaign of information and mass protest in order to expose, condemn and oppose the persistently hostile and aggressive policy of the US against the DPRK and the Korean people, the long-running economic blockade and further sanctions, the military build-up, which has long included nuclear weapons and other weapons of mass destruction and military exercises and other war provocations of US imperialism, its imperialist allies and its South Korean puppets in the Korean Peninsula, in the vicinity and in further areas of the Asia-Pacific region.

Imperialism in Various Global Regions

Study Marx to Resist Imperialism
Message of Solidarity to the Marx@200 Study Conference of the Institute of Political Economy
June 13, 2018

On behalf of the International League of Peoples' Struggle, I convey warmest greetings of solidarity to the Institute of Political Economy and to all the participants in this study conference to celebrate the 200th birth anniversary of Karl Marx. I congratulate the institute for its success in organizing this conference.

The theme of the conference correctly relates the teachings of Marx to the current conditions of the world capitalist system and to the urgent need for revolutionary change by the proletariat and the people: "Continuing relevance of Marx's teachings in social movements and their struggles." The study of Marxism is indispensable for understanding the current status and crisis of global capitalism. It was Marx who first uncovered systematically the laws of motion of capitalism, how the capitalist class extracts surplus value from the working class in the process of social production, overaccumulates capital and shrinks the wage fund and thereby creates the crisis of overproduction relative to the purchasing power of the working people.

Credit may be resorted to bail out the corporations in distress and buoy up the economy but it merely accelerates the concentration and accumulation of capital in the hands of the few. In the name of free trade, the drive for colonial expansion is propelled. Free competition capitalism leads to monopoly capitalism. Old-style colonialism leads to modern imperialism.

Marxism is not a fixed set of dogmas. It has been extended, developed and applied in correspondence to the emergence and growth of free competition capitalism to monopoly capitalism. Thus, Leninism is Marxism in the era of modern imperialism and proletarian revolution. Further, Marxism-Leninism has been further extended, developed and enriched by Maoism in the face of modern revisionism and the danger of capitalist restoration in socialist countries.

The topics lined up for discussion in your study conference cover two necessary points: first, the correct analysis of global capitalism that lays the ground for changing the world and second, the process of changing the world to what is fundamentally better for humankind, socialism, through the anti-imperialist and democratic struggle of the proletariat and the oppressed peoples.

You start on the correct track by analyzing the role of investment liberalization and its impact on labor and production. The limits of abusing monopoly finance capital in order to override the recurrent and worsening crisis of overproduction and continue profit-making and the accumulation of superprofits are exposed by the excessive and unrepayable debts at the level of households, corporations and central banks. Since the financial meltdown of 2008, the economic and financial experts of the capitalist powers have been unable to overcome the prolonged stagnation and depression of the global economy.

The unbridled abuse of investment liberalization has been in combination with labor flexibilization and global subcontracting. The rapid overaccumulation of capital in the hands of the monopoly bourgeoisie has been at the expense of the working class which has been subjected to deprivation of job security, to wage freezes and to violation of trade union and other democratic rights. But the blowback is the now prolonged stagnation and depression of the global economy.

The monopoly capitalists have been able to manipulate to their advantage the reserve army of labor on a global scale and in nearly every country in the world. Moreover, they have used global subcontracting and outsourcing as well as compelling labor migration from the underdeveloped and impoverished countries to attain more intensified forms of exploitation by migrant workers who are deprived of democratic rights and are easier subjected to the worst forms of exploitation.

The adoption of higher technology, from the electro-mechanical processes of the industrial revolution to the current digital age of speedier systems of production and distribution, has enabled the unprecedented acceleration of the concentration and accumulation of monopoly capital, the higher organic composition of capital and diminution of wage income. It has led to the now severe economic and financial crisis and the prolonged depression of the global capitalist economy. As Marx pointed out a long a time ago, capitalism creates the conditions and diggers for its own burial.

Monopoly capitalism profits much from the cheap labor of the migrant workers. And the migrants who suffer from separation from their homelands and families are subjected to further suffering by being deprived of democratic rights and fair wages and being subjected to xenophobic, racist and fascist movements. But they are driven to seek international solidarity with their fellow migrant workers and the workers in the host countries. The monopoly bourgeoisie makes all attempts at mass distraction to conceal or obscure the root causes of capitalist exploitation, socioeconomic crisis, political crisis, social discontent, disorder and wars of aggression, with outright reactionary propaganda as well as opportunism, reformism and revisionism.

But the global workers' movement perseveres in struggle against the evils of monopoly capitalism under the leadership of Marxist-Leninist parties

Study Marx to Resist Imperialism

which uphold the red banner of proletarian internationalism and inspire the proletarian-socialist revolution in the world and in particular countries.

Contrary to its claims of developing the whole world under imperialist neoliberal globalization, monopoly capitalism has generated grossly uneven development, further enriching a few imperialist countries and impoverishing the majority of countries supplying cheap labor and cheap raw materials. In many underdeveloped countries of the world, where there are still significant vestiges of feudalism persisting, the working class and its revolutionary party strive to lead and generate the revolutionary peasant movement and the struggle for land reform.

They build the basic alliance of the working class and peasantry and ensure the mass mobilization of the overwhelming majority of the people, win over the urban petty bourgeoisie and the middle bourgeoisie, and take advantage of the splits among the reactionary classes in order to isolate and destroy the power of the enemy, which is the most reactionary force and most servile to foreign monopoly capitalism.

There are huge sectors of society, such as the women and youth who if aroused, organized and mobilized like the basic exploited basic classes to take the revolutionary road can accelerate the advance of the revolutionary movement and the downfall of any regime or even the entire ruling system.

The broad masses of the people have suffered for so long from the US-instigated neoliberal policy of unbridled greed since the onset of the 1980s and from the neoconservative policy of stepping up war production and continuous wars of aggression since the full restoration of capitalism in the revisionist-ruled countries and the collapse of the Soviet Union.

But such policies have also been far more costly than profitable to the US and has accelerated its strategic decline despite the passing phase of the US having become the sole superpower in a unipolar world from the end of the bipolar world of the Cold War in the 1991 upon the collapse of the Soviet Union.

Since the beginning of the 21st century, it has become obvious that the US has undermined its own global dominance by having financialized its economy and conceded consumer manufacturing to China and squandering at least US$ 5.6 trillion in its wars of aggression. Now, there is conspicuously a multipolar world in which the US increasingly finds itself unable to decide global issues unilaterally and dictate on other capitalist powers.

The rise of new imperialist powers like China and Russia is aggravating the crisis of global capitalism. The interimperialist contradictions sharpen as the US tries to stop its strategic decline from the peak or primacy of the sole superpower and the new imperialist powers strive to obtain dominance. The intensification of the interimperialist contradictions are bringing about worse conditions of economic and financial crisis, oppression and exploitation and wars of aggression.

The broad masses of the people can never accept these conditions which inflict on them terrible and intolerable suffering. We are in a period of transition in which interimperialist contradictions and the revolutionary and counterrevolutionary currents are escalating. The economic crises and wars of global capitalism are pressing on the revolutionary proletariat and broad masses of the people to fight back.

We are therefore moving in the direction of the global resurgence of the revolutionary forces of the people and the advance of the movements for national liberation, democracy and socialism against imperialism, revisionism and reaction. We are living in an increasingly turbulent world of crises, social disorder and wars.

But the proletariat and people in the traditional and new imperialist countries and in the less developed and underdeveloped countries are resisting imperialism and reaction through various forms of social movements and revolutionary struggles. We are once more on the eve of great social upheavals and great revolutionary victories on an unprecedented scale in the people's struggle for greater freedom, democracy and socialism against imperialism and all reaction.

Long live the memory and legacy of Karl Marx!

Long Marxism-Leninism-Maoism!

Carry forward the Philippine revolution!

Contribute to the advance of the world proletarian revolution!

Long live proletarian internationalism!

Author's Preface to *Strengthen the People's Struggle against Imperialism and Reaction*

I thank the editor and the International Network of Philippine Studies for publishing Strengthen the People's Struggle against Imperialism and Reaction, Volume 5, thus completing the book series, The People's Struggle against Oppression and Exploitation: Selected Writings: 2009-2015. This volume is a selection of my writings from 2014 to 2015, a period of crisis, social unrest and political turmoil in the Philippines and the world.

As the founding chairman of the Communist Party of the Philippines (CPP) and as Chief Political Consultant of the National Democratic Front of the Philippines (NDFP) in peace negotiations with the Government of the Republic of the Philippines (GRP), I was expected or sometimes obliged to speak or write on major Philippine issues from a patriotic and progressive viewpoint in line with the new-democratic revolution.

As Chairperson of the International League of Peoples´ Struggle (ILPS) I was required to take initiative in stating the anti-imperialist and democratic position of the League on global issues for the benefit of its International Coordinating Committee, global region committees, national chapters and more than 200 member-organizations in five continents.

The contents of Strengthen the People's Struggle against Imperialism and Reaction include essays (articles and speeches), statements, interviews and messages to various people's organizations and institutions. They are arranged chronologically. But they are interconnected and cohere in connection with major events and issues in the peoples' struggles against US imperialism and local reaction in the Philippines and abroad.

The book contains essays that describe the context of the history and circumstances of the Filipino people's struggle for national liberation and democracy. It examines the implications and consequences of the resurgence of the national democratic movement since the 1960s and the EDSA uprising that overthrew the Marcos fascist dictatorship in 1986. And it focuses on the situation and prospects of the people´s struggle against the US-Aquino regime, characterized as a big comprador-landlord regime servile to US imperialism.

The general line of national democratic revolution is explained by a number of articles on the persistent semicolonial and semifeudal conditions and the latest conditions dictated by the US-imposed neoliberal economic policy regime, on the people's mass struggles for national and social liberation and on the new-democratic revolution through protracted people's war.

The roles of various classes and sectors in the people´s struggle are defined by the essays, statements and messages to the working class, peasantry, the indigenous people, youth, women, teachers, cultural workers and other professionals. I take the opportunity to urge various people's organizations to intensify and raise their struggle to a new and higher level. I share with them my experiences and my continuing study of how to arouse, organize and mobilize the masses.

In a paper I delivered to students and some faculty members in Development Studies at the University of Utrecht, I examine the role of activism in Philippine development. I discuss how the mass movement has endeavored to demand national industrialization and agrarian reform and basic social and economic reforms to solve the problems of underdevelopment, mass poverty, unemployment, low incomes and lack of social services. I also present how the revolutionary forces and the mass movement are undertaking reforms to alleviate these dire conditions.

The book contains a major essay on revolutionary art and literature in the Philippines from the 1960s to the present, which explains comprehensively how far the Filipino artists and creative writers have carried forward the revolutionary struggles and demands of the people. The essay was serialized in the Philippine Collegian for the benefit of the students of the University of the Philippines.

In several articles published in major Philippine and foreign publications, I analyze how the US under the Obama regime has tightened its grip on the Philippines by collaborating with Japan, by carrying out a strategic pivot to Asia, by imposing the Enhanced Defense Cooperation Agreement on the Philippines and by using the Asia-Pacific Economic Cooperation to push the neoliberal offensive further.

While the US remains dominant in the Philippines, China has tried to transgress Philippine sovereign rights over the West Philippine Sea. Several articles explain the maritime dispute between the Philippines and China, the Philippine case filed against China before the International Tribunal on the Law of the Sea (ITLOS) and the Arbitral Tribunal and the relations of the Philippines with the US and China regarding the issue.

Despite the revolutionary necessity of people's war, the NDFP in representation of 18 revolutionary organizations (including the Communist Party of the Philippines and the New People's Army), has shown willingness to engage in peace negotiations with the GRP. In connection with these peace negotiations, I have gone as far as to dialogue with senior officers of the reactionary armed forces who are graduate students of the National Defense College of the GRP.

Several articles explain how GRP President Aquino and his OPAPP secretary Deles sabotaged the peace negotiations by violating existing agreements, preconditioning the peace negotiations with the capitulation and pacification of the revolutionary forces and the people and preventing comprehensive agreements on social, economic and political reforms to address the roots of the armed conflict and lay the basis of a just and lasting peace.

Author's Preface to Strengthen the People's Struggle against Imperialism

The book pays serious attention to the Filipino migrant workers. It exposes and denounces the myth of migration as a way for development. It urges the migrant workers to fight commercialization and enslavement and to strengthen Migrante International. Filipino migrant workers are vulnerable: they are discriminated against, they take jobs far below their education and training, receive lower wages than the locals in the host country and are deprived of basic trade union and democratic rights.

The Filipino migrant workers are more than ten million or ten percent of the entire Philippine population or 20 percent of our national work force. It is necessary for them to develop solidarity with the local people and other migrants in the host countries in order to obtain better wage and living conditions. It is likewise necessary for them to gain the solidarity and support of other peoples of the world for the Filipino people's struggle for national and social liberation. The book calls for international solidarity.

The International League of Peoples' Struggle has become the biggest international organization of its kind, a combination of people's organizations engaged in anti-imperialist and democratic struggle. Filipino and overseas Filipino mass organizations are active here and engage in international solidarity and mutual support through unity, coordination and cooperation with people's organizations in various other countries.

As ILPS Chairperson, I give an overview of ILPS work and call for a socially just world, strengthen the people's solidarity and intensify the struggle against imperialist plunder, crisis and war. By teleconference, I delivered the keynote address at the Fifth International Assembly of ILPS which was held in Manila on November 15-16, 2015.

Strengthen the People's Struggle against Imperialism and Reaction relates the Philippines to the world in several articles on the international situation and the role of the Philippine Revolution in the world proletarian revolution, on the CPP, Maoism, new democratic revolution, China and the current world order. It takes up such problems as climate change and nuclear weapons as the result of imperialism and as threats to human survival.

Complementing the expressions condemning US imperialism are expressions of solidarity and support extended to peoples suffering brutal forms of attacks by imperialism and local reactionaries and waging anti-imperialist and democratic struggles, as in Venezuela, Ukraine, Palestine, Kurdistan, Iraq, Libya, Syria, Afghanistan, Somali, Sudan, Congo and other countries.

The US and NATO allies are held criminally responsible for the surge of refugees to Europe from the Middle East and Africa due to the combination of super-exploitation, wars of aggression and climate change resulting from the plunder of the environment. The US CIA and the Israeli Mossad are condemned for organizing terrorist jihad groups like Daesh and Al-Nusra that engage in senseless killings and other depredations.

In messages to various ILPS member-organizations in the Philippines and abroad, I present the situation upon which they act and exhort them to advance their political and organizational work in order to strengthen themselves and mobilize more people to advance the revolutionary cause for the benefit of a certain oppressed class or sector and for the benefit of the broad masses of the people.

In the book, I do not deal only with large issues but I relate myself to personalities of significance. These include the living and departed heroes. I pay the highest tribute to such martyrs as Comrade Leoncio Pitao (Ka Parago) of Mindanao and Comrade Recca Monte of Northern Luzon. I honor Comrade Primo Rivera (Tang Prime) and others who made sacrifices and devoted their lives to the revolutionary service of the people.

I praise Benito and Wilma Tiamzon for being resolute and effective leaders of the Communist Party of the Philippines, Luis Jalandoni for his long revolutionary dedication and role in the peace negotiations and Prof. Judy Taguiwalo for her rich revolutionary experience and patriotic and progressive academic service. I acknowledge the contributions of the departed ally Alejandro Lichauco, the economist, in espousing anti-imperialism and economic nationalism.

I honor comrades and friends abroad who have fought for greater freedom, equality and social justice in their particular fields, such as the political leader Irene Fernandez with whom I worked in the International League of Peoples' Struggle and the playwright and poet Amiri Baraka with whom I became a friend while participating in the same poetry festivals.

In closing, I urge you to read Strengthen the People's Struggle against Imperialism and Reaction in order to understand the major events and issues in the years 2014 and 2015 in connection with the historical background and with the years from 2016 onwards.

It is of course outrageous that today the Filipino people and other peoples of the world are living under worse conditions. But these are the result of the grave crisis and rotting of the domestic ruling system and the world capitalist system and are pushing the people to struggle harder against imperialism and all reaction in order to achieve national liberation, democracy and socialism.

We are confident that the worsening crisis of the world capitalist system, the escalation of oppression and exploitation and the relentlessness of aggressive wars are resulting in greater people´s resistance and will eventually bring about the resurgence of revolutionary movements on an unprecedented global scale.-

Jose Maria Sison
Utrecht, The Netherlands
August 10, 2018

Latin America and the Anti-imperialist Movement
Interview by Dezurda of Guatemala
November 11, 2018

Please give us your analysis of the progressive governments of Latin America, Cuba, Bolivia, Nicaragua and Ecuador.

JMS: There are progressive governments in Latin America like those of Cuba, Venezuela, Bolivia, and Nicaragua because they stand for national independence, democracy, social justice, economic development, cultural progress and international solidarity.

By history and current manifestations, the Cuban government is the most progressive and most stable government standing for national independence and socialism. It arose under the leadership of the late Fidel Ruiz Castro through the armed overthrow of the oligarchy. Since then, it has been able to defeat imperialist aggression, subversion and blockade and has won political, economic, social and cultural victories and engaged in international solidarity under the leadership of the Communist Party of Cuba.

The Bolivarian Movement led by the late Hugo Chavez in Venezuela was able to establish the current government led by President Maduro through elections on a platform of national independence, economic nationalization and socialism. The Chavista government has won great victories in fulfilling its Bolivarian missions in raising workers' wages, housing, health care and other measures of social welfare. It used well its oil income in benefiting the people of Venezuela and other countries in terms of social welfare and social services.

The US imperialists went so far as to connive with Saudi Arabia in bringing down the price of oil in order to inflict harm on such countries as Venezuela and Russia. They have also manipulated the supply of consumer products from abroad in order to create artificial shortages and inflation of prices. But the Bolivarian government has so far overcome the challenges and provocations of the US and its stooges.

The US persists in threatening to launch a war of aggression and instigating a coup, in imposing trade and financial sanctions on Venezuela and in manipulating needed imports and thus generating hyperinflation. But the Bolivarian government is resilient and has been effective in carrying out its Bolivarian missions. It enjoys the support of a solid mass base within Venezuela. This has allowed it to prevail in previous recent elections, in mass actions and other tests of strength.

The Bolivian government under the leadership of Evo Morales is also steadfast in standing up and fighting for national independence, economic sovereignty, democracy, social justice and international solidarity. The

Nicaraguan government under Daniel Ortega traces its origin to the Sandinista armed revolution and has plenty of experience in fighting the US imperialists and the local reactionaries. Lessons can also be drawn from the compromises with the oligarchs in the peace agreement that was made under the pressure of the US-supported contras.

Like Venezuela, the Bolivian and Nicaraguan governments are now targets of regime change by the US imperialists and the local agents. Elsewhere in Latin America, like Mexico, Ecuador, Venezuela, Colombia and Brazil, the US imperialists are using economic, financial and political means to subvert governments and bring them under the control of right-wing cliques of the big compradors and cacique oligarchs.

On the whole, Latin America is still the backyard of US imperialism. US imperialism is dominant through its unilateralist policies, through bilateral and multilateral regional agreements and through multilateral agencies like the IMF, World Bank and the World Trade Organization. The peoples of Latin America need to build and strengthen the anti-imperialist movement by carrying out various forms of struggle.

Please give us your analysis on the peace process in Guatemala and in the Philippines. What would you have done if you were part of the peace process in Guatemala?

JMS: What is fatal to the people's cause in any peace process is for the leadership of the revolutionary movement to capitulate to the persistent reactionary government and agree to disarm and dismantle the people's army even while there is yet no sufficient implementation of the social, economic and political reforms mutually agreed upon by the negotiating parties.

It is worse if there is a disarming and dismantling of the people's army even before there are mutually satisfactory agreements or if the agreements do not satisfy the demands and interests of the people. When the reactionary government succeeds in disarming and dismantling the people's army before the substantial and sufficient implementation of the agreed social, economic and political reforms, that government and the oligarchy will no longer proceed to carry out the needed reforms but proceed to suppress and deceive the people and all their political formations.

By these considerations, I invite you to review the history of the peace process in Guatemala and discover the essential errors that have led to the end of the people's revolutionary struggle and the frustration of their demands and aspirations for national and social liberation. At any rate, I am aware that the old military and economic structures that generated armed conflict in Guatemala have remained intact and that the so-called constitutional reform package has been rejected through processes still controlled by the oligarchy.

As chief political consultant of the National Democratic Front of the Philippines (NDFP), I can describe the principled position and conduct of the NDFP in the peace process with the reactionary big comprador-landlord

Latin America and the Anti-Imperialist Movement

government of the Philippines through the facilitation of the Royal Norwegian Government. I suggest that we learn some lessons from a comparative study of the peace process in Guatemala and the Philippines even as the latter is terminated for the time being by the Duterte regime.

Whenever the enemy wants to fight the people and does not want peace negotiations, the revolutionary forces of the NDFP, the Communist Party of the Philippines (CPP) and the New People's Army (NPA) are ready to fight the enemy and win victories in all forms of the revolutionary struggle. Whenever the enemy wants to negotiate peace, the NDFP is ready to negotiate and prevent the enemy from claiming to be the champion of peace and from misrepresenting the revolutionary forces as opponents of peace.

In our experience of the Philippine peace process, the enemy plays a series of tactics in order to prevent substantive negotiations and comprehensive agreements on the social, economic and political reforms, which are needed to address the roots of the civil war. These tactics of the reactionary government have included the following: demanding to hold the peace negotiations in a venue under its surveillance and control in the Philippines, negotiating an agreement on prolonged and indefinite ceasefire to paralyze the people's army, offering socioeconomic community projects and sham localized peace talks to break up the revolutionary movement and ceaseless carrying out of occupation, psywar, intelligence and combat operations.

Since 1992, the NDFP has always frustrated these tactics of the enemy. It takes the firm position that the peace process must be used to negotiate and make comprehensive agreements on a series of substantive issues, such as the following: respect for human rights and international humanitarian law, social and economic reforms, political and constitutional reforms and the end of hostilities and disposition of forces. The purpose is to address the roots of the civil war and lay the basis for a just and lasting peace.

So far, the Philippine peace process has resulted since 1998 in the mutual approval of the Comprehensive Agreement on Respect for Human Rights and International Humanitarian Law (CARHRIHL) in accordance with the International Bill of Rights and the International Humanitarian Law, not in accordance with the legal and judicial system of the reactionary government. Since then, however, the reactionary government has resorted to all sorts of tactics in order to frustrate the negotiations and the making of agreements on social, economic and political reforms.

Whenever the reactionary government terminates the peace negotiations, the revolutionary forces and people pursue and intensify the protracted people's war. They assert that it took the Filipino people to defeat Spanish colonialism in more than 300 years, it will take much less time for the people to overthrow the US-dominated reactionary government.

What role should the anti-imperialist organizations play in Guatemala and Latin America?

JMS: There is certainly a need for the anti-imperialist mass movement in Guatemala and in other countries in Latin America to major a decisive role in carrying forward the people's demand for full independence from US imperialism, democracy, social justice, economic development through land reform and national industrialization, cultural progress and a just peace.

In this regard, as Chairperson of the International League of Peoples' Struggle, I am happy to acknowledge the fact that the ILPS has been trying hard since its founding in 2001 to encourage the mass organizations of Latin America to join the ILPS, establish national chapters and wage anti-imperialist and democratic struggles for national and social liberation from US imperialism and the local oligarchy. But it take more than the mass organizations to accomplish the tasks of national and social liberation.

In any country of Latin America, there must be a revolutionary party of the proletariat capable of providing the correct ideological, political and organizational leadership to the revolutionary mass movement of the people in carrying out the new democratic and socialist stages of the revolution. The working class is the only class capable of leading the people from democratic reforms to socialism. But it must rely on various types of mass organizations.

There must be the trade unions, the association of peasants, farm workers and the indigenous peoples and the organizations of the youth, women, teachers, lawyers, scientists and other professionals, the religious and social activists for human rights and a just peace. They are all needed to carry out the various forms of anti-imperialist and democratic struggle. They are the broad base and source of further strength of the revolutionary movement led by the revolutionary party of the proletariat.

The revolution in Guatemala and the rest of Latin America can be successfully carried out with the three weapons of the revolution: the revolutionary party of the proletariat, the people's army and the united front. The modes of existence, the strategy and tactics in the use of these instruments depend on the concrete conditions of any country. In any case, these must respond to the needs, demands and aspirations of the people for national and social liberation.

The people of Guatemala and Latin America have a rich revolutionary experience. They can draw positive and negative lessons from this experience and clarify the tasks for waging revolution more successfully than ever before. They can never agree to the perpetuation of their oppression and exploitation by the US imperialists and the local exploiting classes. They hunger for greater freedom, democracy, social justice and all-round progress and are always ready to fight for these when they are correctly aroused, organized and mobilized by a revolutionary party daring to struggle and daring to win.

Message to Comrade Gabi Fechtner and the Youth in Mass Education on Imperialism during Whitsun
June 9, 2019

I wish to express warmest greetings of comradeship and international solidarity to Comrade Gabi Fechtner and to all the youth in the mass education that she is conducting on the occasion of the Whitsun Youth Festival.

Your topic of discussion, What Is Imperialism?, is of great importance and relevance to the life and struggles of the proletariat and people in Germany and elsewhere in the entire world. Let me give you a few basic points about imperialism in order to describe it in accordance with the teachings of Lenin on imperialism. I am sure that Comrade Gabi will update you on imperialism until the current century.

Imperialism is monopoly capitalism, the highest and final stage of capitalism. It has gained dominance in the industrial capitalist economies, definitely since the late years of the 19th century and beginning of the 20th century. It is an economic system in which bank capital and industrial capitalism have merged to bring forth the financial oligarchy.

The export of surplus capital has gained importance over the export of commodities from the imperialist countries. Loan agreements and direct investments by monopoly corporations in less developed and underdeveloped countries give them the leverage to dominate these countries and extract superprofits.

The monopoly corporations engage in combinations such as cartels and syndicates in order to dominate several countries. The imperialist countries have completed their domination over all other countries as sources of cheap labor and raw materials, markets and fields of investments and as dependent countries, semi-colonies, colonies or spheres of influence.

The imperialist countries engage in economic competition and political rivalry and in alliances against each other. Thus, they tend to outgrow any given balance of forces among them and tend to struggle for a redivision of the world. It is in the very nature of monopoly capitalism to be stricken and upset by economic and financial crisis and to be prone to the use of aggressive wars.

Monopoly capitalism is moribund because the extraction of surplus value from the proletariat is faster than ever before and the crisis of overproduction arises more severely than ever before. The monopoly bourgeoisie uses finance capital to revive the depressed or stagnant economy and bail out the failing companies. But the use of financial credit results in bigger economic and financial crises. These cause further destruction of productive forces and inflict intolerable suffering on the proletariat and people of the world.

Monopoly capitalism is aggressive. The imperialist powers deliberately use war production as a vital part of their economies and launches wars of aggression in order to expand economic territory and geopolitical hegemony. They have used their war capabilities to engage in the two inter-imperialist wars of the 20th century and wars of aggression against underdeveloped countries.

And from the time of the Cold War to the present US imperialism continues to wage wars of aggression and threaten the very existence of humankind with nuclear weapons and other weapons of mass destruction and with the accelerated plunder and ruination of the environment.

In this current message, I can only mention briefly the current balance of imperialist powers since the end of the Cold War between the US and the Soviet Union in 1991. The traditional alliance of the US, the European Union and Japan is arrayed against the tandem of new imperialist powers, China and Russia. The inter-imperialist contradictions are intensifying because of the entry of two new imperialist powers. There is the danger that the imperialist crisis will worsen and produce several fascist governments that are willing to start an inter-imperialist war. However, there is still an interweaving of interimperialist collaborations and debates in the UN, multilateral agencies and bilateral arrangements.

The US tries to rally the old Atlantic alliance against Russia but the latter is avoiding sustained clashes despite provocations instigated mainly by the US in the Ukraine, on the borders of Russia and elsewhere. At the moment, the US and China are conspicuous with their trade war and exchange of complaints over a wide range of economic, technological and security issues. But China is deliberately speaking against war, despite its rapid development of strategic weapons, its expansionist claims over 90 percent of the South China Sea and its Belt and Road Initiative which aimed at creating a new center of world trade and of course despite the strategic aim of the US to upset the Chinese economy and China's Belt and Road Initiative (BRI).

The burden of the crisis of imperialism continues to be shifted to the proletariat and peoples of both imperialist countries and the underdeveloped countries. The wars of aggression instigated by the US imperialism are still mainly directed against underdeveloped countries or are in the form of inter-imperialist proxy wars and avoid being wars of aggression directly among the imperialist powers, although there are already increasing cases of direct collision. Up to now, those who suffer most are the oppressed peoples and nations in the battle grounds in the underdeveloped and poor but resource-rich countries.

The study of imperialism is necessary and urgent. We must understand its evil character and workings in order to be resolute and effective in carrying out the anti-imperialist and democratic struggle and in bringing about the victory of national liberation, democracy and socialism on a global scale. The global victory of socialism is premised on the global defeat of imperialism. But in achieving this goal, we must advance in stages and in various countries.

Message to Comrade Gabi Fechtner and the Youth in Mass Education

It is high time to unite all anti-imperialist, democratic and progressive forces and build the International Anti-Imperialist United Front against imperialist plunder, state terrorism, fascistization, fascism, foreign military intervention, subversion and wars of aggression--for democracy and freedom, national and social liberation and socialism.

Imperialism in Various Global Regions

World Situation: An Outline
August 20, 2019

Introduction

After the proletariat and people took a severe beating from the forces of imperialism, modern revisionism and reaction on a global scale, we live today in a world of intensifying interimperialist contradictions, worsening economic and political crisis, escalating oppression and exploitation, social disorders and wars in imperialist countries and in the less developed and underdeveloped countries.

1. Socioeconomic situation

1.1 The rapid rise of the world population and technology are unprecedentedly straining the socioeconomic relations in the world capitalist system. Contradictions between the social character of the forces and the relations of production under the rule of private appropriation by the capitalist class. The class war between labor and capital is intensifying.

1.2 The neoliberal economic policy has been adopted to press down wages, scrap job tenure, reduce social benefits and curtail democratic rights of the working class. Touted as the creator of wealth and jobs, the monopoly bourgeoisie is privileged to accelerate the accumulation of capital through liberalization of investments and trade, privatization of public assets, deregulation and denationalization of underdeveloped countries.

1.3 From the 1980s, the US found it profitable to outsource consumer manufacturing to China to avail of cheap Chinese labor and to promote the restoration of capitalism in China. After the Tienanmen Incident, which resulted from economic crisis, the US extended in the 1990s more trade and technological concessions to China as its main partner in neoliberal globalization within the WTO framework.

1.4 As a result of the rapid accumulation of capital in the hands of the monopoly bourgeoisie and the shrinkage of the incomes of the working people, the crises of overproduction and finance have become more frequent and worse; and accelerated the concentration of wealth in the hands of a few. Recall the big costs of recurrent and worsening economic and financial crisis, from the Asian financial crisis of 1997 down to the crisis in the traditional imperialist countries in 2008.

1.5 The global economic and financial crises and depression since 2008 has been prolonged until now and can be more damaging to the world capitalist system than the Great Depression of 1929 that led to the outbreak of World War II. Until recently, China seemed to be able to take advantage of the recurrent crises and fulfill its strategic economic and security goals with the use of two-tiered system of state and private capitalism.

1.6 Under the Trump regime US has been pushed by the prolonged crisis since 2008 to adopt protectionist measures against China since last year in contradiction to the previous main partnership with China in the policy of neoliberal globalization. Neoliberalism has practically run to its opposite, protectionism. Now the US is building higher tariff walls and restricting technological transfers to China and wishing to revive its consumer manufacturing by means that are unclear, especially in view of the anti-immigrant campaign.

1.7 In their economic competition, the US and China avail of alliances with fellow imperialist countries. The US and its traditional allies make use of such multilateral agencies as the IMF, World Bank and the WTO. China avails of its alliance with the Russia and they make use of the BRICS bloc, the New Development Bank, the very ambitious Belt and Road Initiative (BRI) and the Asian Infrastructure and Investment Bank (AIIB)1.8 The imperialist powers compete hard economically and avoid direct wars among themselves by shifting the burden of the crisis to the less developed and underdeveloped countries. They have done so since the end of World War II. Thus, there has been no direct interimperialist war for more than 70 years despite the Cold War of 1948 to 1991. Even then, they seek to expand economic territory and have engaged in foreign military intervention and wars of aggression against underdeveloped countries, especially in the form of proxy wars.

1.9 In the US, China and other imperialist countries, the monopoly bourgeoisie requires military buildup not only as a means of national security but as a means of obtaining superprofits. The danger of war arises from the constant drive to increase war production in the name of safeguarding expanding the overseas economic and geopolitical interests of the monopoly bourgeoisie.

1.10 The monopoly bourgeoisie is the fundamental cause and source of threats to the very existence of humankind, such as nuclear war and global warming. The biggest capitalist corporations are engaged in military industrial production and the plunder of natural resources and the perpetuation of the use of fossil fuel. Humankind is threatened today by sudden death and slow death by global warming.

2. Geopolitical situation

2.1 The US has never been able to override the problem stagflation since the mid-1970s when this arose because of the full reconstruction of the capitalist countries devastated in World War II. The strategic decline has been

World Situation: An Outline

aggravated by socioeconomic crisis under the neoliberal policy and by waging ceaseless costly wars under the neoconservative policy. Thus, the US has declined from being the sole superpower from the time of the collapse of the Soviet Union in 1991 to the biggest crisis so far in 2008.

2.2 The US strategic decline has favored the rise of China as an imperialist power. In its desire to promote capitalist restoration in China, the US outsourced consumer manufacturing to China since the 1980s. China gained huge trade surpluses and began to buy US securities. Consequently, the US became the biggest world debtor from being the biggest creditor. Recall the stages of US-China economic cooperation and the series of US-led wars of aggression in Yugoslavia, Afghanistan, Iraq, Libya and Syria.

2.3 But the US is still the No. 1 imperialist power desperately trying to maintain such position, cut down the manufacturing, trade and technological concessions to China and undermine the SCO, BRICS, NDB, AIIB and BRI. China has ambitiously pushed these to grab resources and markets while the US with preoccupied with wars. It has touted the BRI as a reversal of the dominance of Western powers in world trade since the 16th century.

2.4 The US tries to use its traditional alliance with EU and Japan to counter China's back-to-back alliance with Russia in the escalating interimperialist contradictions. The US boasts of augmenting its unilateral military and political strength with the NATO and other multilateral and bilateral security alliances with various countries. By making a strategic pivot to East Asia, the US is exerting pressure on China and challenging its claim to 90 percent of the South China Sea.

2.5 The imperialist powers compete to dominate the less developed and underdeveloped countries in order to obtain sources of cheap labor and raw materials, markets fields of investments and spheres of influence. The highest profits are drawn by the imperialist powers from such countries. The imperialist powers engage in collusion and contention with each other in exploiting and dominating these countries.

2.6 But there are countries whose governments assert national independence and aspire for socialism. The Democratic People's Republic of Korea, Cuba and Vietnam have stood firmly against US imperialism. The Bolivarian Republic of Venezuela has resisted the repeated attempts of the US and its puppets to overthrow its government. Syria has frustrated the war of aggression launched by the US and its puppets. Those subjected to blockades, threats of war and actual war have availed of the cooperation and assistance of China and Russia.

2.7 There are countries where revolutionary struggles are being waged for national and social liberation. The people's war in the Philippines is the most outstanding in being the longest running and covering the entire length and breath of a country. In India, the people's war is developing in various areas and promises to win victory in a big country comparable to Russia and China

225

in the past. People's wars continue to rage in Turkey, Kurdistan, Colombia and other countries.

2.8 Under any circumstances at present, the proletariat and oppressed peoples can take advantage of the interimperialist contradictions to advance the proletarian revolution and the national liberation movements. They can wage various forms of struggle against imperialism and reaction.

2.9 Under conditions of worsening economic and political crisis, the monopoly bourgeoisie in imperialist countries have become even more exploitative and oppressive and are encouraging fascist movements in order to counter the rise of anti-imperialist movements.

2.10 The proletarian revolutionaries are driven to fight back against their oppressors and exploiters. They wage class struggle and forge alliances with all anti-imperialist, antifascist and other progressive forces concerned with the threats of nuclear war and environmental catastrophe.

3. Prospects World Situation: An Outline

3.1 The inter-imperialist conflicts will continue to intensify due to the worsening socioeconomic crisis and the rise of fascist movements.

3.2 The US will continue to decline in a multipolar world, while its current protectionist measures can also impede China's expansion. There is self-damaging effect of protectionism to the US and to the global economy.

3.3 The US-China conflict will be increasingly at the center of interimperialist contradictions. With the collaboration of their respective allies, US and China will strive to block each other's advance.

3.4 The proletariat and oppressed peoples will be subjected to worse forms of exploitation involving a mix of neoliberalism and protectionism and will be driven to join mass movements in defense of human rights and to engage in revolutionary resistance.

3.5 The revolutionary parties of the proletariat will rise against imperialism and fascism for democracy and socialism in imperialist countries and for national and social liberation in other countries.

3.6 The revolutionary parties of the proletariat will have to win the battle for democracy, especially against fascism, before they can take power and realize socialism.

3.7 The oppressed peoples and nations will be able to take the most advantage of the worsening crisis of the world capitalist system and the interimperialist conflicts by waging people's war for national and social liberation. In the imperialist countries, there are advocates of protracted people's war. But they have merely been talking about it as long as the social democrats and other reformists have hoped for the evolution of capitalism to socialism.

World Situation: An Outline

3.8 The existing anti-imperialist governments and their peoples are bound to persevere and resist submission to imperialism. They can take advantage of interimperialist contradictions but must be vigilant towards any imperialist country.

3.9 The peoples of the world will stand against the use of nuclear weapons in the interimperialist wars and will seek to prevent any imperialist government from using them. Proletarian revolutionaries will increasingly forge alliances with movements against wars and nuclear weapons.

3.10 The peoples of the world will increasingly identify and oppose monopoly capitalism as the primary cause of global warming and environmental catastrophe. Proletarian revolutionaries will increasingly forge alliances with ecological movements.

We are in transition to a world in which the revolutionary forces and movements of the proletariat and the people are of unprecedented scale and intensity and are in the process of winning great victories in the struggle for national liberation, democracy and socialism.

Imperialism in Various Global Regions

The World Capitalist System Is Bankrupt and Breaking Down, Causing the Resurgence of the World Proletarian Revolution
Message of Solidarity and Gratitude to the Participants in the Launch of Reflections on Revolution and Prospects and Ein Leben im Widerstand
December 21, 2019

I express to you warmest greetings of solidarity! Thank you for coming to this joint launch of Reflections on Revolution and Prospects and its German version Ein Leben im Widerstand. It is an honor and pleasure to be with you in this event.

I wish to give special thanks to my co-author Dr. Rainer Werning, our editor Julieta de Lima, the publishers International Network for Philippine Studies and the Verlag Neuer Weg, the book reviewers, the moderator Coni Ledesma and the host of this event, the NDF International Office.

I am pleased that on this occasion Rainer has ample opportunity to talk about our cooperation since we were young and his steadfast solidarity with the Filipino people's struggle for national and social liberation.

I am glad that as book reviewer Louie Jalandoni will focus on Philippine issues and refer to the 51st anniversary of the Communist party of the Philippines and Peter Weispfenning will focus on global issues in relation to German-Filipino solidarity.

The two books being launched appear to sum up my life, views and work and to say goodbye to the Philippines and to the world. But not really. I still have some years to go. I am determined to express my views on Philippine and global issues and call for militant actions by the people's mass movement against imperialism and all reaction.

It would be a pity to say goodbye in the year 2019 when the world is on fire and great masses of people are rising up in anti-imperialist and democratic struggles against the depredations of neoliberalism, state terrorism, economic blockades, military intervention and wars of aggression.

The scale and intensity of the mass protests are unprecedented. They manifest the resistance to the extreme oppression and exploitation of the proletariat and people of the world in the hands of the imperialists and local reactionaries. I dare to foretell that these mass protests will lead either to reforms or fascism and on the whole will stimulate the growth of revolutionary movements.

Fifty years ago, it was said during the Great Proletarian Cultural Revolution that if the problem of modern revisionism were solved, then imperialism would be heading towards total collapse and socialism would be marching towards total victory. But Mao cautioned that it would take another 50 to 100 years for such a possibility to become real. Indeed, in the zigzag course of history, the world proletarian-socialist revolution would suffer major setbacks.

After the death of Mao in 1976, the Dengist counterrevolution seized power from the proletariat and enabled the capitalist restoration in China. In 1991, with the collapse of the Soviet Union, US imperialism became the sole superpower. But subsequently, the frequently recurrent economic and financial crisis of the US and world capitalism and the ceaseless US wars of aggression accelerated the strategic decline of US imperialism.

We are now living in a world of intensifying inter-imperialist contradictions, chiefly between the US and China which used to be the main partners in neoliberal globalization from the 1980s to the first decade of this century. But since the economic and financial crash of 2008, the smartest guys of the capitalist world have failed to solve the problem of prolonged global depression. The US is the chief instigator of neoliberalism but is increasingly protectionist and remorseful over its trade and technological concessions to China.

While the traditional and new imperialist powers are locked in a struggle for a redivision of the world, they continue to shift the burden of crisis to the proletariat and people of the world who are made to suffer the ever worsening conditions of oppression and exploitation. The accelerated capital accumulation by a few, bureaucratic corruption, military overspending and the growing tax and debt burden have aggravated the conditions of low income, unemployment and poverty among the toiling masses.

In their own homelands and in the client states, the imperialist powers push the use of state terrorism and fascism to suppress the people's resistance and perpetuate the neoliberal methods of exploitation. They engage in military buildup, foreign military intervention and wars of aggression in order to expand their sources of cheap labor and raw materials, markets, fields of investments and spheres of influence.

Imperialism ruins the lives of the people through class exploitation and threaten the very life of humankind with the degradation of the environment and the proliferation of nuclear and other weapons of mass destruction. But the proletariat and people of the world can rise up and unite to fight imperialism. The current worldwide mass protests against neoliberalism, fascism, war and ruination of the environment expose the rottenness of the world capitalist system and signal the transition to a world of resurgent revolutionary struggles, characterized by mass protests, people's wars and great victories of the cause of national liberation, democracy and socialism.

The Filipino people can be proud that they have persevered in their new democratic revolution through protracted people's war, have overcome adversities from within the Philippines and abroad and have won significant victories. Through their revolutionary struggle, they have served as the torch bearer of the world proletarian revolution at a time that the toiling masses have taken severe punishment as a result of neocolonialism, anti-communism, revisionist betrayal of socialism, neoliberalism, state terrorism, wars of aggression and other weapons in the arsenal of imperialism.

The Filipino people have excelled at waging armed revolution and becoming stronger through struggle against escalating campaigns of military suppression designed by US imperialism and its Filipino puppets. They have overcome the Marcos fascist dictatorship and a series of pseudo-democratic regimes. They have been able to carry out the program of new democratic revolution against the semicolonial and semifeudal ruling system and to build the revolutionary party of the proletariat, the people's army, a wide array of mass organizations, alliances and the organs of democratic political power on a nationwide scale.

But since 2016, there has been a retrogression of the ruling system towards fascist dictatorship by the Duterte regime. The tyrannical, treasonous, genocidal, plundering and swindling policies and acts of this regime can only drive the Filipino people, especially the toiling masses of workers and peasants, to raise their revolutionary strength and intensify their revolutionary struggle, as they did during the Marcos fascist dictatorship. They have the rich experience, the ample strength and abundant international solidarity and support to avail of.

Regarding the recent offer of Duterte to resume peace negotiations with the National Democratic Front of the Philippines, I think that he has made the offer because his military efforts have failed to destroy the revolutionary movement and, by committing grievous crimes against the people, he and his military minions have instead caused this movement to grow in strength and advance. But for the peace negotiations to be resumed, the regime must agree to the reaffirmation of previous joint agreements made since 1992 and must do away with all the presidential issuances that have terminated and prevented said negotiations.

So long as there is no final agreement on a just peace that addresses the roots of the armed conflict through comprehensive agreements on social, economic and political reforms under the principles of national independence, democracy, all-round development and social justice, the Filipino people together with all their revolutionary forces have all the sovereign right to wage all forms of revolutionary struggle until they win complete victory. Sincerity in the GRP-NDFP peace negotiations can be proven only by a willingness to agree on respect for the national and democratic rights of the Filipino people and on what is beneficial to them in clearly substantial and realizable social, economic and political terms.

I hope that the two books being launched today will contribute to the understanding of Philippine and global issues, promote the unity of the Filipino people and inspire them to raise the level of their revolutionary struggle to a new and higher level. The world capitalist system is bankrupt and breaking down, incapable of solving social and environmental problems, and is generating the conditions for anti- imperialist and democratic struggles, the upsurge of militant solidarity of all peoples and the resurgence of the world proletarian-socialist revolution. Thank you.

Terrorist Crimes of Trump and US imperialism Turn the Peoples of the Middle East against Them

The acting Iraqi Prime Minister Adil Abdul-Mahdi revealed in his recent address to the Iraqi Parliament that US President Trump had asked him to "play the mediator's role" between the US and Iran and that consequently General Qassem Soleimani flew to Baghdad with a message from the Iranian government regarding the lowering of tensions between Iran and Saudi Arabia.

General Soleimani was on a peace mission when Trump ordered his military minions to track the flight and arrival of the celebrated Iranian general at the Baghdad airport in order to target him with an air strike by drone and to murder him together with Iraqi Popular Mobilization Units leader Abu Mahdi Al-Muhandis and their Iranian and Iraqi companions.

The revelation of Iraqi Prime Minister Abdul-Mahdi completely belies the claim of Trump and the Pentagon that they took "decisive defensive action" to preempt an attack directed by Soleimani. In fact, Trump knew that Soleimani was traveling to Baghdad in a diplomatic capacity as an emissary of Iran to discuss with the Iraqi Prime Minister the de-escalation of violence involving the US and Saudi Arabia.

Although previously known as a close ally of the US, Abdul-Mahdi is totally offended by the multiple murder of his official guest General Soleimani, PMU leader Al-Muhandis and the accompanying Iraqi and Iranian citizens in brazen violation of Iraqi national sovereignty and territorial integrity and has recommended to the Iraqi Parliament to approve the resolution to kick out the US military forces from Iraq.

As already resolved by the Iraqi Parliament, the US must withdraw its military forces from Iraq. But in reaction, Trump is aggravating his crime of multiple murder and flagrant violation of Iraqi sovereignty by refusing to withdraw US military forces from Iraq, demanding payment for US military bases and threatening to impose sanctions far worse than those on Iran.

In the first place, the US has been in Iraq because of its war of aggression and its illegal occupation on the false pretext of taking out nuclear, chemical and other weapons of mass destruction. The US is under obligation to make war damage payments to Iraq for the large-scale destruction of Iraqi lives, infrastructure and properties.

The US must respect Iraqi sovereignty and territorial integrity. It has no choice but to yield its military bases to Iraq as sovereign owner of the land and pay the rent for the use of said bases for many years. It is the US that has the moral and financial obligations to Iraq and not the other way around. Otherwise, there is just cause for the Iraqi people to rise up against US imperialism and its terrorism.

Far beyond the gangster mentality of Trump, there are far reaching consequences of his criminal acts. He has driven the Iraqi and Iranian governments and peoples to stand together against US imperialism. They can use their own resources, means and alliances to fight US imperialism and its closest allies, Israeli Zionism and the Saudi monarchy. And they can avail of the support of Russia and China in countering the high-tech weaponry of their enemies.

Thanks to the terrorist roguery of Trump and US imperialism, they are becoming further isolated and there is high potential for the Middle East to become a new Vietnam on a much wider scale for US imperialism and its regional puppets and with far worse consequences for them. The ceaseless wars that the US has unleashed in the region under the neoconservative policy are graduating to a grand war between increasingly independent states and US imperialism on accelerated decline.

Under these conditions, the people and their revolutionary forces (especially national liberation movements with a socialist perspective) can gain strength for themselves from the opportunities arising from the inter-imperialist contradictions and contradictions between imperialist powers and recalcitrant or discreditable client-states. The proletariat and people of the world are steadily moving and advancing in the direction of widespread anti-imperialism and the resurgence of the world proletarian revolution.

An Update on the International Situation
March 30, 2020

Dear Colleagues, as Chairperson Emeritus of the International League of Peoples' Struggle, I am happy to share with you my views on the international situation and try to clarify the major events and issues, the trends and direction of the crisis of the world capitalist system and what the peoples of the world can do in order to advance their anti-imperialist and democratic struggles for national liberation, democracy and socialism.

Background to the current situation

The Great Depression of the 1930s led to World War II as basically an interimperialist war in which the Allied Powers had to include the Soviet Union in order to defeat the Axis Powers. As a result of the war, one third of humanity came under the governance of socialist states and the struggles for national liberation broke out in Asia, Africa and Latin America.

But the US also emerged as the strongest imperialist power. It proclaimed the Cold War in 1947 in order to confront the rise of socialism and the national liberation movements. It waved the flag of anti-communism against the socialist challenge and offered neocolonialism as the alternative to decolonization as a process of national liberation from colonialism and imperialism.

The Soviet Union recovered from the death of more than 25 million people and the destruction of 85 percent of its industrial capacity by the Nazi invasion, rebuilt its productive on an unprecedentedly scale and caught up with the US in the development of nuclear weapons in order to put the US in a nuclear stalemate.

After the death of Stalin, however, Krushchov rose to power in order to impose modern revisionism on the Soviet Union in1956. He used methods of decentralization to breach the socialist state and economy. He was followed by Brezhnev who used methods of recentralization in order to further strengthen the monopoly bureaucrat capitalism and engage in social-imperialism.

Under the leadership of Mao, the Communist Party of China and China emerged as the strongest defenders of the socialist cause and the world proletarian revolution against Soviet modern revisionism and social-imperialism, from the start of the Sino-Soviet ideological debate and disruption of state-to-state relations in 1959 to the Great Proletarian Cultural Revolution of 1966 to 1976.

In the meantime, the national liberation movements surged forward. The Korean people fought US imperialism to a standstill in 1953. The Vietnamese people dealt a resounding defeat to US imperialism in 1975. The Cuban people moved out of the orbit of US imperialism in 1961 and inspired the peoples of Latin America to fight US imperialism. The process of decolonization accelerated in Africa from 1950s to the 1980s. The apartheid regime in South Africa came to an end in the 1990s.

Soon after the death of Mao in 1976, the capitalist roaders led by Deng Xiaoping successfully carried out a counterrevolutionary coup in China against the proletarian revolutionaries and the socialist state of the working class. The Dengist counterrevolution carried out capitalist reforms and opening up China for reintegration in the world capitalist system. It was able to suppress the mass uprisings against corruption and inflation in scores of Chinese cities in 1989 and it pleaded to US for further investments, trade and technological concessions in order to stabilize the economy.

In December 1991 the Soviet Union collapsed and its satellite revisionist-ruled states in Eastern Europe disintegrated. The bourgeoisie took full control of all the countries in the Soviet bloc. US imperialism became the sole superpower and sought to fill the vacuum left by Soviet social imperialism in Eastern Europe, Central Asia, the Middle East and Africa. The ideologues and publicists of US imperialism proclaimed the death of socialism and the end of history with the supposed permanence of capitalism and liberal democracy.

Strategic decline of US imperialism as sole superpower

Having become the sole superpower, US was at its strongest in propagating and imposing on the world the policy of neoliberal globalization and unleashing wars of aggression in the Middle East (in Iraq, Libya, and Syria), in Central Asia (Afghanistan) and in the countries near or adjoining Russia (former Yugoslavia, Georgia and Ukraine).

It sought to expand NATO to the borders of Russia and use it for aggression in Central Asia. It overestimated its role and its capabilities as sole superpower and continued to a adopt and implement policies that appeared to advance its interests but which in fact were extremely costly and aggravated the problems that had caused its strategic decline since the middle of the 1970s.

Since becoming the sole superpower, the US has spent more than US$6 trillion to unleash endless wars of aggression that have rapidly increased its public debt. And yet these wars have not resulted in expanding stable economic territory abroad to offset the crisis of overproduction in the imperialist homeland. By assisting China in capitalist restoration and development, the US has also unwittingly aggravated its crisis of overproduction.

This is reminiscent of how the US undermined itself by stepping up war production, building hundreds of military bases abroad and engaging wars of aggression and at the same assisting the reconstruction of the capitalist countries ruined in World War II and thereby bringing about the crisis of

An Update on the International Situation

overproduction of the US and world capitalist system. As a result, the US became afflicted by stagflation in the mid-1970s.

In trying to solve the problem of stagflation, the US adopted neoliberalism and favored the military-industrial complex to strengthen the US military as well as to sell weapons to the oil-producing countries. But neoliberalism never solved the crisis of overproduction and excessive military spending which had been the root causes of stagflation.

The increased production of the military-industrial complex was profitable within the US economy and in sales to oil-producing countries. But it was counterproductive and unprofitable in the failure of the wars of aggression to expand stable economic territory for US imperialism abroad. In assisting the development of capitalism in China, it has ultimately brought about a new economic and political rival, despite the previous notion of the US that it could exploit China as a new big market.

The neoliberal policy regime has abetted the wrong notion of the US that it can without limits accelerate the centralization and accumulation of capital in the hands of the monopoly bourgeoisie supposedly in order to create more jobs by using in its favor tax cutbacks, wage freezes, erosion of social benefits, privatization of profitable public assets, antisocial and anti-environmental deregulation and denationalization of the economies of client-states. But the crisis of overproduction within an imperialist country arises from shrinking the domestic market by pushing down the incomes of the working and consuming public.

Another blinding factor in neoliberal policy is the manipulation of the money supply and interest rates supposedly to expand or contract them in order to prevent inflation or stagnation and to always favor the monopoly bourgeoisie by expanding the public debt and subjecting the working class to further austerity measures and reduction of real wages. At the same time, legal and political measures have been undertaken by the monopoly bourgeoisie to attack job security and curtail trade union and other democratic rights.

Collaboration and contention between US and Chinese imperialism

Because the US was in need of expanding its market due to the recurrent and worsening crisis of overproduction, it adopted China as its main partner in neoliberal globalization and at first conceded to it low technology for sweatshop consumer manufacturing and a big consumer market in the US and elsewhere. The US calculated that it could concentrate on manufacturing the big items (especially by the military-industrial complex), financializing the US economy and ultimately making direct investments in China.

But it was depressing its own consumer manufacturing and disemploying millions of workers. The export income of China swelled as the US suffered trade deficits. From being the biggest creditor of the world, the US became

237

the biggest debtor at the end of the 1980s. Further, the US expanded its foreign investments and technology transfer after China pleaded for these in the aftermath of the nationwide mass protests against inflation and corruption in China in 1989.

The US set preconditions for China to privatize the state-owned enterprises, desist from providing state subsidies to enterprises, liberalize further its policy on foreign investments and imports and enter the World Trade Organization (WTO). China agreed but in fact continued to use state planning and state-owned enterprises and copy without permission US and other foreign technology in order to achieve its own strategic economic and security goals.

The US-China economic and trade partnership appeared to be running smoothly, especially after China joined the WTO in 2001 The US and other imperialist powers and their economic technocrats were glad that every time there was a major global financial and economic crisis the high growth rate of China's GDP served to buffer the stagnant growth rate of the world economy. But when the global financial crash occurred in 2008, the US began to accuse China of unfair economic practices in their relationship.

The crash resulted in a global depression that is still running now and is adversely affecting China's economy. The growth rate has conspicuously slowed down. China experienced in 2015 a stock market crash that wiped out 30 percent of stock values. Foreign investors have transferred their plants to other countries with cheaper labor in the Asian mainland. The huge mountain of unpaid debts by Chinese local governments and corporations and high ratio of public debt to GDP have become exposed even while China deploys capital for its Belt Road Initiative (BRI).

Trump began in 2018 to accuse China of maintaining a two-tiered economy of state monopoly capitalism and private monopoly capitalism, stealing US technology, providing state subsidies to economic enterprises, manipulating finance and the currency, adopting Chinese brands on products previously patented by US and other foreign companies and using both imported and self-developed technology to build the military might of China.

Trump has taken special note of the challenge of Made in China 2025 and has countered with protectionist calls in sharp contrast to the longrunning US line of neoliberal globalization. He has called for raising US consumer manufacturing and imposing high tariffs on imports from China. The obvious objective is also to cut down the export surpluses from which China has drawn the surplus capital for expanding its domestic economy and external economic relations.

US imperialism has been strained by its own stagnant economy, the loss of competitiveness of US products, the extreme cost of overseas US military bases and endless wars of aggressions and the rapid rise of its public debt. The wars of aggression has cost at least US$6 trillion and failed to expand and stabilize the US economic territory abroad. The US strategic decline has accelerated and become more conspicuous.

238

An Update on the International Situation

Despite its emergence as the winner in the Cold War and as sole superpower in 1991, the US has a further declined strategically as a result of the high costs of its military bases overseas and its wars of aggression and its investment, trade and technological concessions to China. Although still the No. 1 imperialist power, the US has become one among several imperialist powers in a multipolar world and has less space for unilateral actions than ever before.

China has become the main economic competitor and political rival of the US. It has become so ambitious as to design and implement the Belt Road Initiative in order to make a radical departure from the pattern of maritime global trade which the Western colonial powers had established since the 16th century. At the same time, it seeks to dominate the Indo-Pacific maritime route. But it has serious economic problems, especially its sitting on a mountain of bad debts by local governments and corporations, the high ratio of public debt to GDP and the onerous terms of Chinese foreign loans which are vulnerable to debtors' default and revolt.

In Southeast Asia, the peoples are confronted with the extraterritorial claims of China over the 90 percent of the South China Sea in violation of the UN Convention on the Law of the Sea. But in other regions of the world, certain governments that assert national independence and the socialist cause, have taken advantage of inter-imperialist contradictions and availed of China's cooperation in order to counter sanctions and acts of aggression instigated by the US and its traditional imperialist allies.

Worsening crisis of world capitalist system and intensification of contradictions

The crisis of the world capitalist system is rapidly worsening and all major contradictions are intensifying. The contradictions are those between labor and capital in imperialist countries, those between the imperialist powers and the oppressed peoples and nations, those between the imperialist powers and states that assert national independence and the socialist cause and those among the imperialist powers.

The contradictions between labor and capital within imperialist countries and among imperialist powers are rising as the crisis of overproduction worsens as a result drastically reduced incomes of the working class and the middle class in imperialist countries and in the rest of the world capitalist system. The workers and the shrinking middle class have become restless and rebellious due to unemployment, reduced incomes, rising prices of basic commodities, austerity measures, the curtailment of democratic rights and the rise of chauvinism, racism and fascism.

Among the imperialist powers, the US and China have emerged as the two main contenders in the struggle for a redivision of the world. Each tries to have its own alliance with other imperialist powers. The traditional alliance of the

US, Europe and Japan is generally effective in such multilateral agencies like the IMF, World Bank and WTO and in NATO and other military alliances. On the other side, China has maintained closest all-round relations with Russia and they have broadened their alliance in BRICS, Shanghai Cooperation Organization, BRICS Development Bank, the Belt and Road Initiative and the Asian Infrastructure Investment Fund.

Afraid of mutual destruction through nuclear warfare, the major imperialist powers continue to avoid direct wars of aggression against each other by undertaking proxy wars despite the frequent US wars of aggression against underdeveloped countries in Asia, Africa and Latin America. They have developed the neocolonial ways and means of shifting the burden of crisis to the underdeveloped countries. They engage in a struggle for a redivision of the world but so far they have not directly warred on each other to acquire or expand their sources of cheap labor and raw materials, markets, fields of investment and spheres of influence.

They make the oppressed peoples and nations of the underdeveloped countries suffer the main brunt of the recurrent and worsening economic and financial crisis of the world capitalist system. They make them the main source of superprofits through direct investments and loans and extractive enterprises. The policy of neoliberal globalization has served to accelerate the rate of exploitation and resource-grabbing. To suppress the people's resistance to oppression and exploitation, they provide their client-states with the means of state terrorism and fascist rule by the bureaucratic comprador bourgeoisie. They also use their respective client-states for proxy wars and counterrevolutionary wars for maintaining and expanding economic territory.

Despite shifting the burden of crisis to the oppressed peoples and nations, the imperialist powers are driven to extract higher profits from their own working class under the neoliberal policy regime.

They suppress the resistance of the proletariat and people to the ever rising rate of exploitation in both the developed and underdeveloped countries. They have escalated oppression by enacting and enforcing so-called anti-terrorist laws and are wantonly using state terrorism and emboldening fascist organizations and movements to counter the growing revolutionary movement of the proletariat and the people.

In the underdeveloped countries, US imperialism and its puppet regimes are unleashing the worst forms of aggression and state terrorism against the people in order to perpetuate the neoliberal policy of unbridled greed. Since the end of World War II, the wars of aggression and campaigns of terror unleashed by US have resulted in 20 to 30 million killed in Korea, Indochina, Indonesia, Afghanistan , Iraq, Libya, Syria and other countries. To complement its neoliberal economic policy, US imperialism has adopted and implemented the so-called neoconservative policy of using the full-spectrum of violent and suasive means, especially its high-tech military weaponry, to maintain global hegemony in the 21st century.

240

An Update on the International Situation

But the US, which is now conspicuously in strategic decline economically and politically, cannot have its way as it pleases. Previously powerful socialist countries, such as the Soviet Union and China, have succumbed to capitalism as a result of modern revisionism. But as new imperialist powers, China and Russia are operating to hem in US imperialism, aggravate the crisis of the world capitalist system, sharpen the inter-imperialist contradictions and generate conditions that are more exploitative and oppressive than before but incite and drive the people to wage revolutionary resistance.

Even when it emerged as the strongest imperialist power after World War II, US imperialism suffered outstanding defeats, such as in China, north Korea, Cuba, Vietnam and other Indochinese countries. It has been unable to stop the decolonization of colonies and semi-colonies which is still an ongoing process. The proletariat and people have persevered in protracted people's war in the Philippines, India, Kurdistan, Turkey, Palestine, Peru, Colombia and elsewhere. The spread of arms where US imperialism have unleashed wars of aggression, such as in the Middle East and Africa, can open the way to the rise of more armed revolutionary movements.

There are effective governments like the Democratic People's Republic of Korea, Cuba, Vietnam, Venezuela and Syria that assert national independence and the socialist cause. They enjoy the support of the people, stand up against US imperialism and take advantage of the contradictions among the imperialist powers in order to counter sanctions, military blockade and aggression. The people and revolutionary forces led by the proletariat can strengthen themselves in the course of anti-imperialist struggles.

Mass protests signify transition to the resurgence of world proletarian revolution

The unprecedented rise and spread of gigantic anti-imperialist mass protests in both the underdeveloped and developed countries since last year is a consequence of the bankruptcy and grave crisis of the world capitalist system and the domestic ruling systems. It manifests the inability of the imperialist powers and their client-states (neocolonies and dependent states) to rule in the old way. It signifies the transition to unprecedentedly greater global anti-imperialist struggles and the resurgence of the world proletarian revolution from major setbacks since 1976.

The massive, sustained and concurrent mass protests in many countries of Europe, North America, Latin America, Asia and Africa bring to the surface the deep-going hatred of the people for the extreme oppression and exploitation that they are suffering. The proletariat and people of the world are fighting back. We are definitely in transition to a great resurgence of anti-imperialist struggles and the world proletarian revolution.

The broad masses of the people are rising up against the worst forms of imperialist oppression and exploitation, such as neoliberalism, austerity measures, gender discrimination, oppression of indigenous peoples, fascism, wars of aggression and environmental destruction. The starting issues and inciting moments for the mass protests may be of wide variability but they always involve the intolerable oppression and exploitation by imperialism and its reactionary agents.

In the last 50 years, we have seen imperialism, neocolonialism, modern revisionism, neoliberalism and neoconservatism attack and put down the proletariat and people of the world. Now, the people are resisting as never before and generating new revolutionary forces, including parties of the proletariat and mass organizations. These will ultimately result in the spread of armed revolutionary movements and the rise of socialist states and people's democracies with a socialist perspective.

The financial crash of 2008 has led to worse crisis of the world capitalist system and to a far bigger fall of the financial and economic system in 2020 at a rate faster than that of the Great Depression of 1929 onwards. The neoliberal policy regime has become more bankrupt than ever resulting in unprecedented overaccumulation and inflation of assets of the financial oligarchy and monopoly bourgeoisie, unsustainable debts of households, corporations and central banks, depression of the economy as the consuming public is impoverished and the escalating contest of the fascist and antifascist currents throughout the world.

The bailouts and lower interest rates are designed to favor the monopoly bourgeoisie at the expense of the proletariat and people. In accordance with the neoliberal bias, more capital is being put into the hands of the monopoly bourgeoisie by the central banks for stimulating the economy from the top. And yet the economy continues to stagnate and fall. The crisis of overproduction keeps on worsening and making the financial bailouts fail. The so-called middle class in all the developed and underdeveloped countries is dwindling faster. The stage is set for the revolt of the 99 percent of the people against the filthy 1 percent.

The current plunge of the world capitalist system coincides with the spread of the Covid-19 pandemic. This has resulted in lockdowns and other repressive measures in many countries. It has resulted in the disemployment of working people and further breakdown of production. While suffering economic and social deprivations, the people do not receive adequate health care because the public health systems have been undermined and drastically weakened by the privatization of hospitals and the unbridled profit-making of drug companies. The economic and social crisis, aggravated by the pandemic, has high potential of causing bigger and more widespread protest mass actions.

Since its founding in 2001 the International League of Peoples' Struggle has played a major role in inspiring and generating the anti-imperialist and democratic struggles of the peoples of the world through mass organizations

An Update on the International Situation

in so many concerns. We have become the largest and strongest international united front against imperialism and fascism and for national liberation, people's democracy and socialism.

We have made significant contributions to the upsurge of mass protest actions on a global scale. And we are further encouraged by this upsurge to further strengthen our ranks and to engage in consultative and consensual relations with similar international formations in order to expand the united front against imperialism and fascism.

We are confident that we are going to become stronger as the world capitalist system continues to break down and generate more favorable conditions for the rise of revolutionary forces. We are determined to invigorate the subjective forces of the anti-imperialist and antifascist mass movement that can bring about the resurgence of the world proletarian revolution and the greater victories of national liberation and socialist movements.

Imperialism in Various Global Regions

On the International Situation, Covid-19 Pandemic and the People's Response
First Series of ILPS Webinars, April 9, 2020

Dear colleagues and fellow activists, I am highly honored and delighted to be the first speaker in this series of webinars, billed as Teach-Ins or Interviews, online discussions on international events and people's struggles, under the auspices of ILPS Solidarity.

The format is simple. I make the presentation. And the audience can react with observations, questions and further discussions. My task today is to present the international situation, the Covid-19 pandemic and the peoples' response.

Let me state at the outset that the world capitalist system was already in trouble even before the Covid-19 pandemic arose. And the pandemic has unmasked and aggravated the crisis of global capitalism. It is of urgent importance to know how the people are affected and how they are responding.

1. Crisis of the world capitalist system

Science has advanced so fast and so far and has provided the technology to raise the productivity of the forces and means of production to such a high degree as to have the capability of eliminating class exploitation, gross inequality and mass poverty and providing a comfortable and fruitful life for at least twice the population of the world today.

The social character of production has risen so high with the adoption of higher technology. But unfortunately, the monopoly bourgeoisie and its financial oligarchy own the means of production, control the relations of production and dictate the terms of employment and the use of the human and material resources for the maximization of private profit and the inflation of the value of private assets.

Abusing bourgeois state power over the toiling masses of workers and peasants and middle social strata, the international bourgeoisie has adopted the neoliberal economic policy in order to accelerate the accumulation and concentration of productive and finance capital in the hands of the few, the mere 1 percent of the population to exploit, deprive and oppress the 99 percent.

The neoliberal economic policy has liberalized trade and investments, provided tax cuts, incentives and bailouts to the monopoly bourgeoisie, pressed down wages and other incomes of the lower classes, privatized public assets, reduced social services, imposed austerity measures, removed

245

social and environmental regulations and denationalized the less developed economies of the world.

The crisis of overproduction has therefore become more frequent and worse every time. The working people have suffered disemployment at so rapid a rate and cannot buy what is produced by the economy. The so-called middle class has dwindled and joined the ranks of the precariat. Yet, the monopoly bourgeoisie has proceeded to make the people suffer and insist on its system of unbridled greed.

Before the financial crisis of 2008 can be solved, another more serious crisis has come on top of it to further prolong and deepen the stagnation and depression of the global economy. All imperialist countries suffer from the crisis of overproduction due to the dwindling incomes of the working people and the underdeveloped countries.

All major contradictions in the world are intensifying: those between capital and labor in the imperialist countries, those among the imperialist powers, those between the imperialist powers and the oppressed peoples and nations and those between the imperialist powers and a number of states assertive of their national independence and socialist aspirations.

I mention first the contradiction between capital and labor in the imperialist countries to stress the point that even in their own national bulwarks of monopoly capitalism the imperialist powers have gone so far in exploiting their working class and diminishing the middle class as they have engaged in one round of austerity measures after another to cope with economic and financial crisis.

US imperialism has complemented the neoliberal policy to maximize profits from the production process and financial markets with the neoconservative policy to ensure government expenditures for the acquisition of weapons from the military-industrial complex for the maintenance of more than 800 overseas military bases and for endless wars of aggression, including proxy wars, and military intervention in support of local reactionary regimes.

After China became monopoly capitalist in 1976, it used to be touted as the main partner of the US in neoliberal globalization and as the exemplar of continuous capitalist growth. But since 2015, it has become conspicuously afflicted with unsustainable national, corporate and household debts and the same economic and financial crises that bedevil the traditional imperialist powers headed by the US.

The interimperialist contradictions are sharpening fast, with China having become the main rival of US imperialism. The US regrets and seeks to overcome the consequences of its previous concessions to China in terms of investments, trade and technology transfers. It is resentful that China has used state planning and state-owned enterprises in order to achieve strategic economic and military goals.

On the International Situation, Covid-19 Pandemic and the People's Response

But of course, China has its own vulnerabilities, like having to deal with the trade war already started by the US and with the mountains of debt it has accumulated, to cite only a few major problems. The US is trying hard to cut the large export surpluses that China gains in trade with the US and reduce the amount of surplus capital that China uses to expand its own fields of investments, markets and sources of raw materials in various countries.

The US and China try to strengthen their respective positions by alliances with other countries. The US still has the main influence in the UN and controls the multilateral agencies (IMF, World Bank and WTO) and the NATO and other military alliances. China has its all-round alliance with Russia and has tried to broaden this alliance with BRICS, SCO, the BRICS Development Bank, the Asian Infrastructure Investment Fund and the Belt and Road Initiative.

The imperialist countries continue to shift the burden of crisis to their reactionary client states in the underdeveloped countries and therefore exacerbate the imperialist contradictions with the oppressed peoples and nations. They are detested for aggravating the underdevelopment of entire countries and continents in contrast with the false promises of development.

Such states are always and increasingly in an untenable position. They suffer from widening deficits in trade and balance of payments because their exports consist of raw materials and semi-manufactures. They have mounting difficulties in servicing previous foreign debts and getting new foreign loans to be able to get by.

The broad masses of the people detest the imperialists and their puppets for the state terrorism that they suffer. The conditions are increasingly becoming favorable for the rise of various anti-imperialist and democratic struggles. There are a number of countries where the revolutionary partied of the proletariat and the people persevere in armed revolution for national and social liberation. These serve as example to all the oppressed peoples and nations in the world

There are states of underdeveloped countries that are assertive of national independence and socialist aspirations. These include the Democratic People's Republic of Korea, Cuba and Venezuela. They are dramatically standing up against US imperialism which is using economic sanctions, military blockades and threats of aggression.

Certain countries in Southeast Asia are also standing up to both the US and China. Vietnam is outstanding in opposing the invalid claim of China over ninety percent of the South China Sea. It is in this part of the world where China is exposing itself as an aggressive violator of the sovereign rights of other countries in violation of international law and the UN Convention of the Law of the Sea.

But US imperialism still has the worst standing as the aggressor and violator of sovereign rights in Asia, Africa and Latin America. But it is paying dearly for its wars of aggression and military intervention. It is on a course of accelerated strategic decline in an increasingly multipolar world in which the

247

inter-imperialist contradictions which incite the proletariat and people of the world to rise up.

Since last year, there has been an outburst of mass protests all over the world, in both underdeveloped and developed countries. This is a clear manifestation of the people's resistance to all the evil workings of imperialism such as neoliberal exploitation, the rise of state terrorism, fascism, austerity measures, racism, gender discrimination and imperialist plunder and destruction of the environment.

We are now in the midst of the transition to the global resurgence of the anti-imperialist and democratic struggles for national liberation, democracy and socialism.

2. The Covid-19 pandemic

Between the two main imperialist powers of today, the US and China, there are accusations and counter-accusations regarding the origin of Covid-19 and the malicious criminal motive behind it. There are speculations that one imperialist power is using the Covid-19 pandemic in order to weaken and defeat the other. These are manifestations of the growing contradictions between the US and China.

China accuses the US of having created Covid-19 in a bio-warfare laboratory in Fort Detrick in Maryland, USA, and having used the US athletic delegation to the World Military Games in Wuhan in October 2019 to bring into Wuhan the highly contagious virus. In turn, the US accuses China of having created the virus in its virological institute only to leak it to the Wuhan wet market through the sale of laboratory test animals.

There is the third view that the Chinese scientists themselves got the virus from a laboratory operated by the US military and somehow leaked the virus to the Wuhan meat market. Still there is the fourth view that Covid-19 is of purely zoonotic origin and has mutated from a previous virus, generated by an environment extremely devastated and imbalanced by imperialist plunder.

We let the independent scientists do their investigation and let the experts on international criminal law use the scientific findings and conclusions to prosecute the culprit if possible. But in the meantime, we can discuss the impact and consequences of Covid-19 to the world capitalist system and to the people.

Covid-19 has exposed and aggravated the antisocial character of the world capitalist system, the unpreparedness of the monopoly bourgeoisie and the harsh consequences to the people who have long suffered class exploitation, gross inequality, mass poverty and deprivation of social services in the fields of public health, education and housing.

Under neoliberal economic policy, the broad masses of the people have become extensively and extremely vulnerable to the recurrent and worsening

On the International Situation, Covid-19 Pandemic and the People's Response

crisis of the world capitalist system, to the imperialist sanctions, threats of war, actual wars of counterrevolution and aggression, natural disasters and pandemics.

The vulnerability of the overwhelming majority of the people consists of having no income and property to tide them over in case of unemployment or being out of work even only for a week for whatever reason of emergency. This is absolutely clear in a lockdown situation in which the people cannot go to work and have no public transport to use in order to obtain medical treatment for Covid-19 or any other illness.

Worst of all, when so many people need testing and treatment in time of a pandemic, the public health system has been eroded by the neoliberal economic policy of privatizing and eroding what remains of the public health system so that there are not enough health personnel, facilities, equipment and medicines. The remaining tokens of the public health system are easily overloaded and break down. And the private hospitals can at will turn away patients because they are not intended to serve the public, they have inadequate facilities or the patients cannot pay for the medical treatment.

We have also seen the tragedy of doctors, nurses and other health workers themselves getting sick and dying from Covid-19 because of the lack of personal protection equipment. The neoliberal state and the hospitals have appreciated the role of private profit but have depreciated the role of the health workers and the social service that they must render to the people.

In quite a number of developed and underdeveloped countries, where neoliberalism has been imposed as a policy, there has been the pseudo-scientific notion that it is enough to do washing of the hands and social distancing and at worst lockdown down on communities or entire regions because after the contagion has run rampant and claimed plenty of victims then the herd immunity develops in the rest of the population.

Thus, quite a number of governments have not made timely and adequate preparations and action plans to fight the pandemic. There is no mass testing for a long while. Thus, the spread of the contagion has not been measured well. And there is a lack or shortage of health personnel and resources for the treatment of those afflicted by Covid-19. The lack or shortage of ventilators has caused the death of many patients suffering from pneumonia, whether they are elderly or younger.

The ruling bourgeoisie and the entire ruling system have deprived the overwhelming majority of the people of the means of fending for themselves in time of lockdowns. And their political agents can only promise food rations and some compensation for the wages lost. But the promise is not kept in a timely and sufficient manner. The most victimized are those who are the millions of jobless and homeless as well those imprisoned in congested jails.

But ahead of any reasonable concession to the people, the monopoly bourgeoisie is assured of financial bailouts and stimulus packages in order

Imperialism in Various Global Regions

to make up for their business losses. We are well aware of the policies and actions being undertaken by the rulers of imperialist countries to override the breakdown of the production chain and the drastic falls in the stock market.

In the underdeveloped countries, especially where the barefaced repressive regimes exist, the tyrannical and corrupt bureaucrats invoke the Covid-10 to divert public funds to their own pockets instead of providing for the urgent needs of the people. Whatever good or service is provided is ascribed to those in power in order to raise their political stock.

Worst of all, the fascist-minded rulers use the lock downs to tighten their command over the military and police forces of the state to promote further the notion through the exercise of repressive measures that they are the saviors of the people. In the meantime, they use state power to aggrandize the private interests of their families, political cohorts and business cronies.

3. The people's response to the Covid-19 pandemic

It is correct for the people to use disinfectants, do social distancing and respect the rules of quarantine and lockdown whenever these are needed in the face of Covid-19. The people must stay safe from the highly contagious virus and avoid prejudicing the health of other people.

But they retain their democratic rights to make demands from the state and health authorities mass testing of the people at the community level and treatment for the sick and the means of survival while they are locked down and deprived of their means of livelihood. They can ventilate their grievances in order to obtain positive results for the common good.

To any positive extent that public officials recognize the urgent needs of the people and try to satisfy them, it is absolutely clear that social needs are being met by policies and actions for the common good and for whoever is dire need. But it is clear from the beginning that capitalism fails in the face of pandemic. What is needed is the spirit of service to the people and the desire for socialism.

In view of the utter bankruptcy and antisocial character of capitalism in a time of pandemic, the people and their anti-imperialist and democratic forces are justly demanding system change from capitalism to socialism and that everyone must be assured of a basic income in order to subsist and the social services like public health, public education and public housing.

Higher economic and social demands can be made in the developed countries, especially the imperialist countries. The level of economic development allows substantial social reforms and even socialism. But of course, the obstacle is the violence-prone rapacity of the monopoly bourgeoisie which would rather repress the people or aggress other countries than agree readily to the just economic and social demands of the people.

On the International Situation, Covid-19 Pandemic and the People's Response

Consider the trillions of dollars wasted by the US on its high-tech armaments, overseas military bases and endless wars of aggression. The US military forces have been far worse than Covid-19 in killing people. They have killed 25 to 30 million people since the end of World War II.

The huge US military expenditures can be redirected towards the expansion and improvement of social services. Best of all, if the American people succeed at system change. They can build a socialist society of plenty, creativity, justice and peace, if the monopoly bourgeoisie ceased to engage in domestic oppression and exploitation and in wars of aggression and mass destruction abroad.

In the case of underdeveloped, especially pre-industrial countries, the tax levied on the exploiting classes can be increased instead of decreased in order to promote economic development through national industrialization and land reform and provide social services in the spheres of education, health, housing and so on.

But substantial reforms can be achieved only if the people have strong patriotic and progressive forces in order to remove from power those who harm the people; and promote those leaders that work for the benefit of the people. Best of all, the people and their revolutionary forces can strive for system change and achieve national and social liberation towards the goal of socialism.

In any kind of crisis such as the Covid-19 pandemic, the best of the people and their organized forces stand out and shine. The people's social activists make the demands in favor of the people and do what they can to arouse, organize and mobilize them for the common good. They gain the experience and strength for carrying out anti-imperialist and democratic struggle toward the goal of socialism.

At the community level, they create ways for the people to have food, shelter and medical care and to engage in mutual aid. They call for donations from those who can give these. And they do not get paid for the volunteer work that they render. The actions that they can carry out for the common good under the circumstances of fighting the pandemic are a means of gaining public support and strengthening the organized forces.

In certain countries, where the people have revolutionary movements against the ruling system, the leading revolutionary parties have responded to the UN secretary general's call for a global ceasefire in order to fight the Covid-19 pandemic. In these countries, the revolutionary movement have their organizations attending to the economic and health needs of the people.

As a result of the pandemic, the vile character and failings of the world capitalist system are exposed. Even after the pandemic, the systemic crisis will continue and worsen in both imperialist and in nonimperialist countries. And the anti-people regimes and leaders in many countries will be held accountable and hated as enemies of the people not only for mishandling and aggravating the pandemic but for continuing an unjust system.

Imperialism in Various Global Regions

But wherever they exist, the revolutionary movements of the people will grow further in strength and will make advances. Where they do not exist, they will rise and wage revolutionary struggles. The world capitalist system will continue to be crisis-stricken economically and politically and its crimes will generate more favorable conditions for the rise of the revolutionary movement for national liberation, democracy and socialism.

On the Relations of the Philippines with US and Chinese Imperialism
Contribution to the webinar titled "Exposing Toxic Relationship: Signs Imperialist US is an Abusive Partner" Hosted by the League of Filipino Students -National and University of Santo Tomas Chapter
July 4, 2020

I thank the League of Filipino Students-National and its University of Santo Tomas chapter for inviting me to participate in this webinar, titled "Exposing Toxic Relationship: Signs Imperialist US is an Abusive Partner" and to discuss the topic, Of Love Triangles and External Affairs: PH Caught between US and China.

Let me discuss the relations of the Philippines with US imperialism and then with Chinese imperialism. In the concluding part of my presentation, I shall consider the sharpening interimperialist contradictions between the US and China and look at the dangers and opportunities that arise from these contradictions.

1. Relations between the Philippines and US imperialism

US imperialism has the monstrous record of successfully waging a war of conquest against the Philippine republic and the Filipino people from 1899 onwards. In the process, it killed at least 1.5 million Filipinos. As a result, it has been able to dominate the Philippines in an all-round way economically, politically, militarily and culturally in violation of national sovereignty and democratic rights of the Filipino people. I agree with you that the relationship between US imperialism and the Philippines is toxic.

With the exception of the Japanese Occupation during World War II from 1942 to 1945, the US was able to impose its colonial rule on the Filipino people from 1902 to 1946 and then granted a bogus kind of independence to the Philippines on July 4, 1946; and thereby shifted from colonial to semicolonial or neocolonial rule over the Philippines, with the Filipino puppet politicians allowed to run all levels of the counterrevolutionary state of the local exploiting classes of big compradors and landlords.

This false kind of independence was preconditioned by the US-RP Treaty of General Relations in 1946, which retained the US military bases on Philippine territory, the property rights of US corporations and US control of foreign trade and diplomatic relations. To this day, the US has been able to dominate the

Philippines by using a series of treaties, agreements and arrangements to bind the country and the people against their own sovereign rights and interests.

For this purpose, the US has been able to use the collaboration of the comprador big bourgeoisie, the landlord class and the bureaucrat capitalists. To adjust the Philippines to the requirements of foreign monopoly capitalism, the US has brought about a semifeudal economy run by the city-based comprador big bourgeoisie and the rural-based landlord class and by training political puppets mainly from these exploiting classes and the middle social strata to do the bidding of the US and become bureaucrat capitalists.

After using such legal devices as the Parity Amendment in the 1935 Constitution, the Bell Trade Act of 1946, the Quirino-Foster Agreement of 1950 and the Laurel-Langley Agreement of 1955 to ensure US economic dominance over the Philippines, the US has taken cover under multilateral foreign investment laws and treaties and all kinds of economic, trade and financial agreements under the auspices of the IMF, World Bank, World Trade Organization and the Asian Development Bank.

To this day, the US remains the No. 1 foreign investor in the Philippines and the No. 1 largest export market. It also accounts for 43 percent of hot money inflow. US corporations are dominant, with the assistance of the comprador big bourgeoisie of Spanish, Chinese and Filipino ancestry which acts as the chief trading and financial agents in a semifeudal economy characterized by the exchange of raw materials and some semimanufactures from the Philippines and capital goods and consumer goods from abroad. Japan is the No. 2 largest foreign investor in the Philippines but is the No. 1 provider of so-called official development assistance (ODA). Yet the largest part of this ODA is tied aid and spent on Japanese materials, equipment and contractors.

China, even including Hong Kong, is only the distant No. 3 largest foreign investor in the country in relation to the US and Japan. It has become the No. 1 trading partner of the Philippines, especially since 2013. It steadily came to this position after it started to dump cheap Chinese consumer goods and after it became the global manufacturing base for semiconductors and other products after the Asian financial crisis of 1997. Most imports from China are not even Chinese but from US, Japanese and other foreign transnational corporations located there to take advantage of its cheap labor. China also enjoys certain advantages in trading due to the collaboration of Chinese and Filipino-Chinese big compradors.

The US-RP Military Bases Agreement of 1947 was not renewed in 1991 as a result of the demand of the broad masses of the Filipino people who were indignant over the fact that the Marcos fascist dictatorship had used economic and military relations with the US in order to maintain autocratic rule. But the US-RP Mutual Defense Treaty of 1951 has continued to bind the Philippines and its military forces to the aggressive policies of US imperialism. The US-RP Military Assistance Agreement of 1947 has also persisted to allow the

US to control the security policy, military planning, indoctrination of military officers, intelligence exchange and armaments of the counterrevolutionary semicolonial state.

Soon enough the US imperialists were able to obtain the series of military agreements to authorize and facilitate the deployment US forces and de facto military bases. The agreements include the Visiting Forces Agreement (VFA, 1999), Mutual Logistics Support Agreement (the latest MLSA, 2002), the Enhanced Defense Cooperation Agreement (EDCA, 2014) and so many operational and supply agreements. US imperialism is the biggest terrorist in the entire history of mankind, responsible for the mass killing of 25 to 30 million people since after World War II. Especially since after September 11, 2001, it has used the term "terrorism" as a pejorative expression against the anti-imperialist and democratic forces and as pretext for unleashing wars of aggression and staging false flag operations by CIA-trained mercenaries posing as Islamic jihadists.

Quite recently on January 11 the Duterte regime made the threat to abrogate the VFA to create the impression that he was favoring China, drawing away from the US and forging an independent foreign policy. It did not take long before Duterte exposed his incorrigible puppetry to US imperialism and his shallow deceptive character by backing out of his false threat after just a few months on June 2. All the while other military agreements aside from the VFA have remained valid and in effect and the regime has continued to receive US military assistance and collaborate with US military forces under Operation Pacific Eagle-Philippines.

Since the moment he set out to take the presidency, Duterte has always been surrounded by bureaucrats and generals who are rabid agents of US imperialism. As president, he has done nothing to undo the all-round US dominance over the Philippines. In fact, he has promised Trump to terminate the peace negotiations with the NDFP, wipe out the revolutionary movement of the people by all means and deliver charter change allowing US corporations the unlimited right to own Philippine land, exploit natural resources and operate public utilities and all kinds of businesses.

Thus, Trump has practically given Duterte the license to form a civilian-military junta called the National Task Force-ELCAC to further militarize his regime, escalate state terrorism in the name of anti-communism and prepare the ground for a full-scale fascist dictatorship. He has already used the Covid-19 pandemic to form the Inter-Agency Task Force to carry out the lockdowns as dress rehearsal for military and police control of population and resources under a projected fascist dictatorship and to railroad a bill of state terrorism that negates democratic rights and makes superfluous the declaration of martial law.

The US does not just use economic and military means to dominate the Philippines. It has also used cultural, educational and other propaganda means to dominate the Philippines. To combat the demand of the youth and the national democratic movement for a national, scientific and mass cultural and educational system, the US uses various ways to control the educational and cultural policy of the Philippine reactionary state and thus perpetuate their influence over the politicians, bureaucracy and professionals and, in effect, among the masses.

As university activists, you are aware of how the US uses its own official agencies and multilateral agencies, private philanthropic foundations, business corporations, the mass media, social media, publications and films and certain subjects and textbooks in the curricula to propagate colonial mentality and influence the thinking of faculty members and students, the entire intelligentsia and broad masses of the people to follow the US imperialist line on historic and current issues.

2. Relations of the Philippines with China

The Philippines established diplomatic and trade relations with the People's Republic of China in 1975. The Marcos fascist dictatorship felt confident to establish such relations because the US and China had been on a path of rapprochement since the Nixon visit to China in 1972. It became easier for Sino-Philippine relations to develop after the Dengist coup in 1976 and China's adoption of capitalist reforms and opening up for integration in the world capitalist system in 1978.

The US established diplomatic relations with China in 1979 and proceeded to concede to it low-tech consumer manufacturing for export to the US by way of weaning China from socialism while continuing to press for more capitalist reforms in favor of foreign monopoly firms. The course of capitalist development in China was increasingly characterized by rampant corruption and inflation, which ultimately resulted in massive protests and their violent suppression in Beijing and many other Chinese cities in 1989.

In the aftermath of such mass protests, the Deng ruling clique begged for more economic, trade and technological concessions from the US and promised to adopt further capitalist reforms, especially the reduction of state-owned enterprises, increase of joint private-state sector enterprises and further loosening of the foreign investment law. The US played hard to please but made enough concessions in investments and technology transfer to help China stabilize its economy in its rapid conversion to capitalism, advance significantly from cheap consumer manufacturing and register high growth rates.

The rapid growth rate of China, especially its expanding production of cheap consumer goods for export to the US market, had an adverse impact on the so-called tiger economies of East Asia and triggered the Asian financial crisis of 1997. When this crisis occurred, China further expanded its production

256

of cheap consumer goods and became the final platform for assembling semimanufactures from the Philippines and other Southeast Asian countries.

The US was pleased to have China as its main partner in carrying out the imperialist policy of neoliberal globalization and to have China's high growth rate cushion the falling global growth rate. During the financial crash of 2008 and consequent Great Recession until recently, China was celebrated as the ever-rising star of the world capitalist economy. It has raised its own level of scientific and technological development, with the help of technology transfer from the US and elsewhere through foreign direct investments, direct purchases of dual-purpose equipment and academic exchanges in science and technology.

By the time China joined the WTO in 2001, the US under Bush junior was pleased with the apparent extent of liberalization of the Chinese economy and the surges of foreign investments there. The Bush regime preoccupied itself with drumming up its so-called war on terror after 9-11, with unleashing wars of aggression in Iraq and elsewhere and with trying in vain to buoy up the US economy through "military Keynesianism", making more and bigger purchase orders from the military-industrial complex.

Obama played the house boy loyal to the interests of US imperialism and continued to pursue wars of aggression. But it was during his regime that US strategy planners began to pay attention to the gravity of the US economic crisis as well as the world capitalist system in the wake of the financial crash of 2008, the high cost of overseas military bases and the wars of aggression away from the Asia-Pacific region and the galloping growth of the public debt burden.

The Obama regime noticed the economic and military rise of China and its growing geopolitical potential and ambitions. Thus, by 2012 it called for a strategic pivot to East Asia and stronger economic and security cooperation among the US, Japan and Australia to hold the line in the Pacific. The US was facing up to the challenge of China as it harped on owning 90 percent of the South China Sea and demanding the return of the Daoyu islands from Japan. It was also around this time that China started to tout its Belt and Road Initiative to reverse Western dominance in maritime trade since the 16th century while consolidating its growing ties with countries across a vast swath of the Asian mainland reminiscent of the ancient Silk Road.

China began to build artificial islands in the exclusive economic zone of the Philippines in the West Philippine Sea and claim even the Panatag Shoal (Scarborough Shoal) in violation of Philippine sovereign rights and the UN Convention on the Law of the Sea. The Philippines was therefore compelled to file a case against China before the Permanent Court of Arbitration on January 22, 2013. It won the case on June 12, 2016.

But the incoming Duterte regime declared that it would lay aside the judgment. He expected his ruling clique to benefit from Chinese loans for infrastructure projects as well as from lucrative connections with Chinese big compradors on both sides of the South China Sea and with criminal syndicates in drug smuggling and casino operations. The Duterte ruling family and its cronies are known to have been stashing away their ill-gotten wealth in China. They are thus tied to China and have to play an ambiguous role whenever issues arise publicly against Chinese policies and actions detrimental to the Philippines.

Under the Duterte regime, China has been able to build and militarize seven artificial islands in the Philippine EEZ in the West Philippine Sea. It has brought Philippine soil from Zambales and northeastern Mindanao in connection with the frequent smuggling out of mineral ores for China and likewise to serve as landfill for its artificial islands. It has also consolidated its control over the national power grid and built cell towers of China Telecom inside AFP military camps in contradiction with EDCA even as China has not delivered on most of its promises of loans for infrastructure projects. But it would be even worse if it fulfilled these promises because the loans carry high interest and require overpriced Chinese contractors, labor and supplies.

In the meantime, the Philippines under the Duterte regime has isolated itself from nearly all other members of the ASEAN, especially Vietnam, Indonesia and Malaysia, in standing up against the aggressive claims and acts of China in their respective EEZs and extended continental shelves. The Duterte regime also runs counter to the position of the US that China must not claim ownership over the high seas, violate the freedom of navigation and take any aggressive action against the ASEAN states.

The position of the Trump regime on China's unlawful claims over the whole of the South China Sea and on keeping free and open the Indo-Pacific maritime route is related to a whole framework of protectionist and punitive measures against China for using state planning and the still dominant state-owned enterprises (supposedly only 3 percent of Chinese corporations but in fact in control of the most strategic 30 percent of the Chinese economy) to achieve strategic economic and military goals. The US has vigorously accused China of using state power to manipulate its economic, trade and financial policies in violation of global market rules and stealing technology from the US and becoming the chief economic competitor and political rival of the US.

3. Dangers and opportunities from the interimperialist contradictions

From time to time, there are naval and air military shows of strength in the South China Sea by China and by the US independently or together with allies. Sometimes, there are expressions of fear by political analysts that war might break out. Frequently, the tyrant Duterte practically gives China the license to occupy the maritime features of the West Philippine Sea by gratuitously saying that he cannot do anything to stop China because he does not have the capability to wage war against China which would wipe out his troops in case of any armed conflict.

On the Relations of the Philippines with US and Chinese Imperialism

There is no immediate danger of direct all-out war breaking out between the US and China because the latter is obsessed with gaining more time for its "peaceful economic rise" and because each of these two imperialist powers has enough nuclear weapons to destroy the other. There is a balance of terror between them, resulting in mutual deterrence. The two imperialist powers are still subject to certain decision-making processes domestically. And under current circumstances in the world, the people have the high potential to counter and defeat a government that is poised to launch a nuclear war and cause a catastrophe of global scope.

For some years to come, the crisis of the world capitalist system, including inter-imperialist rivalries, will worsen but the imperialist powers will avoid a direct war between any of them. As much as possible, they would rather shift the burden of crisis to the underdeveloped countries and launch wars of aggression against them or mire them in regional and local proxy wars. That has been the case for 75 years already since after the end of World II. The nuclear stalemate arose during the Cold War when the Soviet Union developed its own nuclear weapons and delivery system.

Major economists and international institutions, including the IMF, World Bank and OECD, have come to the conclusion that the global economy is now afflicted by a crisis far worse than the still unsolved Great Recession that began in 2008 and even worse than the Great Depression of the 1930s that generated the inter-imperialist contradictions leading to World War II. Covid-19 has aggravated the crisis but the root cause is the ever worsening crisis of overproduction, the bankruptcy of the imperialist policy of neoliberal globalization and the sharpening struggle for a redivision of the world among the imperialist powers.

The inter-imperialist contradictions between the US and China and their respective alliances with other imperialist powers will escalate and will expose the weaknesses of both sides. At the same time, the anti-imperialist and democratic struggles of the proletariat and peoples of the world will intensify and generate the conditions favorable for the resurgence of the world proletarian revolution.

The strategic decline of the US will continue. Meanwhile, the efforts of the US to contain and cut down the economic and military rise of China will have adverse effects on both China and the US. The trade war between the two imperialist powers does not solve but aggravates the crisis of overproduction and sharpens the struggle for a redivision of the world among the imperialist powers. But for some more years to come, the imperialist powers can still find ways of cutting down each other through calibrated adversarial means, including covert cyber or biotech operations and regime-change strategies but short of a direct all-out conventional or nuclear war.

The interimperialist contradictions generate dangers and opportunities. Under current circumstances, the worst kind of danger for a country like the

Imperialism in Various Global Regions

Philippines is to become a complete captive and pawn of any imperialist power, whether the US or China, or to become a confused victim of these two imperialist powers. But on the contrary, the Philippines under a patriotic leadership can take advantage of the opportunities generated by the inter-imperialist contradictions and avail of the ASEAN to counter the most outrageous impositions of any imperialist power.

With regard to problems posed by China's claim of ownership of nearly all of the South China Sea, the ASEAN countries can agree with nearly all countries of the world that the right of free navigation in the high seas must be respected and be so exercised by countries critical of China's expansionist ambitions as to help prevent China from violating said right and from crossing over from its own EEZ and ECS to take over those that belong to the Philippines and other ASEAN states.

In the face of the traitorous character of the Duterte regime, the Filipino people and their patriotic and progressive forces must do everything in their power to oust it as soon as possible and intensify the demand for China to respect the 2016 judgment of the Permanent Court of Arbitration in favor of the Philippines in accordance with the UN Convention on the Law of the Sea, as well as encourage the other ASEAN countries to assert their own sovereign and maritime rights against the expansionist policy and actions of China and avail of the legal precedent set by the 2016 judgment of the Permanent Arbitration Court in favor of the Philippines. The ASEAN countries can take all possible legal and political initiatives to invoke said judgment as precedent and discourage China from violating their rights.

The Philippines and other ASEAN countries can present their respective complaints against China and demand compensation for damages before the appropriate agencies of the UN and file cases in the appropriate courts that can make the assets of China in certain countries answerable for Chinese obligations and liabilities. The point is to require China to withdraw from the artificial islands it has built, militarized and occupied in the West Philippine Sea and to pay for the damages that it has done to the marine environment in the same manner as the US was previously compelled to pay US$ 2 million for the damage done to Tubbataha Reef by the US warship USS Guardian.

The Duterte regime has played up fear of China's military might in making the Philippines desist from exploring and exploiting the hydrocarbon (oil and gas) resources in its own exclusive economic zone. And the traitor, coward and crook Duterte has even gone so far as to offer to China joint ownership of the resources under the guise of joint exploration and exploitation of said resources. He is in fact giving away to China full control of the technology, personnel, the accounting of costs and production and the siphoning of the resources to China.

The utter stupidity of the tyrant Duterte is best demonstrated by his obfuscation of the fact that the Philippines can get the best possible technology and the best possible terms from one of the three companies (Norway's

260

On the Relations of the Philippines with US and Chinese Imperialism

Equinor, previously known as Statoil) Royal Dutch Shell and the US Chevron) that are acknowledged as the best in undersea exploration and exploitation of oil and gas resources. If for instance, the Philippines can get the best possible terms from the Norwegian oil company, China will not dare to make war on the investments of a company belonging to a NATO member-state.

The Duterte regime has utterly failed to assert the sovereign rights of the Philippines over its own exclusive economic zone. The marine resources there have an estimated value of US$1.5 trillion and the oil and gas resources an estimated value of at least US$26 trillion. These are more than enough to industrialize the underdeveloped Philippine economy, engage the revolutionary forces of the people in a just peace agreement, overcome imperialist dominance and bring about a higher quality of life for the Filipino people. Instead, the regime has bowed to the aggressive claims of China and has reduced the Philippines to begging for loans at the most onerous terms for infrastructure projects that are overpriced and undertaken by Chinese companies and their own Chinese employees.

Yet the Duterte regime has the temerity to occasionally claim that its subservience to China is veering away from the US and developing an independent foreign policy. There can be no bigger lie. The regime has a two-faced character. It has not done anything to cut down the all-round dominance of the US over the Philippines. It has backed out of its false threat to abrogate the VFA and it is still hell-bent on fulfilling Duterte's 2017 promise to Trump to wipe out the revolutionary movement of the Filipino people and change the constitution to allow US and other foreign corporation to own up to 100 percent of land, natural resources, public utilities and other business enterprises in the Philippines.

The Duterte regime cannot be trusted to act in the interest of the Philippines and the Filipino people. In fact, it is the fervent desire of the Filipino people to oust this traitorous, tyrannical, murderous and corrupt regime and obtain justice against its so many grievous crimes. The rights of the Filipino people can best be protected by a government that arises from the revolutionary struggle for national and social liberation against imperialist domination and the local exploiting classes of big compradors, landlords and bureaucrat capitalists.

Imperialism in Various Global Regions

US-led Wars and Types of Weapons in the Era of Modern Imperialism
July 21, 2020

Introduction

Since the advent of modern imperialism at the beginning of the 20th century, the monopoly capitalist states have engaged in wars of aggression or counterrevolution of varying scales and such inter-imperialist wars as World War I and II. For the purpose, they have made use of military and private-sector science and technology to research and develop both conventional and nonconventional weapons of mass destruction of various types, including chemical, biological, nuclear and radiological. As one consequence, top US defense corporations emerged bigger and globally dominant and profited from government contracts as well as got "free" technology from government-funded research and development.

Conventional weapons are those weapons deployed primarily for their explosive, kinetic or incendiary potential, especially against combatants in the battlefield. But their scope of destruction can also cause widespread death among the civilians at the same time, such as through carpet bombing, firebombs, and the use of white phosphorous, napalm and cluster bombs. Even if the intended main targets are military force and facilities, the nonconventional weapons of mass destruction have the potential to destroy in one moment entire civilian populations, the social infrastructure and the environment, and damage them in a lasting way.

Because of space constraint, I will give historical backgrounds very briefly and I will try to focus on the wars and weapons of mass destruction for which the imperialist states are responsible in recent times after the Cold War of the US and the now-defunct Soviet Union. The imperialist powers of today, including China, hold the biggest stockpiles of both conventional and nonconventional weapons of mass destruction.

The US stands as the supreme terrorist power in accordance with the Nuremberg principle for having produced both conventional and unconventional weapons of mass destruction and used them for blackmail, military blockade, and wars of aggression in ways similar to or even surpassing those used by Hitlerite Germany. In 2019, the US also remains the number one supplier in the global arms trade.

The US is heir to to the violence and brutality of British colonialism in the conquest of what is the US, which involved genocidal campaigns against the native population. The white settlers used the most advanced conventional weapons of the time and brought smallpox, the bubonic plague, cholera, influenza, chickenpox, scarlet fever, syphilis and other diseases to afflict the Indians. Then they used guns,whips and chains to enslave the African-Americans and to kill them at will with impunity. The ideologues of Nazi Germany admired the white supremacist domination of the Indians and the African slaves.

US imperialism has the distinction of being the first and so far the only power that has used the atomic bomb on the civilian populations of entire cities, such as those of Nagasaki and Hiroshima. It has also used chemical, bacteriological and entomological weapons against the peoples of Korea, Cuba and Vietnam and radiological weapons in the more recent wars of aggression under the fascist and neoconservative policy of full-spectrum dominance, which gives full play to US superiority in high-tech weaponry. Extensive US nuclear tests have also damaged the people's health and environments in many Pacific islands and atolls, while medical tests in its clandestine laboratories have likewise damaged the health of numerous voluntary and involuntary human test subjects.

I shall not be distracted by the ideologues and propagandists of the US and other imperialist powers to ascribe the title of terrorist solely to individuals and small groups that use weapons of no comparison to the weapons of mass destruction in the hands of the imperialist terrorists. These super-terrorists circumvent and violate existing international conventions to produce these weapons and use them to threaten and attack their adversaries. Together with the Israeli Zionists, with whom they share certain weapons of mass destruction, they are also the main suppliers of handy chemical weapons to Al-Nusra, Al Qaida, Salafi and Islamic State (Daesh) as their terrorist agents.

I. World wars and wars of aggression or counterrevolution of varying scales

By themselves, wars fought even without the use of nonconventional weapons have involved the massive destruction of civilian lives, social infrastructures and the environment, creating the conditions for mass hunger and epidemics to arise and spread without sufficient health personnel and facilities to treat the sick and prevent the spread of diseases. In the US-Filipino War from 1899 onwards, US imperialism was responsible for the death of more than 20 percent or 1.5 million of the Philippine population by torture and gunfire as well as by the spread of contagious diseases due to food blockades, forced relocation of people, mass hunger, and lack of medical care.

In the course of World War I, both the Allies and Central Powers used chemical and biological weapons extensively in addition to conventional weapons. Mustard gas, phosgene gas, and other chemical agents were used to cause lung searing, blindness, death and maiming. The army of the

US-Led Wars and Types of Weapons in the Era of Modern Imperialism

Imperial German government inflicted anthrax and glanders on its enemy. The unchivalric use of such unconventional weapons would lead to the postwar Geneva Protocol of 1925 banning chemical weapons. Nevertheless, the massive disruptions in social life caused by World War I brought forth another horrendous but unintended result—the 1918 influenza pandemic that infected one-third of the world's total population and killed more than 50 million people.

During World War II, the Allied Powers and Axis Powers had stockpiles of chemical weapons. But the latter were the ones which used chemical weapons in the battlefield and in gas chambers to exterminate Jews and other adversaries in large numbers. To the German, Italian, Japanese and other fascists belong the discredit for the untimely death of tens of millions of people in the countries that they invaded and occupied, as a result of conventional battlefield violence, organized reprisals against civilian resistance, the lack of food and medical care, mass hunger and the spread of diseases.

But on the side of the victorious Allied forces, the US and its European Allies can be taken to account for disproportionate bombing at the expense mainly of the civilian population in Germany. There is however the rationale of the war victors that the so-called strategic bombing campaign was absolutely required to cripple Germany's cities and industrial belts which produced war materiel and that it was a just punishment for a population that adulated and supported fascist regimes and it was a necessary preemption of the local population from violently resisting the advance of the Allied Forces.

The US, taking advantage of the Allied Forces' having quickly achieved air superiority in the Pacific theatre by 1943 and in the European theatre by 1944, was the most outstanding in the use of firebombs and carpet bombing of fascist-controlled cities in Europe and Asia. Even the bombs used by its allies had been manufactured mostly in the US. But the most unique and most unnecessary use of violence in the closing year of World II was the atom bombing of Hiroshima and Nagasaki despite the offer of surrender already made by Japan. The bombs totally destroyed the two cities and exposed all survivors to lethal radiation that later led to debilitating disease and birth defects. The US argues that the atom bombing was to break decisively the certain resistance of the population to the US invasionary forces and therefore to save the lives of the US troops and ensure their victory.

For a while, the US had a monopoly of nuclear weapons and could use them to blackmail other countries or even as implied umbrella over the deployment of US military bases and forces in various countries of the world. The Soviet Union broke the US nuclear monopoly in 1949. Its arsenal of nuclear bombs was enough to deter the US from using nuclear bombs when it launched wars against the Korean people from 1950 to 1953 and against the Vietnamese and all Indochinese peoples from the 1960s onwards.

The US used extensively and intensively conventional weapons as well as bacteriological and chemical weapons in wars of aggression in Korea and

Indochina. For generations, surviving victims of the germ warfare in Korea and Agent Orange in Vietnam have been living witnesses to the dastardly imperialist attacks on the civilian population. In assisting puppet governments in armed counterrevolution in the Philippines and other countries, the US has supplied chemicals to poison wells and streams used by the guerrilla fighters as well as mosquitoes carrying the deadly falciparum strain of malaria to bite them.

Only after learning about the Soviet research in biological warfare did the US become amenable to the 1972 Biological Weapons Convention prohibiting offensive biological warfare. Despite the long precedence of the Geneva Protocol of 1925 against the use of chemical weapons under any circumstance, the imperialist powers agreed on the Chemical Weapons Convention (CWC) on the Prohibition of the development, production, stockpiling and use of chemical weapons and on their destruction only in 1993.

The Soviet Union reached strategic parity with the US in nuclear and other conventional weapons by the late 1970s during the Brezhnev regime. Between the two superpowers, a situation of nuclear stalemate and balance of terror arose and resulted in a candid recognition of mutual annihilation in case of nuclear war. A series of countries also made their own nuclear weapons: the UK in 1952, France in 1960, China in 1964, India in 1974 and Pakistan shortly thereafter. Later, Israel and the Democratic People's Republic of Korea would be known to have their own nuclear weapons. Several other countries are also known to have the technical capacity to build nuclear weapons.

In 1963 the Treaty Banning Nuclear Weapons Tests in the Atmosphere, in Outer Space and Under Water (otherwise known as the Partial Test Ban Treaty) was signed by the US, the Soviet Union and the UK. In 1968 the two superpowers agreed to the establishment of the UN Treaty on the Non-Proliferation of Nuclear Weapons. The Comprehensive Nuclear Test Ban Treaty was signed in 1996 and would not come into force. The US and its allied imperialist powers are the most insistent on keeping their nuclear stockpiles and the privilege of using them for war. They are most resistant to complete nuclear disarmament.

In May 2020, US President Trump stated publicly his unilateral willingness for the US to restart nuclear weapons testing. The US is continuing also to upgrade its nuclear weapons and delivery systems using the most recent technological advances (related to, for instance, cyberspace integration, artificial intelligence, quantum computing, and human-machine interface), while it develops as well new space weapons and related military hardware to be based in space, the Earth's orbit or outermost atmosphere. Among the biggest profiteering defense corporations making nuclear weapons are Huntington Ingalls Industries (US$28.87 billion in contracts), Lockheed Martin (US$25.1779 billion), Honeywell International (US$16.5488 billion), General Dynamics (US$5.8303 billion), and Jacobs Engineering (US$5.3293 billion).

Conventional weapons, which are allowed by international law to be in the hands of the army, air force and navy of each nation-state, are presumed to be more subject to calibrated and precision targeting and thus less destructive to the lives of the civilian population. But with the use of higher technology these conventional weapons have been enhanced to inflict far more casualties among civilians and destruction of the social infrastructure than ever before.

Even in the absence of a global inter-imperialist war, US imperialism together with its allies has been responsible for the death of 25 to 30 million civilians since the end of World War II. The bulk of the victims perished in the imperialist wars of aggression and imperialist-backed counterrevolution from China and Korea, to Indochina, Indonesia and other countries of Southeast Asia, to South Asia and the Middle East, all the way to Africa and Latin America. And since the end of the Cold War, the US and its NATO allies have used a wide range of weapons to inflict the biggest destruction in the shortest period to the civilian population and social infrastructure as in Iraq, Yugoslavia, Libya and Syria.

They have added to more destructive conventional weapons such new weapons as white phosphorus bombs and depleted-uranium munitions which continue to harm the civilians even after the war. They have also used far more "efficient" delivery systems, like long range as well as intermediate and short-range cruise missiles, supersonic planes, stealth bombers, AWACS surveillance and control planes, tactical drones, and electronic gadgets to trigger planted explosives. While some may consider that they are efficient in hitting their military targets, these systems also target many more unsuspecting civilians in residential, business, and open space locations.

The US cynically dismisses the destruction of civilian lives and infrastructure as mere "collateral damage", despite the explicit and repeated provision in Protocol I for states to avoid such civilian damage. The unspoken mindset among US imperialist policy planners is to utilize such "collateral damage" to send a warning to civilian populations not to support anti-US forces so as not to be treated as fair game.

Apart from civilian deaths, displacement is also a major direct measure of civilian suffering due to imperialist-instigated wars. According to official figures, the number of people uprooted from their ruined homes and communities steadily rose from 1950 onwards, such that by end-2014 there were 19.5 million cross-border refugees and 38 million internally displaced people. A big bulk of these are from Middle East countries torn apart by US-instigated wars.

II. Nonconventional weapons of mass destruction

As in the research and development of conventional weapons, the imperialist states use science and technology to research and develop nonconventional weapons of mass destruction of various types, including chemical, biological, nuclear and radiological. They have taken advantage of the duality in the use of science and technology to serve contradictory purposes, benign and malign, in a sense like the ordinary knife can be used for preparing food in the kitchen or murdering someone.

Whenever they admit to researching and prototyping or manufacturing an instrument of mass destruction, supposedly more deadly to the civilian population than the conventional weapons, they invoke certain non offensive purposes such as self-defense, deterrence or developing antidotes. These are the usual terms used for preempting, preconditioning and then circumventing laws and conventions that ban or control such weapons.

Among the imperialist powers, the US is supreme in the research, development, and use of chemical, biological, nuclear and radiological weapons of mass destruction. According to its own judgement, it collaborates with one or more of its imperialist allies in research, development and use of these nonconventional weapons through treaties of military alliance, joint scientific research programs, academic exchanges, and naturalization of foreign scientists and technologists as US citizens.

It is a matter of history that the US made use of American and foreign scientists and engineers in the Manhattan Project to research and produce the atom bomb. The US also took advantage of its leading role among victorious Allied powers at the end of World War II to recruit German scientists, some of them with Nazi ties, to jumpstart its own rocket technology. At the same time, the US did a parallel scheme to recruit Japanese germ-warfare scientists based in China under Unit 731, exempting them from war crimes prosecution.

In the entire course of the Cold War, the US sought to maintain supremacy in the production of nuclear weapons, especially after the Soviet Union broke the US nuclear monopoly. As a result of the nuclear stalemate, the US strategic planners headed by Kissinger conceived of the idea of producing tactical nukes, which are low-yield nuclear munitions such as short-range missiles and artillery shells designed for battlefield use. Tactical nukes were supposed to make US nuclear power more credible to peoples engaged in revolutionary struggles for national and social liberation and states which were also without any nuclear power but threatened by the US for asserting national independence and socialist aspirations.

As it turned out, the bulk of tactical nukes were deployed in NATO areas facing the former Soviet Union and other Warsaw Bloc countries, supposedly to enhance superiority in case of a shooting war. But then there could only be a short leap from the use of tactical nukes to strategic nukes. Thus, the US adjusted to the battlefield use of depleted-uranium-tipped bombs delivered by planes and artillery, which were used extensively in the Balkan wars and the Middle East under the neoconservative policy proclaimed by the US after the Cold War. The US has openly boasted of possessing and using depleted uranium and lasers as weapons although it denies using caesium which it has in abundant stock.

US-Led Wars and Types of Weapons in the Era of Modern Imperialism

Under the false pretext of self-defense to circumvent the treaties banning the use of chemical and biological warfare, the US has always maintained research laboratories for developing and producing chemical and biological weapons in the US and abroad. It has been notorious in the widespread use of germ warfare in the Korean War and in the use of Agent Orange and other defoliant chemical agents in the Vietnam War.

The use of chemical weapons is attractive to the imperialists because of the low cost of producing them and also because of the instant fatal effects on the victims and the maimed survivors as well as the shock effect on the entire population, whether the weapons be napalm bombs, white phosphorous bombs and aerosol-delivered toxins or pathogens. The US has most recently used these as covert weapons in the hands of its own personnel and terrorist agents like the Islamic State (Daesh) in Afghanistan, Iraq, Syria and elsewhere, and then twists the story by blaming its adversary states as the culprits.

The use of biological weapons is attractive to the imperialists because they are the easiest to develop and produce and likewise they are easiest to ascribe to other states or small groups acting clandestinely as assets of the US, and to further smokescreen their deployment as naturally occurring or accident-caused "viral outbreaks". Biological weapons are in the form of microbes as pathogens, mainly in the form of bacteria and viruses. The only restraint on the user of these weapons is the problem of ensuring the immunity of his own forces from the epidemic.

Covid-19 is the latest type of viral contagion, which has rapidly affected and alarmed the entire world because it is as easily transmitted as the common cold by people who are already infected Covid-19 but show no obvious symptoms for several or even many days. Covid-19 may likely cause severe illness or even death especially among people who are elderly or immuno-compromised. Based on the latest scientific findings, mortality rates in most countries for people below 60 are comparable to or lower than seasonal influenza, and almost nil for people below 20.

It is also potentially far more deadly in poor countries with megacities or congested slum communities with poor nutrition, healthcare and hygiene systems. It is more easily transmitted in community and from country to country and it is potentially far more deadly than any previous epidemic. It has become pandemic and it is still running its course in infecting millions of people and killing hundreds of thousands on a world scale.

It remains to be seen whether it can be promptly checked by a vaccine and to what extent it can be compared to the so-called Spanish flu of 1916 to 1918 which killed at least 50 million up to 65 million people, according to various reports. There is a distinct trend among reactionary states of bloating or misdirecting the real dangers to public health and fanning a parallel pandemic of fear to further their own narrow interests.

The chief imperialist rivals of today are accusing each of other of being culpable for originating and spreading SARS-CoV-2, the virus that causes the

Covid-19. China was the first to claim that the virus came from Fort Detrick in Maryland, USA and that the US military athletic delegation to the World Military Games brought it to Wuhan in October 2019. US President Donald Trump and his State Secretary Mike Pompeo have countered in public that the virus leaked from the Wuhan Institute of Virology and spread in Wuhan and that China suppressed the information, thus allowing Chinese and foreign travelers to pick up the virus in Wuhan and further spread it to many other countries.

Both sides claim to know the general state and pertinent details of biological research and development through previous exchanges of biological scientists and experts in four decades of close US-China cooperation as the main partners of neoliberal globalization. There are third parties that point to either country as the culprit or describe the Covid-19 virus as strictly zoonotic in origin, mutating from previous corona viruses and probably resulting from the imperialist plunder of the environment and disturbing the ecological balance among organisms in their drastically decreased and degraded forest habitat.

Various scientific studies claim that 60 to 70 percent of recognized emerging infectious diseases are zoonotic or originating from forest-dwelling animals. Covid-19 is supposedly traceable to bats as the "ultimate incubator" for the virus because of their strong immune system which make them an excellent host to viral strains that mutate into pathogens that are highly infectious and deadly to humans. There is the claim that the virus leaped from the bats to humans who consumed bat soup or meat at the Wuhan wet market.

Meanwhile, due to the demand of Australia and an overwhelming number of other countries for an independent investigation of the origin and development of Covid-19, the recent assembly of the World Health Organization has resolved that an independent investigation is to be conducted. China and the US have agreed to the investigation. Nevertheless, a recently-revealed secret 15-page research dossier shared among the US-led "Five Eyes" Security Alliance that includes Canada, the UK., Australia and New Zealand claims that the virus was leaked from a Chinese biodefense lab and that China suppressed information on the spread of the virus since December 2019.

Whatever is the outcome of the aforesaid investigation called by the WHO, the US and other imperialist states will continue to engage in bio-warfare research and development under such pretexts as self-defense, deterrence and production of the antidotes. Bio-warfare and pandemics will continue to be potent weapons as the crisis of the world capitalist system worsens and the contradictions among the imperialist powers, those between the imperialist powers and the oppressed peoples and nations and those between the proletariat and the monopoly bourgeoisie in imperialist countries intensify.

Furthermore, to the extent that bio-warfare and pandemics may spin out of control and endanger the entire system especially in the imperialist homelands, monopoly capitalist blocs and financial oligarchies will attempt to further entrench and expand their interests in big infotech, biotech, nanotech, space tech and other high-tech industries as the growing core of their respective military-industrial black holes—which in turn will further sharpen all the contradictions among the imperialist powers and within the entire world capitalist system.

III. Far-reaching consequences and prospects

The Covid-19 pandemic and the various state-enforced lockdowns on vast areas of the world have a strong impact on the world capitalist system, on the imperialist countries and client-states and the relations of the ruling classes, the governments and broad masses of the people. The pandemic and the resulting lockdowns have telescoped so many basic contradictions and defects of global capitalism into one monster storm of global scale. They have disrupted the usual mode of existence of the ruling systems and the population, brought down drastically the level of production and unemployment, caused widespread hunger and disease and generated more social uncertainty and unrest.

It has aggravated what has become the chronic crisis of the world capitalist system which has continued to lurch from one level of economic stagnation and financial volatility to a deeper level since the financial crash of 2008. It has been moving in the direction of a plunge comparable to or even worse than the Great Depression from 1929 onwards, generating on a global scale anti-imperialist and democratic struggles as well as prodding the monopoly bourgeoisie and the reactionaries to adopt fascism and war as desperate ways to overcome their problems.

The imperialist states and their client states have used the Covid-19 pandemic as opportunity for taking and exercising emergency powers, imposing lockdowns, tightening control of the people and institutionalizing repressive measures. In various countries, the lockdowns have been used to suppress the right to free assembly and expression and to unleash harsher campaigns of military suppression where the oppressed peoples and nations are engaged in people's war.

In most of the imperialist countries and in all the client-states, the people are actually deprived of community-based medical surveillance, the effective, prompt and free testing for Covid-19 and the timely and adequate treatment of the virus and other diseases in violation of the supposedly medical reason for the lockdown. In the course of the lockdown, the people are deprived of public transport and the means of livelihood. And yet they do not get the food and economic relief that have been promised to them by their governments. They suffer hunger and lack access to medical testing and treatment, and basic household supplies as well, especially in poor countries and impoverished or migrant communities.

They also have to cope with difficulties of dealing with sudden and imposed physical restrictions and social deprivation especially in Western countries where many elderly people live alone or in institutional homes. The lockdowns have created many instant refugee shelters for migrant workers and other stranded people who are unable to proceed or return home and left to their own devices to survive. The lockdowns have also drastically disrupted production and distribution chains, leading to shortages in many basic goods and services.

The extremely damaging consequences to the 99.9 percent of the world's population of 7.5 billion of more than four decades of neoliberal economic policy are exposed. They include lack of savings for the overwhelming majority of the people to tide them over the crisis, the lack of job security and the prevalence of precarious means of livelihood and the scarcity of social services. The public health system is exposed as too thin or close to nil or skewed in favor of more lucrative fields of medicine, as Covid-19 cases mount and overload it. There are inadequate personal protection gears even for the doctors, nurses and other health workers, no sufficient bed spaces, face masks, respirators, medicine and disinfectants.

While the broad masses of the people suffer, the imperialist and reactionary states assure the big bourgeoisie of financial bailouts and stimulus packages to cover their temporary losses from the stoppage or sharp reduction of production and sales of their production. The ensuing global economic depression also provides a most golden opportunity for the biggest predatory corporations to buy at hefty discounts troubled companies with choice assets and further consolidate their already-awesome economic power. And of course the class exploiters, their political agents and law enforcers enjoy the expanded opportunities for vulture capitalism and corruption yielded by the lockdown as well as the prolonged vacation in the wide spaces of expensive homes and resorts.

The pandemic and its resultant lockdowns have encouraged a stronger fascist trend in many countries, such as imposing stricter police-state measures in the guise of tighter public-health surveillance against new outbreaks; population control measures especially directed against migrant labor and refugees as "carriers of new diseases"; and steamrolling unpopular legislation and budget priorities in the guise of resetting society into a "new normal."

Both pandemic and lockdown have also produced deep cultural and ideological impacts. On one hand, the imperialists and other ruling classes have learned to weaponize the public's fears of a "new, unknown and unseen enemy," reminiscent of the post-9/11 hysteria against "terrorism" and the anticommunist hysteria of the Cold War era. On the other hand, they are now tightening their state-public or corporate-private hold on the digital or online channels of communication, mass media and entertainment which have proved to serve a critical social-control function and enjoyed massive expansion of user base in the last three months.

US-Led Wars and Types of Weapons in the Era of Modern Imperialism

The Covid-19 pandemic has brought about a health crisis and has seriously aggravated the crisis of the world capitalist system. It has exacerbated inter-imperialist rivalry, especially between the US and China. While the US remains as the No. 1 imperialist power especially with regard to military strength, Russia and China are formidable opponents and continue to develop their military capabilities.

The inter-imperialist rivalry is more fraught then ever with the danger of regional wars and even that of direct inter-imperialist war. As Lenin has pointed out, imperialism means war. There is no peace in the world while imperialist powers ride roughshod over the proletariat and the people and they themselves are driven to struggle for a redivision of the world and enlarge their respective shares of economic territory and client states.

Even while the lockdowns are in effect, the broad masses of the people and their organized anti-imperialist and democratic forces have found ways to discuss the implications and consequences of the situation at various levels, draw up conclusions on the most important issues, make collective decisions and carry out concerted actions to make protests and demands. They have electronic and non-electronic means of communications at the level of local communities, countries and the entire world. They have used noise barrages from their homes and yards to make protests and demands.

They have used various Internet platforms such as independent progressive news sites and blogs, the social media and videoconferencing to spell out their position on the pandemic, unjust lockdowns and other issues involving their rights and the violations of these by the rulers who are daily exposed as incompetent, corrupt and repressive.

While the closing of schools and workplaces created conditions for many wasted hours in forced isolation, it also created conditions for intense study, online group interaction, cultural creativity and technical innovation especially among the youth, intellectuals and professionals who lent their talents and time in the service of people and public facilities in dire need, including embattled health workers in the frontlines against Covid-19.

Even under strict lockdown rules or more relaxed quarantine rules, the people in various countries have engaged in mass protest action of varying scales. The masses of Hong Kong have gone back to the streets in great number to fight for democratic autonomy and other demands. Most remarkable of all the mass protests currently are those being held nationwide by African-Americans and the people of all races in the US against racism, police brutality and the unjust economic system as a result of the brazen murder of George Floyd by the police. Mass actions of solidarity have spread worldwide.

For sure, after the lockdowns are lifted and mass assemblies are permitted, the broad masses of the people will rise even more extensively and intensively against their oppressors and exploiters. Since last year, they have been rising up on a world scale to condemn and oppose the most predatory and brutal manifestations of modern imperialism, such as neoliberalism and fascism. Having come under more oppression and exploitation due to the Covid-19 pandemic, excessive lockdowns and states of emergency, they are impelled to undertake ever more resolute and militant acts of protest and demand for the solution of basic social, economic, and political problems.

We can be certain that the proletariat and people in the imperialist countries will carry out all possible forms of struggle to win the battle for democracy against imperialism and all reaction, prevail over the worsening crisis of capitalism, end the rule of unbridled neoliberal greed and fascism and the threat of inter-imperialist wars and to aim for the victory of socialism. The revolutionary struggles of the oppressed peoples for national and social liberation will also grow in strength and advance towards the goal of socialism. This is only way to end imperialism and all reaction in any country and in the whole world.

The imperialist and client-states reject and suppress the people's demands for national liberation, democracy, and socialism. But by doing so, they unwittingly arouse the people to wage revolutionary resistance, which is the most effective counter to imperialism and war. They undermine their own position in using tyrannical power, state terrorism and armed counterrevolution, in getting enmeshed in interimperialist conflicts and unleashing wars of aggression.

As the crisis of the world capitalist system becomes worse, the imperialist and client-states will escalate the oppression and exploitation of the people, and further plunder and degrade the environment. It is therefore necessary to fight for social, racial, and environmental justice in the comprehensive people's struggle for national liberation, democracy, all-round development and socialism.

On the World Situation

On the World Situation
Contribution to the Meeting of the ILPS International Coordinating Committee (ICC) in Phuket, Thailand, September 26-27, 2022

Dear Colleagues, I wish to give you a brief historical background before I discuss our main topic, which is the current world situation. In discussing this situation, I shall present the major contradictions and crises. Then, I shall discuss the prospects of the anti-imperialist struggle and the resurgence of socialism.

Historical background

Free competition capitalism inevitably led to monopoly capitalism in the last three decades of the 19th century in the most advanced capitalist countries. The capitalist class had kept on raising the organic composition of capital by increasing constant capital (plant, equipment and raw materials) and decreasing the variable capital for wages.

Ultimately, monopoly capitalism became dominant in the economy and society. Industrial capital merged with bank capital to form the finance oligarchy. The export of surplus capital gained importance over the export of surplus commodities. The capitalist class formed cartels and syndicates against each other. The capitalist powers formed blocs against other. The division of the world as economic territory (as sources of cheap raw materials and cheap labor, as fields of investments and as markets, as spheres of influence—as colonies, semi-colonies and dependent countries) was completed.

As Lenin pointed out, monopoly capitalism is the highest and final stage of capitalist development. For any bloc of capitalist powers to redivide the world in its favor is to cause a war, such as World Wars I and II. Monopoly capitalism is decadent, moribund, aggressive and prone to war. But the advent of monopoly capitalism in the late decades of the 19th century and early decades of the 20th century introduced not only the era of modern imperialism and the most destructive wars in the history of mankind but also the era of world proletarian-socialist revolution.

As a result of World War I, an interimperialist war of the Allied and Central Powers, the Great October Socialist Revolution won victory and the Soviet Union emerged in one-sixth of the surface of the earth to challenge the world capitalist system. In the course of World War II, the Soviet Union shone as the most decisive force in defeating the fascist Axis powers and enabling the rise of several socialist countries, including those of Eastern Europe and China.

275

Imperialism in Various Global Regions

The victories of the antifascist forces in World War II and the resultant socialist camp contributed as well to the emergence of newly independent countries and powerful national liberation movements in Asia, Africa and Latin America.

By 1956, it could be said that more than one-third of humanity was already governed by communist and workers' parties. But this was also the year that the modern revisionists headed by Khrushchev took power in the Soviet Union, took advantage of the difficult postwar conditions as a result of the deaths of 27 million Soviet people and the grave destruction wrought by World War II to the Soviet economy.

Stalin had practically industrialized the Soviet Union for the second time from 1945 onward and broke the US nuclear monopoly in 1949. But the Soviet modern revisionists chose to play the role of cowards by harping on the line of detente, bourgeois populism and bourgeois pacificism as a craven reaction to the US whipping up the Cold War since 1948. Upon the postwar consolidation of hardliner anticommunists ruling US society with the death of Franklin Delano Roosevelt, the US fortified militarism with the setting up of the Central Intelligence Agency (CIA) and the Pentagon. It sought to intervene in the Chinese civil war and then launched a war against the Korean people in 1950. It was put to a stalemate by the Korean ILPS Newsletter Vol. 2, Issue 2, April-October, 2022. 17 people and the Chinese volunteers. Thus the People's Democratic Republic of Korea stood beside the People's Republic of China to breach the Eastern front of US imperialism.

Further on, the Indochinese people advanced on the road of people's war, with the Vietnamese people taking the lead in defeating the French colonialists in 1954 and ultimately US imperialism in 1975. It became utterly clear that it is impossible for US imperialism to impose its hegemony on the Asian mainland because of the cross-border advantages of the Asian peoples generated by the October Revolution of the great Lenin and Stalin, followed by socialist China in the time of Mao.

At any rate, the US succeeded Nazi Germany as the strongest imperialist power after World War II, and its industrial capacity was expanded due to the war and was also undamaged by the war. It stood up as the fiercest imperialist power, took over the Nazi-led global anticommunist campaign by spearheading the Cold War and continued the world capitalist counterrevolution against the cause of national liberation, democracy and socialism.

It decided to reconstruct and rehabilitate the capitalist countries that belonged to the Allied and Axis powers in order to confront and fight the socialist cause and the strong wave of national liberation movements. It employed the twin domestic policy of suppressing rising American anti-capitalist and antifascist trends among the workers', youth, civil rights, anti-racist, anti-war, anti-nuclear, social justice and socialist movements and placating the American populace with the highest of living standards from 1945 to 1975 among the imperialist powers even as it was spending heavily for maintaining overseas military bases and waging wars of aggression.

276

On the World Situation

It continued to strengthen the overall imperialist front against the Soviet Union and other revolutionary forces and to face the problem of stagflation that had arisen as a result of the economic recovery of its fellow imperialist powers. Towards the end of the 1970s, it decided to adopt the neoliberal policy in order to bring about economic expansion as if without limit and even use the policy to entice revisionist-ruled countries to take loans from the West and import high-grade consumer goods.

The US found it opportune to take advantage of the Sino-Soviet ideological dispute to advance US interests and global capitalism. Although in the aforesaid dispute China and Mao Zedong were on the Marxist-Leninist and socialist side, against the Khrushchovite capitalist reformers in the Soviet Union and thereafter the social capitalist, social fascist and social-imperialist under Brezhnev, the US strategists found breaches among the Leftists in China and between them and the Centrist-Rightist side to take advantage of.

Thus, by 1971, there was a severe split between the Group of Four and the Chen Boda-Lin Biao alliance which allowed the Centrist-Rightist faction to rise and become dominant with the line of diplomatic prudence and "modernization" through capitalist-oriented reforms and opening up to the US and the world capitalist system. The Nixon visit of 1972 concurred with the counteroffensive to the Great Proletarian Cultural Revolution and rise of the Dengist counterrevolution.

The capitalist romance of the US and China started with sweat-shop operations and gross exploitation of cheap Chinese labor from the late 1970s to the 1980s. This coincided with the dismantling of the communes and privatization of the rural industrial cooperatives. The US was at first careful in giving concessions to China with regard to technology transfer but loosened up steadily after the outburst of the Chinese uprisings against inflation and corruption in 1989. From the early 1990s onward, the US increased its concessions to China as the latter made further concessions on the liberalization of trade and investments and joined the WTO in 2001. The rise of capitalism in China became conspicuous in the last four decades.

The US-China economic and political relations appeared to be going along well until the financial meltdown of 2008. Shortly thereafter, during the Obama regime, the US started to complain of China's economic and military rise and excluded China from the Trans-Pacific Partnership Agreement (TPPA). It drummed up the strategic pivot of the US forces to East Asia in order to contain China. When the Trump regime took over, the US declared a trade war on China, withdrew trade and investment concessions from China and condemned her for stealing high technology from US companies and research institutes. It identified China as the chief economic competitor and political rival of the US

In the case of the Soviet Union, the US induced Brezhnev to plunge into the Afghan quagmire from the late 1970s onward. Biased by its long-running class hatred of the Soviet Union as the first socialist country and its intense rivalry

277

in the Cold War, the main goal of the US was to subvert the Soviet Union and make it rot, lose control over Eastern Europe and ultimately dissolve itself. The Soviet Union collapsed in 1991.

Before the collapse of the Soviet Union, the Soviet revisionist rulers received assurances from the US and other Western powers that NATO would not recruit former members of the Warsaw Pact after its dissolution. But the US and NATO proceeded to expand the NATO in Eastern Europe and tried to extend it to former Soviet republics. They intensified their war of aggression in Iraq in the name of a "new world order" in the 1990s. And before the end of the 20th century, they destroyed Yugoslavia and punished it for being a stalwart of the Non-Aligned Movement.

Subsequently, the US announced its neoconservative policy of taking advantage of its being sole superpower and using the full spectrum of its power to dominate the world. In the name of the "war on terror", the US unleashed wars of aggression in Central Asia, Middle East and the Balkans. In the name of the global war on terror, it carried out wars of aggression with impunity on a global scale. These are the worst forms of terrorism condemned by the Nuremberg principles.

In trying to take advantage of its moment of being sole superpower since 1991, the US has aggravated and accelerated its strategic decline, incurring more than US$ 10 trillion without obtaining more significant amounts of stable economic territory to exploit. It has been compelled to leave Afghanistan after failing to conquer it after 20 years of occupation.

In the meantime, China has moved forward in growing its economy even as this is capitalist and has gained space for maneuver with the BRICS, Shanghai Cooperation Organization, the Eurasian Economic Union and the Belt and Road Initiative, the New Development Bank, and the AIIB as alternatives or supplements to such traditional multilateral agencies as the IMF, World Bank, the WTO, OECD, the G-7 and so on.

II. The world situation: major contradictions and crises

The major contradictions in the world capitalist system are intensifying. They include those between monopoly capital and labor in the imperialist countries, those among the imperialist countries, those between the imperialist powers and the oppressed peoples and nations, and those between the imperialist powers and the countries assertive of national independence and socialist program and aspirations.

It is of great importance to recognize the contradictions of monopoly capital and labor within the imperialist countries in order to understand the limits to the economic and political expansion of those countries. Within these countries, there are limits to capital expansion as exposed by the recurrent crises of overproduction or cycles of boom and bust. These also set limits to global

On the World Situation

capital expansion, contrary to the claims of the neoliberal economists that there are no such limits.

There are limits to cutting down wages and social services to make more capital available to the capitalist class, to enable it to privatize profitable public assets, to flourish in liberalized trade and investments, to plunder the environment, to denationalize national economies and to resort to public borrowing to bail out corporations and entire economies in trouble. Global public debt has leapt from US$ 226 trillion in 2020 to US$303 trillion in 2021. The global debt is more than 320 percent of global GDP and is growing faster.

The US has persuaded its traditional imperialist allies that China is its chief economic competitor and chief political rival; and that the combination of China and Russia as the new capitalist and imperialist powers is their adversary. After casting away socialism in favor of capitalism, why should these two countries be treated by the US and its allies as their enemy?

It is in the nature of imperialist powers to seek world hegemony and to form blocs for the purpose of gaining profits according to the balance of forces gained at every given stage. This is also the obsession of the most powerful imperialist powers to gain control and hegemony over the weaker imperialist powers. The traditional imperialist powers have the notion that they should be at the top of the new imperialist powers.

At the moment, the consensus of the traditional imperialist powers is that Russia is the weakest of the new imperialist powers because it has it has disintegrated its previous Soviet industrial prowess and lagged behind in industrial development and has an oligarchy that depends on the production of energy, raw materials and agricultural products (wheat, corn, barley, and sunflower oil) in exchange for foreign manufactures.

However, the traditional imperialist powers continue to be wary over Russia's stockpile of nuclear weapons and missile delivery systems. They hope to weaken Russia economically and politically by violating their own dogma of neoliberalism and adopting sanctions against Russia and by instigating proxy wars against it on the basis of the expansion of NATO. Thus the US and the EU have pushed Ukraine to serve as their pawn in their proxy war against Russia and have taken the initiative in imposing sanctions against Russia.

To conjure the illusion that it is still powerful in the whole world, including East Asia, the US has taken the initiative to make provocations against China concurrent with the hot war that has started between Russia and Ukraine. But the shallowness and puerility of the provocations, such as the unwanted visit of Pelosi to Taiwan, have been easily exposed. The US threat to drop the One-China policy is futile, if the goal is to use the Taiwan-ROC flag to justify an imperialist project to retake mainland China, because it has long been proven that any US military expedition to the Asian mainland is futile and is bound to fail.

279

The more effective attack by the US on China has been its ceasing of their long-running neoliberal partnership on a global scale and their bilateral relations as the biggest US economic and trade partner, with China being able to access previously well guarded US technology. As a result of the US-China contradictions, China has suffered internal economic and financial setbacks and adverse consequences on its Belt and Road Initiative (BRI). The US is vigorously opposing the BRI with the AUKUS military alliance of Australia, UK and US, with the QUAD Indo-Pacific Initiative (US, Japan, Australia and India) and with the Partnership for Global Infrastructure and Investment, which involves G-7 support.

The crisis of overproduction in the capitalist system is still investigated and measured within the bounds of every imperialist country. And consequently on a global scale, the overconcentration of capital, the deteriorating conditions of employment and life, the overproduction of goods can be determined. As science and technology raise productivity, the proletariat are compelled to live in poverty amidst the plenty that they create for the capitalists to make profit on.

Even without the necessary tools of Marxist analysis, global economic inequality is starkly obvious in just a cursory review of infographics-style indicators: The ten richest countries in the world are as follows: 1. United States US$18.62 Tn, 2. China US$11.22 Tn, 3. Japan US$4.94 Tn, 4. Germany US$3.48 Tn, 5. United Kingdom US$2.65 Tn, 6. France US$2.47 Tn, 7. India US$2.26 Tn, 8. Italy US$1.86 Tn, 9. Brazil US$1.80 Tn and 10. Canada US$1.53. Half of the world's net wealth belongs to the top 1 percent, top 10 percent of adults hold 85 percent, while the bottom 90 percent hold the remaining 15 percent of the world's total wealth.

The top 30 percent of adults hold 97 percent of total wealth

The total of 2,153 billionaires in the world have more wealth than the 4.6 billion people who make up 60 percent of the planet's population, according to Oxfam. Neoliberal globalization by the rise of the so-called transnational capitalist class or US-led global monopoly bourgeoisie—actually, new and evolving forms of the same basic imperialist bourgeoisies and their financial oligarchies ruling jointly through international cartels and blocs—has accelerated the overaccumulation of capital in the hands of a few and the immiseration of the overwhelming majority of the people.

It was supposed to solve the problem of stagflation for the US and the whole world by freeing capital from nation-state constraints to profitmaking and to buoy up big and small boats by raising the water level. And as the Oxfam report said, we end up with just one percent of humanity owning over one-half of the world's wealth, the top 20 percent owning 94.5 percent and 80 percent of the people sharing just 5.5 percent.

On the World Situation

The extreme overconcentration of wealth in the hands of the capitalist class and the expanded impoverishment of the majority of the people proves that the capitalist class has no way to dispose nationally of the huge amounts of surplus that it has accumulated. The gross disparities have merely led to more financial bubbles, which in turn result in even more mind-boggling economic inequalities when the bubbles burst, to be gradually replaced by new bubbles. This has been exposed by the Great Depression that has unfolded since the financial meltdown of 2008. This has hit hard the imperialist countries and far worse the oppressed peoples and nations of Asia, Africa and Latin America.

Neoliberalism has appeared in imperialist countries as the handmaiden of fascism. The imperialist states prepare themselves to use fascism in order to suppress the mass protests and strikes engendered by unemployment, low wages and decreased social services. We notice now that the traditional and new imperialist powers are prone to use fascism to suppress the mass resistance of the proletariat. In addition, there are factional struggles within each imperialist states which the system can no longer easily do regularly as before. This further drives up the tendency for one ambitious faction of the ruling class to use fascism to further monopolize power, keep itself at the top, and suppress all but the mildest forms of dissent.

New democratic and socialist revolutions are vilified as "communist terrorism" to justify state terrorism or fascism. The danger of a third world war and nuclear war comes mainly from the rise of fascism in both imperialist states and their client states. Unable to solve the serious economic and social problems brought about by neoliberalism, the states of monopoly bourgeoisie engage in fascism to suppress democratic rights and the restive proletariat and other working people. Even the forms of resistance by the spontaneous masses against specific abuses are likewise demonized as "terrorist" or, ironically, "Rightist-led." These are increasingly met with police surveillance and violence, to further hone the swords and stir the bloodlust of the fascist butchers.

The worst of exploitation and oppression transpire in the intensifying contradictions of the imperialist powers and the impoverished peoples and nations of Asia, Africa and Latin America. In times of global depression or not, these peoples are victimized in their own countries by foreign monopoly capital using them as cheap sources of raw materials and cheap labor, markets of surplus goods, fields of investments for surplus capital and as spheres of influence.

In the past decade, and especially at the height of the Covid pandemic and global lockdowns, the dominant monopoly capitalist groups took advantage of the complex tangle of trade and supply-chain disruptions and depleted finances to further tie down and squeeze the poor countries. Sri Lanka's recent economic collapse and political convulsion is just a foretaste of a worsening global foreign-debt bubble. Nearly 20 countries have been listed as on the verge of a debt default.

The oppressed peoples and nations are the most motivated to fight for national liberation and democracy and socialism. The most important armed revolutionary struggles against imperialism are being waged today in such countries as India, the Philippines, Turkey, Kurdistan and Palestine. They are in the main waging people's war along the line of the new democratic revolution with a socialist perspective.

In the countries where the people are still waging the new democratic revolution, the imperialist powers and their puppets use the neoliberal forms of exploitation and the most brutal forms of fascism to oppress the people. The imperialist powers use either puppet regimes to dominate these countries or unleash wars of aggression. In an increasing number of cases, the imperialists are also cunning enough to dress up their interventionist meddling by whipping up certain restive sectors to launch so-called "color revolutions" in order to implement regime change.

Since the end of World War II, the imperialist powers have so far avoided direct wars among themselves because of their fear of nuclear war in both its shortterm and long-term effects, including the still barely understood long-term effects on health, environment, and continued viability of most forms of life on the planet. Also, the US made doubly sure to minimize nuclear rearmament by assuring Germany and Japan of its nuclear umbrella and imposing strict bans on nuclear proliferation.

Thus far, the US and its imperialists allies have succeeded in channeling their economic and political rivalries, including territorial redivisions, through negotiated deals within international and regional bodies, while constricting Russia and China. But they have gone into proxy wars to dominate the underdeveloped countries or gain positions of strength. Thus, the imperialist powers have decreased the chances of direct inter-imperialist wars. But for the first time, the US and NATO have openly emboldened Ukraine to provoke a war with Russia, a country with nuclear power, which has put on maximum alert its nuclear forces. Unlike in earlier Cold War-era crises, there are now so many tiers of "tactical nuke" weaponry pre-deployed in hot spots, which further raises the risks of runaway military escalation.

While for many decades since the end of the US nuclear bomb monopoly, the US has been conspicuously frightened by the nuclear arsenal of the Soviet Union and then of Russia, the US and all other imperialist powers have mindlessly engaged in the plunder and devastation of the environment, especially in the underdeveloped countries, bringing about the current problem of global warming or global heating, which also threatens the very existence of humanity.

The attack on the environment is multi-pronged. It includes the extremely high dependence of capitalist industries on fossil fuels, which emit carbon dioxide and other "greenhouse gases" that hasten climate change, and the use of various extractive and industrial processes that produce toxic industrial wastes, destroy the forests, marine and other biomes, especially those with rich biodiversity, destroy and disturb the various organisms there, and poison the air, water and soil used by local populations and agriculture in order to make way for logging, mining and plantations.

Couple these with the obvious environmental devastation wrought by US-led wars of aggression and maintenance of history's largest global network of military facilities and globally-deployed armed forces. The US military has in fact been condemned as the world's single biggest polluter. Not to be discounted as well is the completely unaudited impact on the earth of the indulgence of the world's military powers in the active but completely covert diabolical weaponization of the weather.

The imperialist powers have also engaged in laboratory research for the purpose of chemical and biological warfare and serious out of control leaks have also occurred, causing pandemics like SARS and Covid-19 in the US, China, and much of the world. Most Western scientific, academic and serious media circles are now saying that the SARS-Cov2 virus is a product of "gain-of-function research"—a euphemism for biowarfare research and development. Russia has recently accused the US of having secretly funded bioweapons laboratories in Ukraine and elsewhere.

Countries assertive of national independence and socialist programs and aspirations still play an important role in resisting the impositions of imperialist powers and the machinations of their local puppets. As they persevere in their revolutionary commitment and struggle, countries like the Democratic People's Republic of Korea, Socialist Republic of Vietnam, Cuba and other anti-imperialist countries can make important contributions to upholding, defending and advancing the cause of national liberation, democracy and socialism on a world scale.

These countries can rely on their own strength, ally themselves with the oppressed peoples and nations still fighting for national and social liberation and take advantage of the splits between the traditional and the new imperialist powers. We are reminded of historical lessons, both positive and negative, in grasping the class character and the objective balance of forces within such countries and their states. The proletarian revolutionaries in China, for example, saw the class logic and had to learn priceless lessons in united-front tactics in dealing with Sun Yatsen's Guomindang in the 1921-27 period. There are other examples among the national liberation movements in the post-World War II period. It is a matter of political wisdom for the revolutionary forces of the world today to do everything possible in order to develop anti-imperialist solidarity with such countries and states and to make up for the deleterious consequences of modern revisionism in subverting and destroying the socialist states in the 20th century.

III. Prospects of anti-imperialist struggle and resurgence of socialism

The conditions are exceedingly favorable for the advance of the anti-imperialist and democratic mass struggles in all types of countries, be they imperialist or imperialist-dominated. They arise as a result of the intensifying major contradictions in the world capitalist system. Once more they lay the ground for great disorder and turbulence in this system and the resurgence of the world proletarian socialist revolution.

Confounded by the rapidly worsening crisis of their system as a result of the unraveling of the neoliberal policy regime, the traditional and new imperialist powers are prone to seek solutions through intensified economic plunder and predation, fascism and wars of aggression. The proletariat and the rest of the people in the imperialist countries are suffering grievously the socioeconomic crisis of the system and now fascism is being imposed on them to aggravate their suffering.

Even now, there is already a strong trend towards another globally devastating economic crash. The revolutionary forces of the people ought to sharply point out the criminal all-sided accountabilities of the predatory classes for the currently worsening global economic super crisis, and condemn any obfuscations of their accountability, like making Covid-19 and any ensuing pandemic as the cop-out reason. They have no choice but to fight back with all vigor.

In the US, while the incumbent president Biden is using democratic jargon and wooing other Right and Center forces to dress up the growing fascist werewolf that is the imperialist Deep State, Trump is trying hard to whip up his followers into a frenzy of white supremacist slogans in order to bring him back to the White House in order to use the same Deep State to govern a more unruly and divided empire. In the rest of the imperialist countries, there are trends which favor Rightist, including ultra-Rightist, positions. We must also be carefully exercise class analysis to expose the many forms of Rightist positions masquerading as Center or Left. At the same time, these rouse the proletariat and people to rise up against their worsening conditions of mass unemployment, low income and dearth of social services.

In the new imperialist countries there is a rising wave of discontent and hatred against the oligarchs who have privatized the social wealth created by the proletariat and other working people. The promises of greater efficiency and prosperity through the adoption of capitalism have been unfulfilled for so long. In former socialist countries, which have not been strong enough to become imperialist powers, the conditions have sunk to the level of the third world countries.

The current mass uprisings in Czechoslovakia are a positive signal for the people in Eastern and Central Europe to rise up against the US and NATO and the entire world capitalist system even as Ukraine is manifesting what

On the World Situation

has gone terribly wrong since the rise of fascism on the back of a chauvinism against the sizeable Russian minority population. Now the oligarchs of both Russia and Ukraine are locked in a prolonged war and the US and NATO are using Ukraine to ensure that Russia is further weakened and become unable to cope with the further advances of US imperialism and NATO in what used to be a wider sphere of the former Soviet Union. All the turbulence that is occurring and is likely to occur further in the Russian Federation and Eastern Europe will serve to agitate the proletariat and the people to review their history and to recover and reassert their revolutionary will. It is therefore necessary for communists all over the world to encourage the formation of the revolutionary party of the proletariat in these countries.

For a while, the US and its traditional imperialist allies might be able to contain and reduce the economic rise of China even if they entertain the dream of deteriorating economic and political conditions in China, which will cause class struggle to intensify between the dominant Chinese capitalist oligarchy and the proletariat for the purpose of repeating history a la the overthrow of the Communist Party of the Soviet Union. At the same time, the US-led Western ruling elite is actively mobilizing important and strategically-placed pro-Western assets within China to undermine it from within, and to gain from new effective counterrevolutionary measures imposed in China. Within China, the use of fascism against the people will only serve to sharpen the battle for democracy, broaden the revolutionary mass movement, and push the proletarian revolutionaries to assert the theory and practice of Marxism-Leninism-Maoism.

The ever fertile ground for waging armed revolution is in the underdeveloped countries of Asia, Africa and Latin America under the domination of imperialist powers and their puppet regimes. They are the most victimized by imperialist and local reactionary oppression and exploitation. They have their own grounds and circumstances for waging revolution and will certainly be encouraged to wage revolution if the proletariat and the people in supposedly more developed countries are already rising up.

On a global scale, the subjective forces of the proletarian revolution can be established and developed faster than ever before. Optimally, the communist party as genuine revolutionary party of the proletariat must adhere to the theory and practice of Marxism-Leninism-Maoism, and sum up the most vital lessons of the particular revolutionary history and experience, to be able to lead the people in any country where revolution is being waged.

In the course of political struggle, it must be able to unite with the basic masses of the oppressed and exploited people, win over the middle forces, take advantage of the splits among the reactionaries, and isolate and destroy the power of the class enemy or foreign aggressor. It must have a people's army to be able to wage the armed revolution and seize political power.

Those interested in waging revolution in any country must avail of the history and experience of communist parties that have won victories in Russia, China, DPRK, and Eastern Europe. It is not necessary for an International of Communist and Workers' parties to exist for a country to start the development of the armed revolution. Lenin spent time debating with and exposing the revisionists, the social chauvinists, social pacifists, social fascists and social imperialists of the Second International to be able to clear the road of revolution in Russia.

He had first to win the Great October Socialist Revolution in 1917 to be able to build the most effective International so far in the history of the revolutionary proletariat. He founded the Third International in 1919. The lack of an international should not be an excuse for failure to start and develop the revolution in any country. Since the dissolution of the Comintern in 1943, because of the inability of the Executive Committee to give directives to so many parties under conditions of World War II, communist parties that could communicate with each other could cooperate bilaterally and even multilaterally.

There is a far longer history of communist and workers' parties that are equal to each other and independent of each other under proletarian internationalism and anti-imperialist solidarity. If there is yet no bulwark of socialism as strong as the Soviet Union or China in the past, the revolutionary parties of the proletariat can devise ways of conferences, consultations and communications in order to exchange information, experiences and ideas and raise the level of revolutionary struggle among the proletariat and the people.

After the success of the modern revisionists in the Soviet Union, they held international conferences of communist parties to spread their revisionist line. For a while, the Communist Party of China had to contend with the pro-revisionist conferences sponsored by the Soviet party by engaging in bilateral relations and hosting Central Committee delegations in China. But alas these were dissolved soon after the success of the Dengist counterrevolution.

Attempts were made by the Revolutionary Internationalist Movement (RIM) and subsequently by the International Conference of Marxist-Leninist Parties and Organizations (ICMLPO) to build an international conference of communist and workers parties. But they dissolved after attempts were made to make the host party the center of the world proletarian revolution despite failure to win revolution in their own country. And groups of small parties also took the fancy of naming their theories after revolutionaries who have not yet won a revolution in their own countries, such as Gonzalo Thought, Prachanda Path, Avakian's New Synthesis and the like. Such cultist groups are in a hurry to claim some kind of global franchise or hegemony.

Since the undeniable successes of the modern revisionists to sabotage the socialist revolutions in the Soviet Union, China and Eastern Europe, restore capitalism and disintegrate the international communist movement, the most

On the World Situation

successful anti-imperialist formations have had a mass character, among them the International League of Peoples' Struggle. These can be powerful mass bases for promoting the establishment and development of the revolutionary parties of the proletariat.

Let us not forget that while the Third International existed, Stalin developed the Popular Front as an international democratic and antifascist force starting in 1935. Thus, he helped the communist parties in various countries to prepare against the imperialist and fascist preparations for war by encouraging various types of mass formations according to class and sectoral democratic interests.

There is a big difference between the circumstances of the founding of the Third International and the circumstances when attempts were made to organize an International as successor to the Comintern outside of any country as the bulwark of socialist revolution. The problem is not merely the lack of a socialist bulwark but also the inadequacies of programs to fight the continuing influences of modern revisionism, all sorts of reformism and subjective idealism propagated by the ideologues and publicists of the imperialist powers.

Since then, significant advances have occurred in the objective conditions for waging the revolution and developing the subjective forces of the revolution. And it is not surprising if there are now renewed efforts to organize a new communist international. But let us first evaluate how much advances need to be made by the initiating parties in terms of ideological, political and organizational victories in the revolutionary struggles of the proletariat and people in their own countries.

Imperialism in Various Global Regions

Milton Keynes UK
Ingram Content Group UK Ltd.
UKHW020829191223
434651UK00015B/794